Cosmopolitan English and Transliteracy

四海之内

Cosmopolitan English & Transliteracy

Xiaoye You

Southern Illinois University Press
Carbondale

Southern Illinois University Press
www.siupress.com

Substantial revisions of the following previously published essays appear in this book: chapter 2, Xiaoye You (2013), "The arts of dwelling places: Building ethos in an online community," in *Critical and corpus-based approaches to intercultural rhetoric*, edited by Diane Belcher and Gayle Nelson (Ann Arbor: University of Michigan Press); chapter 3, Xiaoye You (2011), "Chinese white-collar workers and multilingual creativity in the diaspora," *World Englishes, 30*(3), 409–427; and chapter 5, Xiaoye You and Xiaoqiong You (2013), "American content teachers' literacy brokerage in multilingual university classrooms," *Journal of Second Language Writing*, 22(3), 260–276.

19 18 17 16 4 3 2 1

Library of Congress Cataloging-in-Publication Data
Names: You, Xiaoye, [date] author.
Title: Cosmopolitan English and transliteracy / Xiaoye You.
Description: Carbondale : Southern Illinois University Press, [2016] | Includes bibliographical references and index.
Identifiers: LCCN 2016007228 | ISBN 9780809335244 (paperback) | ISBN 9780809335251 (e-book)
Subjects: LCSH: English language—Rhetoric—Study and teaching—United States. | English language—Rhetoric—Study and teaching—Foreign speakers. | Creative writing—Study and teaching—United States. | Language and culture—Globalization—United States. | Identity (Psychology)—United States. | Multiculturalism—United States. | Literacy—United States. | BISAC: LANGUAGE ARTS & DISCIPLINES / Composition & Creative Writing. | LANGUAGE ARTS & DISCIPLINES / Literacy. | FOREIGN LANGUAGE STUDY / English as a Second Language.
Classification: LCC PE1405.U6 Y66 2016 | DDC 808/.042071173—dc23 LC record available at https://lccn.loc.gov/2016007228

Printed on recycled paper. ♻

To Hsiao-Hui, Tianhuan, and Tianle

Contents

Preface

The proliferation of symbols and meanings due to colonization, migration, trade, and communication technologies is a defining feature of our times. Scholars in applied linguistics, literacy studies, and writing studies have responded to this reality with new conceptualizations of language and literacy. In North American writing studies, for instance, an influential perspective is translingualism. With variations among its proponents, the perspective emphasizes language as dynamic and malleable rather than discrete or static. Some further underscore not only fluid boundaries between languages but also between modalities. Some also argue that translingual practice necessarily involves transacting between the material and the symbolic worlds. The translingual perspective views language differences as resources and promotes an agentive use of symbolic resources for constructing and negotiating meaning in the teaching of writing. At the same time, however, the translingual perspective has led to tensions within writing studies. Some are concerned that the perspective has marginalized traditional but worthy ways of research, teaching, and program administration in the university.

In reflections on the translingual perspective, the most alarming criticism may be that its proponents have unwittingly aligned themselves with neoliberal multiculturalism "that celebrates individual cosmopolitanism and plurilingualism for socioeconomic mobility" (Kubota, 2014, p. 2). The critics are concerned that the perspective has not seriously considered how racial and other power relations might affect the ways people use, learn, and teach language. They are worried that the perspective does not improve the life of those who are linguistically, racially, and economically marginalized in globalization. Responding to the neoliberalism charge, Canagarajah (2015) suggested that while neoliberals use translingualism as a product and as a commodified branding mechanism, proponents of the translingual perspective view it as a practice that is politically savvy and socially conscious, and sensitive to power, social norms, and audience. This critical exchange is productive. It has posed two fundamental questions for language scholars and teachers: First, how do we understand meaning making in a local-global context? Second, what is our moral obligation in globalization?

This book embodies my wrestling with these questions, questions that deal with identity, language, nation, and literacy education. Growing up in China, I developed a communist-influenced utopian vision of the world. I saw the pursuit of equality and justice for every human being through communism as a worthy course. When I studied applied linguistics in graduate school during the post–Cultural Revolution, however, my utopianism was dampened. China moved into a market economy through which global capitalism forced the nation to join neocolonial forces to expand its market both domestically and abroad. Communist discourse, or the discourse of socialism with Chinese characteristics, often came to serve the interests of the nouveau riche. Language education focused on disciplining students (by emphasizing standards and correctness) and cultivating national citizens. Studying and then working in the United States, I was disappointed by the multiculturalist discourse in the academy. Broadly speaking, like contemporary Chinese communist discourse, multiculturalism, following Villanueva (1997), is a discourse intended to solve internal contradictions in a colonizing nation. Inadvertently, I joined the colonizer in reinforcing its politico-cultural hegemony in the world. This book is a reflection on this ambivalence and a personal struggle for social justice on a global scale.

In the process of drafting this book, my daughter, Joy, was born. I soon realized that she might very well face this politico-cultural conundrum. Born into the center of global neocolonialism and growing up with "resident alien" parents, my children could be torn between national, cultural, and linguistic allegiances. This fear was confirmed when Joy was two years old. When I told her day-care teacher that she was developing two languages, the teacher smiled, saying, "That's great. So she can speak English in public and Chinese at home." Like everyone else, the teacher held a particular view of language and social space. At first, Joy seemed to share her teacher's view. She spoke English in school, in church, and in shopping malls and Chinese at home. However, shortly I discovered that she renegotiated this rule. At home, for example, under the parental gaze, she talked to her stuffed animals and dolls in English. And she imported an authoritarian school discourse into the home space: she lined up her animals and dolls on the stairs, talking to them like this—"You bite. You time out. Sit. Be quiet." Her teacher told us that when Joy pinched other children, she was given time-outs in day care. Joy was aware of the linguistic and spatial boundaries that society had constructed for her, and she both conformed to and resisted the expectations (see similar examples in Orellana, 2015). In addition, she learned to exercise linguistic power by modeling her teacher. This is translingualism as a social practice, as Canagarajah has called it. Nevertheless, I still cannot help wondering to what extent and for how long she will be able to resist the temptation to follow the societal norms as a first-generation American, or resist the lure of the American Dream or of neoliberal discourse.

Thus, this book is the response of a migrant intellectual and a father to the translingual conversations and to the issues of identity, nation, and literacy in neocolonialism and globalization. While my thinking on these issues started as early as graduate school, most prominently the book was inspired by several conversations in which I participated. In 2009 Suresh Canagarajah, Maria Jerskey, and I organized a workshop called Toward a Rhetoric of Multilingual Writing at the Rhetoric Society of America Summer Institute. In the ensuing years, Suresh and I team-taught three graduate seminars at Penn State: Rhetoric in Contact Zones, Translingual Writing and Transcultural Communication in Globalization, and Global Rhet/Comp Inc. These conversations familiarized me with theories of cosmopolitanism, multilingualism, and literacy education. They prompted me to reflect on my identities, research, and teaching. They also gave me a venue to test my thoughts on those issues by soliciting responses from interlocutors. To take some of those thoughts into practice, I designed literacy pedagogies in different courses that I taught in China and the United States. My students often challenged me to modify my thinking. I want to thank those students who participated in my studies and granted me permission to reproduce their work.

When I was drafting the book manuscript, several colleagues offered generous and encouraging feedback. Suresh Canagarajah, Steve Fraiberg, Alissa Hartig, Joel Heng Hartse, Yumi Matsumoto, Shakil Rabbi, Brooke Ricker Schreiber, and Dorothy Worden made valuable suggestions to strengthen my arguments and to enhance their coherence. Keith Gilyard recommended *Push* by Sapphire to me as a transliterate work. Robin Becker, Emily Harrington, and Janet Lyon shared with me their insights about undergraduate education in English studies. Southern Illinois University Press reviewers Christiane Donahue and Paul Prior asked thought-provoking questions and made expert suggestions. I am deeply grateful for their patience and guidance with this project. I also want to thank Paul Prior, Liu Yichun, Luo Jing, Yang Shizhou, and Wang Jingjun for inviting me to share my thoughts on Cosmopolitan English and transliteracy at their institutions. My research intern Justin Hatch read two iterations of the manuscript and made insightful editorial suggestions.

The two universities that I inhabit also provided me with valuable support. The College of Liberal Arts at Penn State granted me a half-year sabbatical to draft the manuscript. In the process, Dean Susan Welch and English Department Head Mark Morrisson provided me with guidance and encouragement. Colleagues Cheryl Glenn, Jack Selzer, Richard Doyle, Brian Lennon, and Mya Poe were my best consultants. The faculty of English language and culture at the Guangdong University of Foreign Studies gave me opportunities to explore issues of English-language teaching in China. I used my time as a Yunshan Scholar to complete the last revisions of the manuscript. Professors Zheng Chao, Ouyang Huhua, Liu Ping, Liu Huiying, and Liu Xinfang have been my big supporters at Guangwai.

I am also thankful to the Southern Illinois University Press staff. Editor in chief Karl Kageff offered me encouragement and guidance when I prepared the manuscript. Copy editor Robert Brown was patient with me.

I also want to express gratitude to my family. My wife, Hsiao-Hui Yang, sacrificed tremendously to allow me to focus on my research and teaching. My children, Joy Tianhuan and Felix Tianle, encouraged me to get the writing done even before they were born. They grew up along with this project. My family also extended material and spiritual support. My parents, You Mingkeng and Liu Meixiang, and my sister, You Xiaoqiong, helped me collect source materials in China. My father created the Chinese calligraphy for the book cover.

Early versions of portions of this book were previously published in *World Englishes* ("Chinese White-Collar Workers and Multilingual Creativity in the Diaspora," 30.3, copyright © 2011 by Wiley, http://www.wiley.com, adapted with permission), the *Journal of Second Language Writing* ("American Content Teachers' Literacy Brokerage in Multilingual University Classrooms," 22.3, copyright © 2013 by Elsevier, http://www.elsevier.com/, adapted by permission), and *Critical and Corpus-Based Approaches to Intercultural Rhetoric*, edited by Diane Belcher and Gayle Nelson ("The Arts of Dwelling Places: Building Ethos in an Online Community," 47–71, copyright © 2013 by the University of Michigan Press, adapted by permission).

Cosmopolitan English and Transliteracy

1

Cosmopolitanism and the Future of Writing Studies

> Worst teacher ever. Can't understand what he says sometimes. SO BORING. i look at the clock about 23409834 times a class. the essay examples he gives are written by exchange students, so they don't even make sense. . . . [*sic*]
>
> —www.ratemyprofessors.com, September 21, 2005

> look at the name . . . look at the class . . . enough said . . . kicked my *** [*sic*]
>
> —www.ratemyprofessors.com, December 11, 2005

Judging people by their accents hasn't become obsolete in the cybernetic age. I was so judged by a disgruntled student in my first year as an assistant professor at Penn State. I taught an honors first-year writing course in the fall of 2005. The demographics of our classroom were predominantly white, an immigrant student from Korea and I being the only exceptions. The Korean student and I must have sounded foreign to the rest of the students. In class I used sample essays written by students from Chile, Japan, Malaysia, and Turkey who had explored cultural issues in both their home countries and the United States. After ten years of teaching in both China and the United States, I received my first ratings and comments on ratemyprofessors.com. This American student delivered the first of these after only four weeks of class, the second one at the end of the semester.

Linguistic and ethnic differences evidently caused this student great discomfort and anxiety. From his or her words, the student's mental state vis-à-vis these differences is easily discernible. The student felt uneasy, annoyed, and impatient at first, and was exasperated in the end. His or her discontent came explicitly from one source—foreign accent—for which international instructors are often criticized by American undergraduates (Bailey, 1984;

Kang & Rubin, 2009; Rubin, 1992; Rubin & Smith, 1990; Subtirelu, 2015).[1] Certainly, the international student writers I assigned wrote accented English ("so they don't even make sense"), and the professor spoke accented English ("can't understand what he says sometimes"); even the professor's name sounded bizarrely foreign ("look at the name"). Calling international students "exchange students" indicates that the student might have previously interacted with them in high school. However, that experience obviously had not made this student comfortable or patient with foreignness. Even a semester's exposure to accented speakers and multicultural texts didn't soften his or her attitude: "look at the name . . . look at the class . . . enough said . . . kicked my ***." The student didn't confront me face to face, so I never did find out who this person was. I always wondered whether the student was the only troubled one in class; however, because the students always showed respect in our interactions, I wasn't able to tell.

But honestly I was troubled too; it felt like a slap in the face, one that I had received many times before from others. I had been ashamed of my accent over the years. I have been corrected and punished by teachers, unfairly evaluated on standardized exams, and ridiculed by hiring committees. The outlook I developed as a result of these unjust interactions may be termed "double consciousness," a concept created by W. E. B. Du Bois (1994) to describe the imposition of white America's perceptions of black people on black consciousness. Writing in the early twentieth century, Du Bois referred to double consciousness as "a world which yields him no true self-consciousness, but only lets him see himself through the revelation of the others, measuring one's soul by the tape of a world that looks on in amused contempt and pity" (p. 2). It was this "contempt and pity" that the American student had projected in his or her piercing comments. The student hadn't acted alone but instead joined the amassed voices of countless others that had planted this double consciousness, not only in me, but also in myriad other individuals from marginalized groups. This "contempt and pity" has been perpetuated historically by colonial and semicolonial institutions and is now mobilized through neocolonialism, racism, sexism, nationalism, and the global hegemony of English monolingualism. So-called non-native speakers habitually look at themselves through the lens of "native speakers," to borrow a set of terms derived from monolingualism (Davis, 2003, 2013; Hackert, 2012), just as ethnic minorities look at themselves through the lens of the majority.

People are often judged by their accents, a dialogically co-constructed difference, just as they are by their gender and skin color. Historically, the fact that people traveled little preceded parochial attitudes, ethnocentric perceptions, and racial prejudice. What deeply disturbs me, however, is that in the age of information technologies and globalization a young person continued to embrace this colonialist and racist logic (see Cisneros & Nakayama, 2015, for a similar observation on prevailing cultural logics of race in the new media in the United States). Even a semester's exposure to accented speech and texts failed to alter his or her attitudes toward the Other. The student showed no appreciation for styles of English that were somewhat unfamiliar even though his or her online postings were clearly, in another way, accented. The student adopted elements of "netspeak" that are widely used by the younger generation, such as subjectless sentences, lowercase spellings, and profane expressions. The student feigned positive attitudes toward linguistic and ethnic differences the whole time he or she was in class. Impression management allowed the student to hide his or her disapproval and to complete assignments simply to get away with a good grade. Behind this mask, though, the student held steadfast to his or her prejudice against the linguistic and cultural Other.[2]

Such prejudice, latent also among some of this student's compatriots (see Cabrera, 2009, 2014; Sue, Bucceri, Lin, Nadal, & Torino, 2007), stands in sharp relief against the sea change in the world of English users. First, recent studies show that the number of "non-native speakers" in the world has surpassed that of "native speakers," making non-Anglo-American styles of English the new norm (Crystal, 2003; Graddol, 1997). Certainly, the division between "native" and "non-native" speakers and the use of terms such as "ESL learners" and "second-language writers" are problematic and sometimes offensive. These terms label people based on imagined or artificial boundaries between nations, peoples, and languages. Second, economic development has propelled significant cross-national travel and transnational flows of labor. English speakers of different nationalities and ethnicities mingle in almost all realms of life—marketplaces, workspaces, schools, hospitals, and military bases to name just a few. Third, as did the student in my class, the typical American undergraduate will share spaces with an increasing number of "exchange students" and take courses taught by teachers with unfamiliar accents. These students will be besieged not only by unfamiliar styles of English but also by the alien noises of Arabic, French, Spanish, etc., as well as by those of East Asian languages caricatured as "ching chong ling long" in a racist Youtube rant by a University of California, Los Angeles, student complaining about Asian students talking on the phone in the library (Wallace, 2011). Undergraduate students now live in multilingual and multicultural habitats.

Indeed, universities are increasingly transnational and multilingual, not only those in metropolitan centers, but also those that used to be isolated by the iron curtain. The most notable example of transnationalization is probably the Bologna Process, which intends to harmonize higher education systems in forty-seven European nations to make them more compatible and coherent across international lines (Lazerson, 2015). Universities worldwide have increased English-medium instruction to internationalize higher education and to seize a share of the lucrative education market (Coleman, 2006; Kirkpatrick, 2011; Preece, 2011). Students use differing styles of English to learn, and professors use them to teach. How should we in writing studies understand the use of English in school settings where diverse English accents and styles mingle and sometimes collide with other languages? If we recognize literacy practice as not just local (Brandt & Clinton, 2002; Surma, 2013), how can we add the global dimension to our teaching of meaning making and conveying? The racial microaggressions of the disgruntled first-year student also raise a moral question for the field: if we focused in the past on cultivating good national citizens (Crowley, 1998; Hesford, 2006; Horner & Trimbur, 2002; Mao, 2006; Villanueva, 1997; Wan, 2014; M. Young, 2004), what are our moral obligations in a time of globalization, and how can we fulfill them?

In U.S. writing studies, pedagogies dealing with linguistic and cultural differences have been framed predominantly within theories of multiculturalism (Ball & Lardner, 2005; Duffy, 2007; Fishman & McCarthy, 2002; Flower, Long, & Higgins, 2000; Fox, 1994; Lunsford & Ouzgane, 2004; Richardson, 2002; Schaafsma, 1993; Severino, Guerra, & Butler, 1997). The rise of the discourse of multiculturalism in American academia has been tied to the civil rights movement and to college open admissions in the 1960s. Multiculturalists emphasize the importance of recognizing the distinct cultural practices represented in texts produced by minority authors and students. They focus on the authentic representation of minority cultures in literature and try to identify and appreciate culturally based rhetorical practices among minority students. Teachers try to accommodate students from outside the United States by recognizing their colonial and postcolonial heritage and by identifying and appreciating their culturally based rhetorical practices. However, much of the multiculturalist approach to differences is rooted in and tied up with the nationalist project, which is to guard cultural and ethnic sovereignty within the nation-state. Emphasis is typically placed on marking the boundaries between cultures and ethnicities, often creating essentialized views of these entities and their rhetorical and literary traditions. Transnational flows of capital, labor, and cultural products make the sovereignty-anchored approach hardly adequate for dealing with differences in research and teaching. At least the disgruntled first-year student in my class did not seem touched by my multiculturalist orientation to writing instruction.

In recent years U.S. writing studies scholars have taken feminist and translingual perspectives to issues of difference, doing so, however, without uprooting nationalism in the field. The feminist perspective recognizes the intricate connections between the personal and the political. Scholars taking this perspective have challenged our understanding of intersectional identities and have performed systemic analyses of inequality in the production of knowledge and meaning in particular contexts. They have promoted diverse discourses, effectively drawing students away from the all-familiar thesis-driven, logocentric argumentation essays (Jung, 2005; Lamb, 1991; Meyer, 1993; Zawacki, 1992). They have sought ways to engage conflicts arising from racial, gender, and power differences in the classroom (Bauer, 1990; Jarratt, 1991; Pough, 2006), and they have theorized the arts of silence and rhetorical listening and practiced them in the classroom (Glenn & Ratcliffe, 2011; Ratcliffe, 2006; Dalke, 2002). Practicing queer pedagogies, Alexander (2008) and DiGrazia and Boucher (2005) provoked their students to question the process of normalizing dominant assumptions and beliefs in American society. The translingual perspective, on the other hand, has highlighted the problem of English monolingualism in teaching writing within the multilingual reality of American universities. Canagarajah (2013a); Horner, Lu, Royster, and Trimbur (2012); and Young (2007) have suggested that languages are neither discrete nor stable but rather dynamic and negotiated, and that writing necessarily involves the negotiation of language differences. Both the feminist and the translingual perspectives have underscored negotiations that individuals perform in meaning making and have provided useful pedagogical strategies. However, with relatively few exceptions (Dingo, 2012, 2013; Hesford, 2011; Hesford & Kozol, 2005; Wang, 2013), neither of these perspectives has dislodged the nationalism that underpins English monolingual ideology nor tackled ethical use of language in local-global contexts. Writing studies needs alternative frames and approaches that both acknowledge the usefulness of national, cultural, and linguistic boundaries and at the same time interrogate and break them down.

A candidate for this purpose is cosmopolitanism, a millennia-old notion that has become increasingly relevant for dealing with issues of the present. Of its various formulations across time and geographical space, cosmopolitanism carries a fundamental meaning: though sometimes defined by kindred relations, ethnicity, nation, race, or class, all people are first and foremost members of the human race and as such are morally obligated to those outside their categories; further, they have the agency to develop and sustain new allegiances across cultures, communities, and languages. Taking an antiessentialist stand, the cosmopolitan perspective reminds us of the historicity, artificiality, and rhetoricity of these cultural categories. In writing studies this perspective enables us to perceive human connectedness as being deeply underpinned in the various accents, styles, and uses of language in everyday life and literary culture. Linguistic, cultural, and ethnic differences are not things to be contained but are matters to be respected and appreciated. They need to be explored to recover and protect the multifaceted, intricate human connections severed by various artificial borders. Cosmopolitanism challenges us to acknowledge but also go beyond the interests of people who traditionally claim entitlement to a language. Combining a humanistic vision with the vigor of social science research, this book seeks to understand English-mediated meaning making in globalization and to reimagine literacy education in the university and beyond.

Cosmopolitanism and the Ethics of Globalization

The world is large, but becoming small. Globalization can be viewed as a complex multidimensional set of cross-border processes with multiple origins involving economy, culture, religion, and politics (Holton, 1998, 2005; Scholte, 2005). Globalization has made cosmopolites, or cultural citizens of the world, out of those who once were simply citizens of nations (Gidden, 1990; Keohane & Nye, 2000; Modelski, 1972). Cosmopolitan ideals, however, predate contemporary globalization and have been articulated in various cultures. For example, two and a half millennia ago, Sima Niu, one of Confucius's disciples, was tormented by a politico-ideological divide between him and his brother. He grieved over his loss, saying, "Everyone else has brothers; I alone have none." Zixia, his cohort, comforted him, saying,

> I have heard this saying: "Death and life are the decree of Heaven; wealth and rank depend upon the will of Heaven. If a gentleman attends to business and does not idle away his time, if he behaves with courtesy to others and observes the rules of ritual, then all within the Four Seas are his brothers (四海之内皆兄弟)." How can any true gentleman grieve that he is without brothers? (Confucius, 1989, pp. 163–164)

This passage, containing a central Confucian teaching, for centuries has offered Confucian disciples and East Asian intellectuals a personal ethic for handling conflicts within and across their communities: while politico-ideological differences drive people apart, by respecting others and practicing the rules of ritual, a gentleperson can bring people from far away together like brothers and sisters.

This Eastern ethic compares intriguingly with the notion of cosmopolitanism evoked by Diogenes the Cynic. Of him it is said, "Asked where he came from, he answered: 'I am a citizen of the world (kosmopolitês)'" (Laertius, 1972, passage 63). Articulating a groundbreaking concept, Diogenes challenged the basis of social identity in Greece at that time, which would have been either the individual city-state or Greek society as a whole. The Stoics, who later built upon and developed Diogenes's idea, typically stressed that each person lives in both a local community and a wide community of human ideals, arguments, and aspirations. The basis of the wide community lies in what is fundamental to all—the equal worth of reason and humanity in every person. Allegiance is owed first to the moral realm of all humanity, not to the contingent groupings of nation, ethnicity, and class (Held, 2010).

Articulated in different historical contexts, the two notions—"brothers [and sisters] within the Four Seas" and "citizen of the world"—share some fundamental ideals and values concerning human relations. The most prominent one is that in addition to natural, contingent human groupings such as clans, states, and ethnicities, a person is intricately connected to out-group members by virtue of humanity. Both notions also place confidence in individual agency—one's ability to behave with reason and aspiration and to live peacefully with people from afar. Expanding on these fundamental values, later intellectuals such as Immanuel Kant, Hannah Arendt, and Martha Nussbaum identified further principles and values of cosmopolitanism (Fine & Cohen, 2002). For example, Kant measured the advance of enlightenment in terms of the removal of constraints on "the public use of reason," or the open-ended use of reason and communication to secure the possibility of intersubjectivity; "[l]ocked into the roles, practices, and organization of civil society, people, Kant argued, do not have the opportunity to explore fully the nature and limits of existing rules, prejudices, and beliefs" (Held, 2010, p. 42). While the notions of "brothers [and sisters] within the Four Seas" and "citizen of the world" both value reason and aspiration, the former emphasizes moral cultivation in the individual, treating humility, trust, knowledge, and appreciation of customs and morale (仁、义、信、智、礼) in East Asian communities as the condition for converting all into brothers and sisters within the Four Seas.

In addition to these philosophical articulations, historically cosmopolitanism took various forms, involving actually and imaginatively crossing borders and engaging with cultural differences. For example, cosmopolitanism is evident in early Christianity, Buddhism, Islam, and medieval European literature (Edwards, 2001), the eighteenth-century Enlightenment, the twentieth-century communist movement, and more recent global movements for international laws based on human rights, environmental sustainability, and greater global democracy (Held, 2010). Cosmopolitanism has often been evoked as a way of managing cross-border processes and interdependences from above by empires, powerful nation-states, and global regulatory institutions such as the United Nations and the World Trade Organization. It can equally be seen in terms of cross-border forms of cultural life and politics that operate from below. These forms include globally oriented social movements and networks of intellectuals, professionals, political activists, workers, migrants, and artists linking cities and communities. While these days one may often associate cosmopolitanism with privileged world travelers, there are unprivileged travelers as well, including migrant laborers and refugees. The unprivileged experience is what some have called working-class, vernacular, or plebian cosmopolitanism (Clifford, 1992; Gidwani & Sivaramakrishnan, 2004; Gilroy, 1993; Werbner, 1999, 2006; Waxer, 2001). As world travelers, international students are both privileged and unprivileged. They are privileged thanks to their financial resources but often unprivileged due to their lack of the linguistic and cultural capital valued in host countries.

Cosmopolitanism has been recognized by scholars as existing in multiple modalities, or in different types of social structures and social actions. According to the conceptual mapping by Holton (2009), cosmopolitanism has been articulated relative to four types of social action. First, it is viewed as instrumental for achieving given ends. It exists as a sociocultural condition (such as colonialism and anticolonialism, capitalism and socialism, migration and movement, cities and urban living, institutions of knowledge and beliefs), a political project to build transnational institutions, a project for recognizing multiple identities, and a set of cross-cultural competences. Second, cosmopolitanism is viewed as value relevant, meaning that it might appear as a philosophical worldview, as introduced earlier, or as a mode of orientation to the world emphasizing openness to cultural differences. Third, it is viewed as expressive, referring to "feelings and emotions that engender cross-cultural solidarities in personal or community life." Fourth, cosmopolitanism is viewed as habitual, referring to "habitual openness as a taken-for-granted feature of everyday life" (p. 31).

In the epoch of globalization, scholars and politicians have proposed cosmopolitan visions and outlined principles for achieving those visions (Brown & Held, 2010; Held, 2010).[3] But above all these principles is the willingness and ability to communicate across differences, be they ideological, religious, political, racial, or linguistic, which is variously understood as critical, reflective, or dialogical cosmopolitanism (Appiah, 2007; Mendieta, 2009; Mignolo, 2000; Nussbaum, 2010). Appiah (2007) suggests that despite ineradicable differences, it is important that we keep the channels of communication open and stand ready and willing to listen and to engage with strangers. Similarly, Mao (2006) proposes a creative, dialectical form of meaning making that practices "togetherness-in-difference" in intercultural exchanges. He advocates "reflective encounters," or actively reflecting on and imagining what it is like from another's perspective when two people or two communicative traditions are entangled on a borderland. More specifically he suggests, "We should seize such encounters or moments of co-presence as an opportunity to trace the complex past that has informed their respective experiences, and to recover the different paths each has traveled to arrive at this borderland destination" (p. 28). The imperative to develop both a mentality and an ability to engage strangers through creative meaning making defines the ethics of globalization.

To communicate across differences, divergent styles of English and other languages can provide exactly those channels and forms needed. Certainly, from the perspective of the uninformed and the intolerant, nonstandard and accented language use has been viewed, historically, as a hindrance to communication and meaning. Thanks to modern technology, however, despite their accents and styles, people are conversing across geographic locations and cultures on matters of common interest at an accelerated rate. As Gilyard (2016) suggests, a word is "a microcosm of human history" because "every utterance contains tracings of migration, mixing, negotiation, or conquest" (p. 284). Through the window of divergent styles of English and other languages, people can sample diverse values, identities, and voices from outside their communities. Furthermore, these divergent styles, arising from the interplay of different dialects and languages, offer a heuristic to explore the history of linguistic differences and, in Mao's words, "to trace the complex past that has informed their respective experiences, and to recover the different paths each has traveled." The historical formation of languages, dialects, and the human attitudes and prejudice surrounding these linguistic differences is a fruitful site for cosmopolitan education, where students "learn enough about the different to recognize common aims, aspirations, and values, and enough about these common ends to see how variously they are instantiated in the many cultures and their histories" (Nussbaum, 2010, p. 158). Linguistic differences are so intricately bound up with personal history and issues related to class, race, gender, and sexuality that they can serve as a gateway to in-depth discussions of these perennial issues.

The ultimate purpose of exploring these social issues via the entry point of linguistic differences is to find ways to live with them with heightened understanding, appreciation, and tolerance—to cultivate what Sommer (2004) calls "bilingual aesthetics." Exploring translingual and transcultural possibilities will potentially lead to such noble ends. This book features a series of studies on how multilingual speakers juggle diverse styles of English with other languages in building bridges, sharing personal visions and feelings, and performing academic exercises. These styles constitute part of their communicative repertoire. Therefore, translingual and transcultural possibilities can be defined as the arts of crossing and appropriating multiple languages, cultures, and identities in these individuals' social practices. Furthermore, these possibilities also refer to the fruits resulting from people conversing across borders to form new alliances on specific issues and to develop regional or global affiliations. Such conversations, alliances, and affiliations will conceivably break down the borders between nations and between cultures, enabling one to embrace his or her moral obligations to neighbors and strangers. This is the pathway towards a true cosmopolitanism.

Cosmopolitan English

I refer to these diverse styles of English as Cosmopolitan English (CE). By deemphasizing accentedness, CE bypasses linguistic differences defined by birthright, nation, region, race, and ethnicity. In a sense, every English speaker is a "native speaker," native to one or multiple speech communities or to certain established norms. At the same time, every speaker sounds different to interlocutors outside his or her communities. CE is English as it is actually used by individuals across the globe, each with differences inflected in his or her pronunciation, vocabulary, syntax, and/or discourse structures. With its inherent connections to multiple languages and cultures, CE has the potential to create alliances across borders. Thus, CE is both descriptive and heuristic. It is descriptive because it acknowledges and intends to capture the multiplicity of ways that individuals use English within and across communities. It is heuristic because, first, it requires that we understand the characteristics and functions of English beyond any single cultural category and, second, it challenges us to promote cosmopolitan awareness and practice by privileging or denouncing particular ways of thinking about English uses.

Before elaborating on CE, I want to emphasize that cultural and linguistic boundaries are real, both materially and psychologically. The boundaries have been instilled in our consciousness through nationalist discourses imparted by the media and public education. Every time we go through customs, watch the evening news, or take a language test, we experience these boundaries firsthand, often inexplicitly and unwittingly. They are also embodied in our scholarly language. For example, "native speaker" and "non-native speaker" are defined along the lines of birthright and nation. Conceived as a system, language is often understood along national and ethnic lines, sometimes to the extent that a single regional variety will come to be identified as two separate languages, as with the familiar cases along the borders of France, Italy, and Spain. Or, mutually unintelligible languages (sometimes called "dialects") are clustered as one, as with Chinese in China. Similarly, "monolingual," "bilingual," and "multilingual" are sometimes marked along national and ethnic lines as well. These terms indicate an ability for using, or the attribute of being written or expressed in, a certain number of natural languages. In the U.S. context, Americans are often viewed as monolingual speakers of English as opposed to immigrants, international students, and foreign tourists, who are often bilingual or multilingual speakers. When "code" refers to letters or words of a language (such as "English code") or a style of language use (such as "code-switching"), it also marks national, cultural, or social boundaries. In this book I will evoke, but not to endorse, these boundary-marking terms in my critique of current practices in language studies and literacy education. I will use, for example, *multilingual* throughout this book to signify "the multiplicity and complexity of individual and group repertoires" (Martin-Jones & Jones, 2000, p. 5) instead of simply multiple natural languages. The concept of CE recognizes, engages, and deconstructs these artificial yet still quite real boundaries.

In language studies there are two boundary-marking terms that CE intends to counter. These two terms, along with their derivatives, are commonly used in literacy and writing studies to conceptualize diverse English styles along national and ethnic lines. One is *interlanguage*, often evoked by writing scholars drawing insights from applied linguistics (see Connor, 1996; Ferris, 2014; Rafoth, 2015; Silva, Leki, & Carson, 1997). Originating from second-language acquisition research, interlanguage refers to the language spoken by a language learner in the process of acquisition, and it comes with the assumption that the learner will gradually approach "native speaker" norms. It is often conceived as an emerging linguistic system developed by the learner who has not yet become fully proficient but is approximating the target language (Bardovi-Harlig, 2006; Barron, 2012; Han & Tarone, 2014; James, 2007; Selinker, 1972; Skehan, 2008). Language learners either preserve some features of their first language (L1), or they overgeneralize target language rules when speaking or writing the target language, resulting in creative and innovative linguistic adaptations. Thus a learner's use of language can be observed to vary in different contexts; for example, the learner may be more accurate, complex, and fluent in one discourse domain than in another (Tarone, 1979; Selinker & Douglas, 1985). A learner may produce a target-like variant (e.g., "He doesn't like it") in one context and a nontarget-like variant (e.g., "He don't like it") in another. Pedagogically the interlanguage construct was developed to teach "non-native" speakers "native" standards; they will, hypothetically, learn to think and speak like native speakers. The problem, however, is that with this construct, native speaker norms are reified as the target, and non-native speakers pursuing that target are automatically subjugated by native speakers and by monoglot ideologies, though in reality they may use interlanguage effectively for various purposes (Cook, 1997, 1999). This interlanguage perspective is also present in L1 literacy education. For quite some time, African American students have been told that their vernacular is a transitional language, or interlanguage, a stage in their progression towards acquiring Standard English. In reality, a majority of African American students are able to acquire both and use them skillfully across contexts (Gilyard, 1991, 1996, 2011; Smitherman, 1999).

The other boundary-marking term is *World Englishes* (WE). Kachru (1985, 1990, 1992) suggests that due to colonialism, English spread from the inner-circle nations (such as Australia, Britain, Canada, and the United States) to the outer-circle nations (largely former colonial countries, such as Nigeria, South Africa, Malaysia, the Philippines, and India) and then to the expanding-circle nations (such as China, Japan, Indonesia, and Russia). Proponents of WE tend to favor description of the linguistic forms and uses of English in different parts of the world across domains (such as Bautista & Bolton, 2008; Berns, 1988, 1995; Bolton, 2002, 2006; Mesthrie & Bhatt,

2008; Xu, 2010). Some of them propose codifying and teaching local students these locally developed forms and uses instead of native speaker norms. The problem with the WE construct is that its proponents have continued to favor a modernist conceptualization of nation and language. That is, a nation needs a national language and national literature to cohere its people; English serves as an additional national language for many modern nations, particularly the outer-circle countries. Thus WE proponents become invested in describing, some in codifying, English as it is used in different countries and regions. Their effort is not so different from the monolingual movements in modern nations, which privilege one regional dialect of a majority language by marginalizing other dialects and minority languages in the name of nation building. Influenced by structural linguistics, WE proponents often view language as a system of symbols, and they downplay the fluidity, instability, and multiplicity of language practices by individual users.

As studies of WE have multiplied, a few theoretical views have arisen, distancing themselves from Kachru's historical view of three concentric circles (inner circle, outer circle, and expanding circle), such as the notions of Global Englishes (Pennycook, 2007), English as an international language (Jenkins, 2000; A. Matsuda, 2012), and English as a lingua franca, or ELF (Canagarajah, 2007, 2009a; Jenkins, 2007, 2011, 2014; Mauranen & Metsä-Ketelä, 2006; Mauranen & Ranta, 2009; Seidlhofer 2001, 2003, 2004). These WE derivatives typically leave native speaker norms behind and focus on the situated use of English among non-native speakers or between non-native and native speakers. The most popular view probably has been ELF, which Jenkins (2011) introduces as "an additionally acquired language system" (p. 928) used for communication among speakers of different first languages.[4] It is different from native speaker English, and native speakers also need to learn it when communicating with non-native speakers. The ELF perspective emphasizes English as multiply sui generis instead of evaluating it against native speaker norms. The majority of ELF studies so far have focused on oral interactions, with a few exceptions (such as Aaltonen, 2006; Canagarajah, 2009b, 2011, 2013a; Horner, 2011; Lavelle & Shima, 2014). As the ELF perspective categorizes English into systems or varieties based on the native and non-native speaker distinction, it continues to reify artificial boundaries based on birthright and nation.

CE, in contrast, refers to English as it emerges from contexts of interaction, used by individuals regardless of their birthright, geographic locations, language, and educational backgrounds, and it is often free from the prescriptions imposed by institutions. The concept distances itself from both interlanguage and WE. Compared with the eventual native speaker proficiency assumed in interlanguage, CE users do not necessarily intend to, or may never, reach standard native speaker norms. However, they often communicate effectively in various contexts by constructing local or temporary norms. Compared with linguistic structuralism embedded in the WE construct, while local systems of English may in effect arise from within geopolitical contexts, CE underscores the constant flows of people, languages, and dialects across geopolitical borders, be they regional or national. Users of English, including so-called native speakers, may have, through vigorous studies and stringent exams, acquired standard native speaker norms in schools, but they do not necessarily follow the norms in their actual language use. They live in a world of nonstandard languages, both of English and of other languages and dialects. It is this conception of language in situated practice that the CE construct intends to capture.

CE shares major assumptions with a few concepts already in circulation. One of them is "living-English" proposed by Min-Zhan Lu. In the context of countering the American English-only movement in literacy education, Lu (2010) emphasizes the sociohistorically situated, diverse ways of English use—"English as kept alive by many and having many different ways of using it, each of which is itself a living process in-the-forming: informing and informed by the specific different and dynamic historical and social contexts of individual acts" (p. 45). Thus Lu argues that living-English begs the question of whether one's ease with a particular usage, such as Standard English, might inadvertently sponsor systems and relations of injustice. Like living-English, CE is sociohistorically situated and deeply connected to local and translocal cultural practices. This notion also intends to sensitize teachers and students to the systems and relations of injustice behind linguistic differences with the intent of seeking justice within and across borders.

While Lu proposes living-English to counter the institutional imposition of Standard English and some individuals' unreflective use of it, I view Standard English as cosmopolitan when it is in use, even in unreflective use. It was a historical construct arising from modernist endeavors in Anglophone nations. It emerged through various codification processes, and it is now, with some variation, being taught in schools, assessed in high-stakes exams, used in news media, and reinforced by the publishing industry. Along with other dialects, languages, and media, Standard English has been widely adopted by individuals for home and professional contexts. It is just one among the many styles that people resort to, depending on their communicative context, purpose, and audience. Thanks to colonialism and now global capitalism, Standard English (in its various forms, norms, and modes) has reached peoples outside English-dominant nations and become one of their communication resources. It is one of the lingua franca styles of English. However, as I will show throughout the book, in these contexts Standard English is often spottily used and blended with other dialects and local languages at various linguistic levels, thus taking on accents in each of its users. It is through this blending and spotty use, defying the original modernist intent, that Standard English has become cosmopolitan.

CE also shares major assumptions with the concept of English as a local practice. Revolting against the dominance of structuralism in some strands of linguistics, Pennycook (2010) argues that language is "a product of the deeply social and cultural activities in which people engage" rather than a pregiven structure (p. 1). Thus language should be understood as a social practice within a specific locality, time, and space. Echoing Heller (2007), Pennycook (2012) further illustrates that when we examine real people in real places, language tends to turn up in unexpected places and takes unexpected forms. Focusing on English as a local practice, Higgins (2009) studied the ways in which English participates in local linguistic activities and how "East Africans exploit the heteroglossia of language to perform modern identities through localizing global linguistic and cultural resources while generally maintaining the multiple layers of meaning from both the global and the local" (p. 148). Like living-English and English as a local practice, CE emphasizes the situatedness of English in a specific location and time with intricate connections to local languages and cultural meanings. Nevertheless, CE also recognizes a local-global connection as the character of any social activity (Latour, 1996).

Finally, CE shares major assumptions with the notion of translingual practice. When proposing a translingual, instead of a monolingual, bilingual, or multilingual, orientation for understanding language practice, Canagarajah (2013a) emphasizes two key points. First, communication transcends individual languages because languages are always in contact, mutually influencing each other. Second, communication transcends words and involves diverse semiotic resources and ecological affordances. The notion of translingual practice intends to break down the boundaries of linguistic codes in a speaker's communicative repertoire. In this sense both *translingual* and *multilingual* (as used in this book) emphasize the multiplicity and complexity of individual and group repertoires. In this book I will limit the use of *translingual* to refer to situated language practice. In descriptive terms, CE is a translingual practice. When English is in use, it always mingles with other linguistic and nonlinguistic systems. Drawing resources from these systems, users of English construct meanings in context. As a heuristic, CE emphasizes the potential for boundary crossings and transgressions when marked styles of English are in use. Having had prior translingual and transcultural experiences, English speakers may engage in conversations with each other, and through interactions they develop new communities, identities, and voices. Defying certain linguistic norms and expectations, their styles mark their having crossed linguistic differences in the first place, resulting in their taking on hybrid linguistic identities. As they speak or compose, their marked styles may enable them to cross additional national, racial, class, ethnic, and gender boundaries.

CE is used in both speech and writing. In spoken discourse its phonological features stand out in accents. According to Lippi-Green (2012), technically the word *accent* distinguishes stress in words or intonation in sentences. In the minds of speakers, two phonological elements—prosodic and segmental features—help to differentiate one CE style from another. In addition to phonological features, a CE style may also be distinct in the speaker's choices made at lexical, syntactic, and pragmatic levels. CE will manifest in students' and teachers' speech quoted throughout this book. In written discourse, CE can have "accents" too (Ashcroft, 2010; Blommaert, 2008; Montgomery & Fuller, 1996; Montgomery, Fuller, & Demarse, 1993; Schneider, 1989; Yao, 2010; Zawacki, Hajabbasi, Habib, Antram, & Das, 2007). For example, in his study of a Zairean farmer's writing in Shaba Swahili and French, Blommaert (2008) identified accents as the writer's deviations from standard orthographical and literacy conventions, including alternations between uppercase and lowercase as well as nonstandard uses of punctuation. Studying "foreign accents" in Chinese American poetry, Yao (2010) recognized a series of hybridization strategies that give rise to accented vocabulary, syntax, and discourse. These strategies include cross-fertilization, mimicry, grafting, transplantation (code-switching), and mutation (pp. 21–28). These hybridization strategies can also be used in academic prose, as the reader will notice both in the writing style of this book and the writing styles of the students and scholars cited in this book.

As a translingual practice, CE often manifests itself in the alternation of languages, language varieties, registers, and styles in both speech and writing, described as code-switching, code-mixing, or code-meshing. In linguistics, code-switching refers to the alternation between two or more languages, or language varieties, in a conversation at both inter- and intra-sentential levels (Eastman, 1992; Gardner-Chloros, 2009). In sociolinguistics and literacy studies, code-switching sometimes refers to switching among dialects, styles, or registers, as a speaker moves between informal and formal settings (Debose, 1992; Gilyard, 2011; Gregory & Carroll, 1978; Gumperz, 1972). Code-switching is also widely used in the study of writing, particularly the study of literary texts, to refer to the co-presence of languages, dialects, registers, and styles (Callahan, 2003; Giaimo, 2010; Hess, 1996). While often used interchangeably with code-switching, in sociolinguistics and language acquisition studies, code-mixing suggests a hybrid form used by children or language learners when the latter draw from distinct grammars in their speech (Greene, Pena, & Bedore, 2012; Grosjean, 1989; King, 2006; Sridhar & Sridhar, 1980). Recently, code-meshing has been used to refer to speakers or writers collapsing the boundaries between languages, language varieties, or styles as a way of performing identity or as a language pedagogy (V. A. Young, 2004; Canagarajah, 2006, 2011). With different focuses, these three "code" terms have shared, except where code-meshing challenges, the assumption that languages are discrete systems that a speaker or writer can move between or draw elements from.[5] While CE is full of instances of such language uses, it does not embrace the view of language as a discrete system typically defined by nation or ethnicity. Instead, based on their assessment of the rhetorical situation, CE users marshal the available resources from their repertoires to realize different designs in speech or writing, including potentially forming identifications with the Other.

As a translingual practice, CE naturally involves translation, leading to the transformation of English, the interlocutors, and space-times (Ashcroft, 2010). Translation is commonly understood as the movement of a text from a source language to a target language. More broadly it refers to texts standing in the place of, speaking for, or appearing to mobilize bodies, objects, or other texts (Leander & Lovvorn, 2006). When we view translingual practice as transcending individual languages, involving diverse semiotic resources (Canagarajah, 2013a), and transacting between symbolic and material ecologies (Jordan, 2015; Leander & Boldt, 2012), an English user both translates and is translated by negotiating meanings across languages, other semiotic systems, and the material world. If we view translingual practice as also taking place within one language, as some scholars do (Horner, Lu, Royster,

& Trimbur, 2011), "all writing always involves rewriting and translation, inevitably engaging the labor of recontextualizing (and renewing) language, language practices, users, conventions and contexts" (Lu & Horner, 2013, p. 485). However one understands translingual practice, CE is always translated, transforming subjects, objects, and texts either in English or in other languages or in a mixture of English and other languages. English users sometimes form ideas and feelings in other languages first and transpose them into spoken or written English. Certainly, these speakers may refuse to translate in order to legitimize a certain type of text and a certain type of identity and power relationship between languages and cultures.

The CE construct emphasizes not only English used in naturalistic settings but also the new alliances it may help to forge in a world of constant change. English, with its many dialects and styles, has allowed people from across the world to speak to one another. Historically, however, those afforded the opportunity to speak English across borders have often been social elites—intellectuals, lawyers, businesspersons, and political leaders attempting Standard English, which has led to the unfortunate privileging of native speaker norms. Now, as English education develops in many parts of the world, facilitated by modern technologies, English connects people from all walks of life and from all across the globe F2F (face to face), allowing them to discuss matters of common interest. For example, the antigovernment demonstrations in the spring of 2011 in the Arabic world infectiously spread to other parts of the globe, sparking local antiestablishment responses such as the Occupy Wall Street and #BlackLivesMatter movements in the United States. This grassroots discontent spread from one locale to another largely by means of CE and various local languages and dialects aided by mass media and social media networks. By emphasizing this language-in-use (Halliday, 1970; Hasan, 1984; Labov, 1970; Schieffelin & Ochs, 1986; Bhatia, 1993), with its diverse linguistic and cultural connections, and with the assistance of new technologies, CE has the potential to highlight and bring forth new cultural meanings and affiliations.

In the end, I am calling for a cosmopolitan turn in writing studies, a turn toward taking on cultivating global citizens as our shared mission. As a first step, we can recognize CE as the norm, with all the linguistic, school-based, and *social* benefits that it entails. Taking an antiessentialist stand, we can cease defining English along the lines of birthright, nation, ethnicity, or region, and we can instead understand it as a multiplicity of local practices constantly converging and intermingling with other linguistic and cultural forces. English mediates actions and ideals oriented both to the universal and the particular, the global and the local. Thanks to their cross-lingual and cross-cultural connections, users of English and other languages are able to create variously complex repertoires of allegiance, identity, and interest, which will potentially enable them to communicate across communities and even nations. The cosmopolitan turn demands that writing studies reassess and modify its assumptions, scholarship, and pedagogies. Rather than being bounded by the interests of the state or a particular community, the field ought to develop ethical approaches, pursuing justice for every user of English, as well as for users of all languages.

If we, in writing studies, don't respond quickly and thoughtfully to the cosmopolitan ways of English use, there will be negative consequences. Watching familiar boundaries crumble, one might respond with an ambivalence, which could turn into insecurity or agony. In the name of nationalism, ethnic minorities are often forced to give up their home styles of speaking and reasoning to pursue state-sanctioned ways at a cultural and emotional cost (Gilyard, 1991; Mejia, 2004; Rodriguez, 1983; Villanueva, 1993). On the other hand, pursuing cosmopolitan ways of speaking and reasoning may also lead to cultural loss and psychological trauma for some individuals. A sense of loss may occur in the scholarly community: as scholars recognize that terms such as "native speaker," "non-native speaker," "ESL learner," "second-language writer," and "code-switching" are boundary marking and incompatible with cosmopolitan ideals, they may feel paralyzed, as new terms are yet to be fully developed. Language teachers and program directors may be at loss as well. Standard English used to be at the center of literacy curriculum and assessment. With it now decentered, new literacy standards need to be formulated. Let us be sensitive to and guard against these potential losses as we embrace CE as the new norm.

A Pedagogy of Transliteracy

A cosmopolitan perspective to English requires a new orientation to English literacy education. Literacy is always rooted in local political and ideological formations (Gee, 1990; Street, 1984, 1993). In the United States, for example, since the mid-nineteenth century, school-based literacy has been identified with "character, intellect, morality, and good taste . . . literacy skills co-occurred with moral patriotic character" (Heath, 1981, pp. 35–36). English literacy in Anglophone nations has historically meant the ability and practice of reading and writing in Standard English, with dialects and other languages being relegated to the margins. A cosmopolitan orientation suggests that English users will interact with diverse dialects and languages in addition to Standard English. Furthermore, they will encounter diverse cultural discourses and, through deep engagement with them, potentially form affinities with the communities and groups behind these discourses. The cosmopolitan orientation demands that we seek to cultivate in English users the ability to engage with these cultural discourses through reading and writing using Standard English, other CE styles, other languages, and other semiotic resources. This ability necessarily requires that English users negotiate across language differences and "consciously and effectively move back and forth between as well as in and out of . . . communities they belong to or will belong to" (Guerra, 1997, p. 258). I call this ability and its enactment *transliteracy*. Ultimately, transliteracy should foster in English users "a cultural disposition involving an intellectual and aesthetic stance of 'openness' towards peoples, places, and experiences from different cultures, especially those from different nations" (Szerszynski & Urry, 2002, p. 469). While institutionally they remain citizens of a certain nation, morally and culturally they become citizens of the world. In other words, transliteracy is a translingual and transcultural practice with a cosmopolitan imperative.

The construct of transliteracy has been built upon the perspective of transculturalism (Connal, 2004; Gilyard, 1997; Guerra, 1997, 2015; Mejia, 2004; Pratt, 1991). First defined by the South American scholar Fernando Ortiz, transculturalism refers to the process of *métissage* (mixing of peoples) as a distinctive character of a culture in the Americas, which developed from both native and immigrant populations. Ortiz views transculturalism in its earliest stage as a synthesis of two phases taking place at the same time: a deculturalization of the past and a métissage with the present. As a biological and cultural métis, one is always part of the dialectic with the Other. Cuccioletta (2001) suggests that the process of recognizing oneself in the Other will lead to a cosmopolitan citizenship: "This citizenship, independent of political structures and institutions, develops each individual in the understanding that one's culture is multiple, métis, and that each human experience and existence is due to the contact with *other*, who in reality is like, oneself" (p. 9, emphasis in the original). The construct of transliteracy emphasizes that in globalization everyone is a cultural and linguistic métis. When being respected and taken seriously, one has to, and can, come to recognize oneself in the Other through reading and writing across languages and through engaging diverse cultural discourses.

To cultivate true cosmopolites, schooling remains a powerful mechanism. As formal education is increasingly made available to citizens of most nations, schools become a critical site for the cultivation of a cosmopolitan disposition. Students are exposed to multiple dialects and languages, and they develop different English proficiencies. What we need is to value their English styles and create a space for them to be used for talking with people beyond their communities. And more importantly, we must educate those who speak socially privileged styles about those who speak less-privileged ones, and vice versa. Reading and writing will come to play a major role in this endeavor because, in the cybernetic age, people, particularly youths, increasingly use written symbols and images in meaning making (Baron, 2008; Crystal, 2008). Written English captures well how one manages the multilingual and multicultural shades inherent in the use of English. We can bring CE into the center of one's schooling, making it both a vehicle for border-crossing communication and a launching pad for in-depth interrogations of social issues intricately mingled with language difference and prejudice.

However, in language classes and English-medium programs across the globe, an indiscriminate emphasis on Standard English has been the norm, a practice that promotes one style of CE at the expense of other styles. Whether in Anglophone or non-Anglophone nations, pragmatism fueled by economic opportunity and neoliberal discourse tends to value Standard English as premium cultural capital. Teachers in nations where languages other than English dominate often valorize high-stakes examinations, textbooks, and grammar books, many of which emphasize Standard English to such an extent that they penalize students for any deviations from it. They often dismiss nonstandard variants of English without understanding their social complexity and educational value. Along the same lines, to pursue the cultural capital of Standard English writing, influenced by American composition pedagogy, they typically place emphasis on exposition, relegating narration and argumentation to the margins (Connors, 1981; You, 2010). Students are consequently exposed to limited genres, writing skills (academic, technical, and business), and registers (standard, formal, and semiformal) that are marketable but typically impersonal. They are deprived of the textual spaces where their individual voices and styles can be heard and valued, where their diverse accents can be recognized and respected.

Conceptual obstacles, undoubtedly, stand in the way for those who wish to bring CE to the center. For one thing, many CE styles are what educational institutions and teachers want their students to get rid of or get over. They want to instill Standard English in their students for the alleged purpose of broader communication and, sometimes, national integrity. In Anglophone countries, some CE speakers are viewed as less educated and lower class, thus inferior. Such an attitude has been best illustrated by the Ebonics controversy surrounding the Oakland school board resolution in the late 1990s in the United States. When the school board initially recognized African American vernacular as a unique language system as well as the need to teach it along with Standard English, the resolution met with strong opposition in the national media and in education circles (Perry & Delpit, 1998; Rickford & Rickford, 2000). In contexts where languages other than English dominate, schools conceive most CE styles as barriers to, or interference with, one's educational achievement. To challenge these conceptualizations, three issues need to be tackled in order to legitimize the place of CE in schooling.

First, what are the characteristics of CE, and how do speakers use it for cross-border meaning making, particularly in educational contexts and contexts where languages other than English dominate? A rich understanding of CE is the first step toward altering pedagogical practice and policy in literacy education. Studies of English as an interlanguage are abundant; nevertheless, most of them deal with experimental, controlled settings. From the perspective of those promoting interlanguage, CE has typically been spoken of only in reference to native speaker norms (Bardovi-Harlig, 2006; Barron, 2012; Han & Tarone, 2014; James, 2007; Skehan, 2008), a practice that perpetuates a deficiency model among educators dealing with ethnic minority and non-native speaker students. Scholars in the WE camp, by contrast, while less judgmental, tend to view an individual's use of CE as part of a local speech community, forming a linguistic system of its own. Most recently, proponents of the ELF perspective have studied English in cross-border meaning making; however, they continue to work within the mystified and essentialized divisions of native and non-native speakers. While studying CE in a much broader context than scholars of second-language acquisition, these WE and ELF proponents seldom observe firsthand how English is used in written communication in educational contexts. In reality, CE mediates students' everyday life, in speech and writing, for both curricular and noncurricular purposes. What we need is to describe CE on its own terms in both educational and noneducational contexts. Recognizing that an abundant body of research in Anglophone nations already exists, studying CE in contexts where languages other than English dominate can broaden our knowledge of its characteristics and border-crossing functions.

Second, how can CE enable students' literacy development and subject learning simultaneously? With multiple symbol systems (each at a different proficiency level) at their disposal, students will use them in their reading, writing, speech, and subject learning. CE mediates these important processes in schools. Both language and subject teachers have the responsibility to help students develop their English ability and subject learning while enhancing their literacy in other languages and dialects, leading to what I call transliteracy. Despite the dynamic nature of each, CE styles are not equally used or valued across "literacy regimes," or structures of distribution, access, value, and use of literacy resources. Students encounter daunting challenges when they attempt to move from one regime to another using certain CE styles (Blommaert, 2010). In addition, as multilingual students juggle different CE styles, they often witness the attrition of their local language/dialect competence across domains. Recent years have witnessed an increasing number of studies that address the issues of crossing literacy regimes and language maintenance in kindergarten through twelfth grade (K-12) contexts (Cook, 2004; Gutierrez, Baquedano-Lopez, & Tejeda, 1999; Kenner, 2000; Moll & Gonzalez, 1994; Rampton, 1995; Vaish, 2008; Zisselsberger, Assaf, & Singh, 2012). Investigating these issues in postsecondary school situations will shed further light on the central role that CE can play in enabling or hindering transliterate skills and subject learning.

Third, when American teachers and students are formally introduced to CE, what might happen to their assumptions and attitudes about language, nation, and culture? In other words, can this informed exposure effect individual and collective transformations, moving them towards a cosmopolitan disposition? For a long time, American teachers and students have been subjugated to the monolingualist ideology concerning English: English is the default national language, and learning Standard English is critical to national integrity (Horner & Trimbur, 2002; Matsuda, 2006). The disgruntled first-year student in my class was victimized by this ideology. The CE construct places all speakers of English on equal footing despite their different statuses relative to power, class, race, and gender relations. It emphasizes the fact that everyone speaks with an accent, whether it be in an English-dominant style or non-English-dominant style. Certainly, language perceptions and receptions are indexical of widespread and deep-seated social inequalities. CE does not itself erase these very real differences and inequalities. Can this informed exposure engender in-depth conversations across borders, however one defines them, and create a cosmopolitan public sphere? Can this informed exposure and its ensuing conversations enhance literacy pedagogy at the same time? To promote and implement CE in school settings and society at large is to hold out hope that it can.

Book Overview

To address these three issues critical to literacy education, this book features a series of studies that examine cases where cosmopolitan practices are discernible. I have adopted Holton's (2009) working definition of cosmopolitanism to identify these cases: "Cosmopolitanism involves inter-cultural openness on a trans-national stage. . . . Openness may be combined in practice with elements of cultural or institutional closure, but the more closed the less cosmopolitan. . . . Trans-national openness . . . does entail some kind of mobility whether of the imagination, or through activities that engage with the wider world" (p. 117). In the first half of the book, I will examine English-mediated meaning making in online communities. Although the majority of the community members live in a certain nation, they demonstrate empathy, fraternity, and responsibility for people in other places within and outside their national boundaries. Pertinent to the interests of writing studies, I will focus on how they use English along with other symbolic resources to construct a cosmopolitan ethos and hybrid identities amidst emergent cultural formations. I also will study cross-border imaginations in works that have been celebrated primarily as national or ethnic literature. The writers of these works draw linguistic and cultural expressions from outside their nations and ethnicities to address both universal and local concerns. In the second half of the book, I will examine processes of border crossing in classrooms located in China and the United States. Guided by experienced teachers, students increasingly show openness to other ways of thinking and other ways of life, and so move away from cultural or institutional provincialism.

To study CE in these contexts, a single research method is hardly adequate. I have adopted a mixture of linguistic and rhetorical analysis to explore the characteristics of CE that emerge when it is enacted by users to achieve their communicative purposes. Because CE is a social practice, its features are necessarily strategic linguistic and rhetorical choices and negotiation strategies across local and translocal scales, instead of decontextualized linguistic forms. Using a linguistic method, I will analyze CE for its lexical, syntactic, and discoursal manifestations at individual and group levels. I am especially interested in how English users' particular language relations, past and present, have crystallized in features of their English. Unlike many WE scholars, however, I am not interested in establishing nativized or ELF norms based on native and non-native speaker divisions; instead, I challenge these norms. In terms of rhetorical analysis, by weighing communicative intents, contexts, audiences, and discursive choices, I will investigate how one makes meaning using CE. I will analyze the effects a speaker or a writer intends and the kinds of interpretations an audience may render. It is critical that I locate the use of CE in local and global systems of power and examine how the user negotiates with various power relations, including political, economic, racial, sexual, and class relations. The interweaving of linguistic and rhetorical analysis will allow me to explore how CE users wrestle with and sometimes cross linguistic, national, and other cultural boundaries.

As I move into pedagogical practices in the second half of the book, I will present empirical case studies, some of them ethnographic. To address how CE may mediate students' literacy practices and subject learning, case studies will allow me to focus on a single educational setting and observe students' reading and writing activities and teachers' pedagogical strategies. To address the possible transformations among American teachers and students following their informed exposure to and engagement with CE, I will examine English studies courses at my own institution. As a teacher-researcher, I will tread the borders between insider and outsider. I will not hide my assumptions and biases. I do not intend for my studies to have broad generalizability, but I hope that literacy teachers will find them interesting and relevant to their own contexts. To mitigate my biases in interpreting students' literacy practices, I showed my findings to them for member checking. Case studies do not exclude linguistic and rhetorical lenses. Both are indispensable when it comes to analyzing oral and textual interactions. Every utterance, every text achieves its meanings in specific contexts of interaction.

Selecting and implementing a methodology for exploring a cosmopolitan perspective is not without its potential dangers, though. In my analysis I will pay special attention to cosmopolitan moments, moments where individuals have crossed linguistic and cultural boundaries. Such moments lay bare the intricate human connections amidst these boundaries and reveal the transliterate arts that individuals have adopted in online communications, in literary creativity, in academic exercises, and in pedagogy. However, if I'm not careful, my research could easily stay at a superficial level, focusing on certain linguistic features, rhetorical strategies, or pedagogical techniques. It could render the lived experiences of individuals and of their communities obscure, and it could easily neglect the importance of community affiliations and social positioning that make one's voices authentic (Gilyard, 2016; Lyons, 2000; Royster, 1996). Therefore, in my research I have adopted a historical-materialistic attitude. I will consider the history, the sociopolitical relations, and the material effects involved in individuals' and communities' literacy practices. I will listen to their voices with the intent of situating them within their unique personal and community histories and experiences.

In alignment with the cosmopolitan perspective, this book practices academic transliteracy. It involves endeavors deployed in both translingual and transcultural dimensions. To highlight the translingual nature of English, I have examined CE practices where English is intermingled with Japanese, Chinese, French, or other languages with the boundaries blurred. Since part of the premise of the book is embracing language difference, all excerpts from CE texts will be reproduced "as is," with nonstandard spellings and grammar intact. I translated non-English elements in these texts, trying to maintain both their meanings and forms. Further, in developing my arguments, I drew expressions, metaphors, and tropes from different languages and rhetorical traditions. In the transcultural dimension, I consciously worked across disciplinary boundaries. I joined conversations in writing studies, cosmopolitan studies, migration studies, comparative literature, and applied linguistics (sociolinguistics, WE, ELF). I have tried to foreground conversations and concerns in these fields rather than cherry-pick theories and concepts developed therein in a decontextualized fashion. Translating across languages and disciplines has pushed me, and hopefully will push the reader as well, to reassess and modify my assumptions and practices in writing studies as I encountered unfamiliar languages, research traditions, and institutional frames. In short, and as also advocated by Horner, NeCamp, and Donahue (2011), practicing transliteracy helps us move beyond English monolingualism in both our scholarship and teaching.

This book emphasizes local-global connections, and the data analyzed were gathered across geopolitical locations. "Local," as well as "global," can be understood in different ways. Local can refer to locality, meaning geographic and cultural localness of sites and contexts. Or when used in relation to global, it refers more generally to the property of being isolated or individual. For example, Latour (1996) identifies globalizing "with the shifting out of individuals as well as the knitting together of interactions" (p. 240). Thus, local and global may not describe pregiven social structures but perspectives on networks to which circulating bodies, texts, and objects give rise. In literacy practices, local refers to reading and writing activities among individuals within a certain cultural group or a particular social or cultural formation; global refers to literacy practices moving beyond these local formations and interactions and being knitted together. Modern communication technologies as well as communication systems, such as English, are globalizing instruments (Brandt & Clinton, 2002). In the notion of "sociolinguistic scales," or semiotized space-times, local (micro) refers to personal, contextualized, storied, and affective, while global (macro) refers to abstract, general, categorical, timeless, and spaceless (Blommaert, 2007, 2010; Leander & Lovvorn, 2006). In this book, local refers to locality, individuality, insularity, provincialism, or nationalism.

When writers use English, a globalizing instrument, they may evoke a cosmopolitan audience, an audience beyond local groups. Whether composing on social media or in classrooms, writers usually assume their intended or invoked audiences can understand them. Of course once their texts are made public, they must entertain the possibility of being (mis)read by both geographically and culturally distant audiences. Their composing activities are always local, and global as well, due to the use of globalizing instruments and the writers' implication in global sociopolitical and economic market forces (Engelson, 2011). Their activities are deeply wedded to and constitutive of local-global cultural practices. While constructing local-global meanings, CE may also enable such writers to gain perspectives unrestrained by the boundaries of class, gender, race, and sexuality. It is the omnipresent use of CE and its ability to transform human relations locally and globally that begs a more in-depth understanding of it.

This book, while focusing on postsecondary situations, forges connections between in-school and out-of-school literacy practices. Previous Anglophone studies on CE-related practices have focused on out-of-school contexts (e.g., Higgins, 2009; Martin-Jones & Jones, 2000; Lee, 2007a, 2007b; Sebba, Mahootian, & Jonsson, 2012; Yi, 2010; You, 2011); some have also examined CE styles practiced in K-12 settings (e.g., Skerrett & Bomer, 2013). I have crossed these boundaries by, first, studying CE in both in-school and out-of-school literacy practices and by, second, conscientiously bringing out-of-school textual practices into English studies courses in my own teaching. The book endeavors to capture the kinds of crossing that are taking place among CE users. For example, I will describe transliterate practices among Japanese adults, Chinese white collar workers, and literary writers in out-of-school contexts (chapters 2, 3, and 4). Then I will introduce how I have connected out-of-school literacy practices to a series of writing-related undergraduate and graduate courses (chapters 6, 7, and 8). In a transpacific virtual exchange project described in chapter 8, for instance, some Chinese college students were connected with American writing teachers through modern information technologies. The former not only exposed the latter to the ways English is used outside the United States, but they also profoundly challenged these teachers' assumptions about teaching writing.

Like a string, English connects people of different cultures, ethnicities, and classes, and creates local-global communities as it penetrates different regions and social sectors. Scholarly discussions on cultural rhetoric arising in and between these communities tend to focus on tensions and conflicts, casting cultures and languages as discrete and bounded. In chapter 2, I argue that once English enters local cultural practice, it mediates conflicts and tensions and creates cultural synthesis. To account for the ethical use of language in local-global contexts, I propose ethos as a theoretical lens. Taking as an example the online communicative practices of a group of Japanese adult readers of English books, I show how they construct ethos through website configurations and contexts of interaction. Drawing on diverse linguistic and cultural resources, they develop themes, rhetorical modes, and unique styles in their sharing of reading experiences. Their transliterate practices subvert language and cultural norms defined by nation and ethnicity, giving rise to new cultural formations. With its potential to construct ethos, or "dwelling places" where the inhabitants can feel at home while constructing knowledge, identities, and alliances beyond those of their homes, English becomes cosmopolitan.

While this Japanese reading group offers us a glimpse of how English mediates the formation of a small local-global community, it also begs an understanding of English in a broader context. Indeed, the nearly universal requirement of English studies in schools has given rise to an increasingly English-literate public in nations where languages other than English dominate. Scholars have widely accepted English used in these contexts as a national or ethnic variety, one of many World Englishes. In chapter 3, I argue that the WE construct has failed to capture the constant and fluid movement of peoples, languages, and cultural practices in the world at present. Adopting the lens of domestic diaspora, I examine Chinese white collar workers' English use as they seek to represent themselves as a distinct group and to articulate their diasporic consciousness on a popular website. Their communication reveals not only patterns of social and personal behaviors belonging to the new Chinese workforce but also the symbolic strategies they develop for achieving agency. Rather than confining themselves to bilingual resources, they actively draw from multiple languages, multiple cultures, and the multimodal functions of digital technologies. Their idiosyncratic, fluid use of English defies the time-honored view of Chinese English as a discrete national variety.

Transliteracy is also used by writers for literary creativity. Braj B. Kachru's (1990) mapping of "bilingual creativity" has been a powerful theoretical construct for understanding how multilingual authors write in English. From a historical perspective, his exploration into contact literature has fallen primarily within the discourse of postcolonial nation building and multiculturalism, favoring a bounded, structuralist perspective on nation, culture, and language. In chapter 4, I propose an alternative, less-bounded approach to complicate the Kachruvian one. This alternative focuses on how writers draw resources from fluid cultural forms and processes; how they capitalize on the multiple languages, dialects, and media available to them; and how they develop their own CE styles to achieve intended literary effects. To illustrate this less-bounded approach to understanding transliterate creativity, I will examine Raja Rao's *Kanthapura* (1938), Xiaolu Guo's A *Concise Chinese-English Dictionary for Lovers* (2007), and Sapphire's *Push* (1997). Embracing a less-bounded approach, we can better account for the contradictions and paradoxes that multilingual writers have to wrestle with when publishing in English.

After establishing the parameters within which multilingual speakers have used CE, one cannot help wondering how far their meaning-making practices can travel as they or their texts move across communities and nations. Along with other scholars, Blommaert (2008) highlights the existence of literacy regimes that may facilitate or impede the migration of texts and language practices. In chapter 5, I argue that by emphasizing the rigidity and normality of regimes, Blommaert has failed to give adequate account of the agency of the parties involved in local literacy practice. In school contexts little is known about how subject teachers, being literacy brokers and representing elite literacy regimes, accommodate multilingual students' literacy challenges in non-English-dominant contexts. Therefore I will examine American professors' brokerage in an English-medium summer school in Shanghai, China, where they taught courses in the humanities and social sciences. The study reveals that some subject teachers appreciated unfamiliar meanings and voices in student texts, which exhibited features of grassroots literacy. In addition, they developed strategies for helping students expand their linguistic and rhetorical repertoires, enabling them to negotiate between literacy regimes. Years of transliterate training and practice had prepared these teachers to cross literacy regimes and to meet their students halfway.

English education for multilingual students should never deter the development of the literacy skills valued in their homes or local communities. Because of the symbiosis of English and other languages in use in multilingual societies, clear demarcations between languages are often difficult to make (Blackledge & Creese, 2010; Canagarajah, 2013a; Garcia, 2009; Jørgensen, 2008). The ability to function literately in discrete languages is an ideal supported by monolingual, nationalist assumptions. English writing, as a local practice, involves multiple languages and cultures; hence it is a site for the development of transliteracy. In chapter 6, I examine the ways that multilingual students address diverse audiences in an academic writing course. The communications involved in their composing processes strongly support the idea that languages don't function as discrete systems in the multilingual mind. Student-teacher conferences held during the course offer ample examples of translingual practice in speaking and writing where this is the case. My students' literacy practices show both the challenges and possibilities of crossing cultural boundaries and assuming multiple identities in academic discourse. Their literacy practices also highlight the ethical values of teaching writing: teachers can and should help students address issues that matter both to them as intelligent beings and to local communities. Inquiry into academic transliteracy matters not only for students' abilities to cross linguistic and cultural boundaries but also for their abilities to cause material consequences in local and translocal contexts.

Writing scholars and teachers have debated how to address language diversity in American universities for decades. However, the majority sentiment in writing studies has continued to hover over issues of nationhood and disciplinary boundaries. In our study and teaching of language issues, we continue to focus on English—its varieties, styles, and genres—and its fictive relations with other languages within a nation (Trimbur, 2010). To attend to cross-language relations in academia and in our lives, we need to transcend our localities and engage students in language relations across disciplines and nations. To that end, in chapter 7, I introduce a transliteracy pedagogy that I have practiced with my American students over the last few years. Starting with code-switching, this pedagogy teaches students language analysis and engages them in studying and practicing transliteracy. Tracing two students' reading and writing activities outside my class reveals that my pedagogy was actually part of a transliteracy pedagogy already at work in English studies at my institution, a finding that challenges writing studies to quicken its translingual turn. We must attend more seriously to transliterate practices within and across disciplines.

We need to find ways to bring writing teachers into direct contact with multilingual students of different cultural backgrounds. Research shows that teachers tend to demonstrate more confidence in working with language learners when provided with opportunities to link conceptual tools with practical tools in their training. After reviewing current practices in writing-teacher development, in chapter 8, I propose a border-crossing model for writing programs and graduate education. Through communication technologies, writing teachers are introduced to multilingual students and their writing from outside the United States. After a period of intense interaction, teachers can gain valuable practical knowledge about the needs and resources of these writers and the characteristics of their writing, an assertion tested and found to be true as I implemented this model in my collaborative teaching with colleagues in China. This chapter explains how an infrastructure can be established in local programs and how this model, mediated by theoretical concepts and CE styles, may help teachers develop expertise in teaching multilingual writers from both inside and outside the nation.

2

Arts of the Dwelling Place

The relationship between English and culture, ethnicity, and nation has long concerned language scholars, giving rise to a series of theoretical constructs. Among them, contrastive rhetoric and contact zone are probably the most widely used in writing studies. Initiated by Kaplan (1966), contrastive rhetoric seeks to understand the thought patterns exhibited in texts by writers of different cultural backgrounds. Contrastive rhetoricians are interested in these writers' cultural upbringing and literate experiences, which are purported to influence the ways in which they use English and other languages. Contrastive rhetoric research has heightened our awareness of cultural factors that may impact writers from countries where languages other than English dominate. At the same time, however, Donahue (2009), Kubota (1997, 1999, 2001a, 2002), Spack (1997b), and Zamel (1997) critiqued contrastive rhetoric research for having essentialized cultures and languages, viewing them as bounded, static, and deterministic. Owing to these criticisms, dynamic views of culture, language, and text have been proposed to account for these writers' composing acts (Atkinson, 2004; Connor, 1996, 2008; Matsuda, 1997; Zamel, 1997). For example, Matsuda (1997) proposed a dynamic model of second-language writing, in which meaning for both writer and reader is mediated by the text in a particular writing situation. In a shared discourse community, the two parties bring their distant and immediate backgrounds to bear on a text. By focusing on contextual factors rather than on broad, abstract cultural and language categories, Matsuda understands English users as engaged in a transliterate activity: writer and reader marshal resources from languages and cultures when composing and interpreting a text. Building on a dynamic understanding of culture, Connor (2008) proposed an intercultural-rhetoric framework in which culture is particularized to include "small cultures" and texts are studied as part of dynamic, interactive patterns of communication in their social and institutional contexts.

Contrastingly, English has also been examined along cultural, ethnical, and national lines using a spatial metaphor, "contact zones," which are defined by Pratt (1991) as "social spaces where cultures meet, clash, and grapple with each other, often in contexts of highly asymmetrical relations of power, such as colonialism, slavery, or their aftermaths as they are lived out in many parts of the world today" (p. 34). Analyzing two historiographic texts written by Peruvians in the early seventeenth century, Pratt identifies the strategies, or the "arts of the contact zone," that the colonized developed for addressing the Spaniards, the colonizer, in the latter's language. Strategies that she identifies include transculturation, critique, autoethnography, collaboration, bilingualism, mediation, parody, denunciation, imaginary dialogue, and vernacular expression. Scholars in rhetoric and writing studies have adopted contact zones to explore critical issues arising from class, race, and gender differences in the United States (Bizzell, 1994; Canagarajah, 1997; Cooper, 2004; Wolff, 2002) and across national borders (You, 2010). For example, Canagarajah (1997) studied how, in one of his university writing classes, African American students used vernacular to celebrate their ethnic solidarity and resist the hegemonic thrusts of academic discourses. The study highlights how strategic uses of various forms of English have helped to mediate and reconcile cultural conflicts in the classroom.

To understand Cosmopolitan English (CE) in context, contrastive rhetoric and contact zone can be both helpful and limiting. Contrastive rhetoric offers explanations of how writers from non-English-dominant nations make textual choices in English-dominant contexts. Contact zone theory is instrumental when examining social spaces where cultures conflict and clash. While *contact* suggests touching, unity, or a genial relationship, as in the literate arts of transculturation and collaboration, as Hall and Rosner (2004) point out, Pratt's definition of a contact zone in several of her publications highlights "the breach, break, rupture, or split that results from the clashing and grappling" that she imagined (p. 107). English has today entered the linguistic repertoires of communities in different parts of the world, communities not easily definable by nation, culture, or ethnicity. These communities can be learning communities, advocacy groups, transnational corporations, or online gaming societies who adopt English as a shared language. When studying the English use and cultural discourse generated in these current and emergent communities, the constructs of contrastive rhetoric or contact zone alone can be limiting. From a procedural and dialectic perspective, the conflicts, contradictions, and paradoxes generated as cultures initially collide and entangle will in general give rise to, if not be resolved through, a synthesis of these cultures, manifesting in the birth of a new culture. In any social space, residents may use the arts of the contact zone to negotiate and resolve tensions and conflicts as they move toward cultural synthesis. Highlighting differences, tensions, and conflicts in cultural encounters, neither contrastive rhetoric nor contact zone theory has given adequate attention to cultural synthesis mediated by a globalizing language.

Further, both constructs have given limited attention to ethics as critical for studying language use. Ethics refers to the body of moral principles or values that govern or distinguish a particular community, which contributes to the formation of its collective identity and serves to guide its practices. In the scholarship on both contrastive rhetoric and contact zones, ethics has been subsumed under discourse conventions. For example, contrastive rhetoricians believe that if they help students recognize and acquire the conventions of a discourse community, the students will succeed in joining that community. These conventions index the moral principles and values of the target community; joining the community means accepting these principles and values. Similarly, in contact zone studies, ethics always stands behind the literate arts of marginalized groups, which reflect (and often serve to negotiate) the tensions between moral value systems of different cultures. When attention shifts to how English enables or hinders the formation of a cosmopolitan disposition and practice, ethics should be studied alongside, rather than under, discourse conventions.

We need a different theory capable of accounting for the ways in which speakers and writers construct discursive spaces through an ethical use of language. To study English in current and emergent communities, and more particularly to study English's ability to effect cultural synthesis and cross-border attitudes and practices, I propose the ancient Greek term *ethos*—meaning both "moral character" and "dwelling places"—as such a broader theory.[1] In feminist studies Reynolds (1993, 2004) also suggested the potential of ethos to open up spaces in which to study writers' subject positions or identity formation, especially to understand how they establish authority and enact responsibility from positions not traditionally considered authoritative. Centering on how individuals and groups construct credibility based on moral values specific to new cultural formations, ethos theory compels us to focus on how communities carve new spaces for their members, both to occupy and to deliberate on matters of common interest.

Ethos as the Dwelling Place

The ancient Greeks never agreed upon a single definition of ethos nor the means to achieve it. For Isocrates (1982), ethos refers to an honorable name and reputation that a speaker has gained among his fellow citizens. It is also one's inherent ability to use language ethically, an ability cultivated through rhetorical training. It is both a legitimating source for and a praiseworthy effect of the ethical practices of the speaker's art. In contrast, Aristotle (2007) views ethos as constructed by the speaker's artful language. He identifies three means of securing persuasion in public discourse: appeal to logical reasoning (logos), appeal to the audience's emotions (pathos), and appeal to the speaker's intelligence and goodwill (ethos). He places the ethical burden largely on the speaker. To establish ethos, the speaker must demonstrate three characteristics in his or her speech: good sense or practical wisdom, good moral character (virtue), and goodwill toward the audience. Apparently, for Aristotle, ethos is inseparable from logos and pathos: without logical reasoning, one does not form accurate opinions; without knowing the audience's values, temperament, and predisposition, one can hardly determine what type of goodwill to express. Aristotle's concept of ethos, however, has two major limitations. First, he values only artistic means to building ethos. He maintains that ethos must be established by the speech itself and may not depend on the actual, historical, and personal characteristics of the speaker. Second, because Greek rhetorical education focused on verbal persuasion, he, of course, excluded nonverbal acts in his discussion of ethos.

The Greek theories of ethos can be enriched by Confucian thoughts on communication. In Confucianism, an individual establishes his or her ethos by exemplifying virtuous traits, such as humility, wisdom, and good character in daily ritualistic behaviors. Confucius holds that a harmonious community is built when individuals perform rituals, including speaking and writing, appropriate to their unequal social status and the social context. As multimodal symbolic configurations, rituals work only if a strong, universal societal bond exists despite all of a society's hierarchical and segmentary oppositions and contradictions. Ritual performance impresses on both performers and receivers a realization of a common human bond among members of a society, thus potentially undoing the ordinary ties of social structure. As rituals carry community-shared values, by participating in or performing rituals, one can easily recognize and become identified with those respective values; thus, persuasion is automatic (Confucius, 1989; You, 2006). In Zixia's conceptualization of a gentleman, introduced in chapter 1, a cultivated individual can potentially transcend the structures and boundaries of the community and turn all within the Four Seas into brothers and sisters. Further, for Confucius, individuals with higher social status, such as ancient sages, rulers, and parents, carry rhetorical authority, that is, ethos, when they speak. The same could be said to hold in a close-knit community, where widely practiced verbal and nonverbal behaviors become rituals for community building. They are ethical practices conducive to making the cultural space livable.

More recently, twentieth-century philosopher Heidegger (1993) reminded us that *ethos* in fact means abode, dwelling place, or the open region that humans inhabit. The spatiotemporal character of human beings is the place where "being" discloses and shows itself as something that can be thought about, understood, and expressed in symbolic form. According to Heidegger, there is a perpetual calling for humans to assume ethical responsibility, through thought and action, for bringing a sense of order and meaning to our lives. Everyone is called upon to act as rhetorical architects, using symbolic construction to create and invite others into a place where they can live and feel at home. Extending the architecture metaphor, "one might also speak of the work as an 'edifying' discourse . . . whose communal character takes form as the artist uses materials (e.g., tropes, figures, topics, arguments, narratives, emotions) to attract attention, maintain our interest, and encourage us to judge the work as praiseworthy and persuasive" (Hyde, 2004, p. xxi). These discursive and nondiscursive "materials" constitute the arts of the dwelling places.

To account for the ethics of communication in cyberspace, Fleckenstein (1999) developed the useful concept of CyberEthos. She argues that, in modern times, it is difficult to locate ethos in a single definition or speech act. The origin of ethos has been attributed dissimilarly in different historical periods and across various cultures. Just as Aristotelian and Confucian theories of ethos have demonstrated, its point of origin shifted from speaker to both speaker and audience, and from within speech to by/through/beyond speech. In a world where boundaries between reality and virtuality are blurred, Fleckenstein argues that "ethos is composed of and by permeable boundaries, subject to the limits of both time and space, resisting allocation to anything but its context and the constancy of its own relationships" (1999, p. 191). Specifically, she views ethos as "a living network consisting of rhetor, text, audience, and context" (2005, p. 326). Ethos in cyberspace transcends any single element of a rhetorical situation; it is derived instead from the interaction and relationships among all its elements. CyberEthos becomes a strategy for securing communal and individual survival in cyberspace; it becomes a heuristic that encourages us to live virtuous virtual lives. Virtue in the cybernetic age manifests in our various efforts to establish a healthy balance, or harmonious human relations.

CyberEthos requires that we understand ethos as systemic. According to Fleckenstein (1999), we can ask questions about the ways in which the network, or "the fluid superordinate systemic sign-reality," is constituted; the means in which certain new information is recognized and transformed in the network; and the "key" by which the network can be read by its initiates. Further, she suggests investigating the adaptive controls (feedback/feedforward loops) created by the system to maintain its CyberEthos (p. 195). In short, CyberEthos requires that we examine the intersection among all elements of the network to understand the network's character, which will lend persuasive power to discourse in the network.

Thus, to understand ethos in an online community, we can observe how community members use linguistic and nonlinguistic resources to construct a cultural space where they can live, feel at home, and deliberate on matters of interest. It is a space where cultures may meet, clash, and synthesize. Specifically, we can examine the relationships within the network, or how members construct the network and maintain its healthy balance using adaptive controls. The way the network is constituted, controlled, and regulated can suggest to us the community ethics, or the communally valued principles of practice. However, individuals may not always embrace this communal ethics. Instead they may negotiate or even contest it. Therefore, in the meantime we can observe the interactions among members, studying how they demonstrate, or not, practical wisdom, virtue, and goodwill through both verbal and nonverbal means, including those of a communal and ritualistic nature. An investigation of both the relationship within the network and interactions among the members can offer a vantage point for observing how English along with other languages participates in the "edifying discourse," particularly how it helps to build or collapse cultural "walls."

The SSS Community

In the rest of the chapter, I will examine ethos in an online community. A majority of the community members reside in Japan, a country where English is commonly viewed as imported, as foreign. Of a voluntary nature, the community consists of Anglo-American authors, Japanese university professors, high school teachers, businessmen, and housewives who are interested in the "Start with Simple Stories (SSS)" method of reading English. According to this method, readers start by reading picture books with only a few words on each page, and they gradually read more difficult books. Reading a wide range of fictional and nonfictional books from outside Japan evidently helped the Japanese members develop understanding of and empathy with other peoples. They are taught "Three Golden Rules": avoid using dictionaries while reading, skip over difficult words, and stop reading when the book is boring or too difficult (Furukawa, 2006). In 2001, Professor Kunihide Sakai and his colleagues established an SSS extensive reading study group to spread this reading method. The group runs a website for readers across Japan. The website hosts a bulletin board system (BBS) consisting of a number of Japanese and English boards, where the 2,200 registered members "can write what they think of a book they have read, and discuss problems faced while reading books" (Kawate & Furukawa, 2005, para. 9).

I will focus on a single English board that Professor Akio Furukawa started in December 2002. By the end of 2014, a total of 1,198 messages had been posted by more than one hundred individuals, forming around 270 threads. The relatively steady member participation on the board indicates that ethos played a crucial role in holding the members together and in encouraging them to keep reading. The ethos of the board became a dwelling place for members to construct communal knowledge and achieve shared goals. The rise and development of the board offers us an opportunity to observe how an English-using community deals with conflicts and tensions arising in cultural encounters and how the cultural entanglement leads to cultural synthesis. At a microlevel it also presents a case for observing how English along with other symbol systems, while maintaining local solidarity, generates translocal, cosmopolitan consciousness, practice, and connections at the same time.

The data to be examined consist of the website (http://www.seg.co.jp/sss/), members' online posts, and other materials published on the website. I observed the English board for several years without taking part in any discussion to avoid influencing the community's discursive activities. To study how the network is constituted, I examined the site map by clicking all the hyperlinks on the index page as well as links on pages immediately under the index page. To understand how the information flows in the network, I studied the message-posting mechanism and the message structure. I also studied the information pages written for the community members and performed open thematic coding to understand the established community regulations (virtue).

To identify the ethos-building "materials" used by the members, I examined all of the 270 threads. Following the general steps for developing a grounded theory, I went through the data and marked each thread with a series of codes related to theme (topics), genre (modes of discourse), and rhetorical strategy (tropes and figures). I assigned each theme a code, such as "reading experience" [1], "response to a book" [2], "English writing" [3], "family/personal issues" [4], and "announcing events" [5]. Genres also received codes, such as "narrative" [1], "poetry" [2], "rhymes" [3], "short story" [4], and "script for talk shows" [5]. For rhetorical strategies, I coded them this way: "call-response" [1], "compliment" [2], "code-meshing" [3], "cultural trope" [4], "metaphor" [5], "simile" [6], "rhyming" [7], and "alliteration" [8]. To illustrate, I coded a thread starting with post 78, to be discussed in a later section, as follows:

> Theme: response to a book [2]
> Genre: narrative [1], poetry [2]
> Rhetorical strategies: call-response [1], compliment [2], rhyming [7], alliteration [8].

Thus the codes for this thread are [2]—[1, 2]—[1, 2, 7, 8]. The codes for all threads were grouped first based on theme and then based on genre. Under a certain theme or genre, the widely used rhetorical strategies thus came into relief. While performing thematic coding, I watched out for instances and moments indicative of cultural conflicts and tensions and of cultural synthesis. To help me see what I otherwise would miss as important ethos-building resources, I showed those moments to a Japanese scholar residing in the United States for her reading.

Next we will consider how ethos is derived from both the relationship within the network and the interactions between members. Specifically, we will look into the way the network system was constituted, the adaptive controls used to sustain the system, and the discursive strategies used by members to construct ethos. An examination of these three areas will show that ethos as dwelling place and moral character is variously constructed through cultural synthesis, or the blending of languages, values, experiences, and emotions with or without reconciliation among them.

Mapping the Network

One way to understand how the network is constituted is to map out the website that the English board members all visit. The site architecture blends both universal/global and local design features. Like organizations and businesses seeking to globalize their web presence (Singh & Boughton, 2005), the SSS study group designed webpages for audiences of different linguistic backgrounds. In grasping how the entire superordinate system maps out, it may be helpful to understand the Japanese index page as a parent page and both the English index page and the bulletin boards as sibling pages. One could also understand the Japanese index page as an entry point for accessing the spaces occupied by the bulletin boards. Either way, the English board cannot be separated from the larger network; English is controlled, neatly connected to both Japanese and web-authorizing codes, such as html and xhtml.

The Japanese index page displays some universal design features. Like many other websites, it uses a two-frame structure, with the left frame reserved for navigation. In the left frame are three groups of navigation links: exchanges between extensive reading learners, a book guide for extensive reading, and various materials concerning the SSS method. In the right frame are a brief introduction to the SSS method and updates on the study group's activities. Most members, particularly first-time visitors to the board, start from the Japanese index page and browse its linked pages. As shown in figure 2.1, except for two links in English in the top corners, all other navigation links and information on the page are provided in Japanese. Such a Japanese-dominant site map creates a familiar, comfortable feel for the Japanese members, who can browse most linked pages easily and, if they desire, converse with other members on the Japanese bulletin board.

In contrast, the English index page shows more local design features. When organization and business websites provide their index page in a different

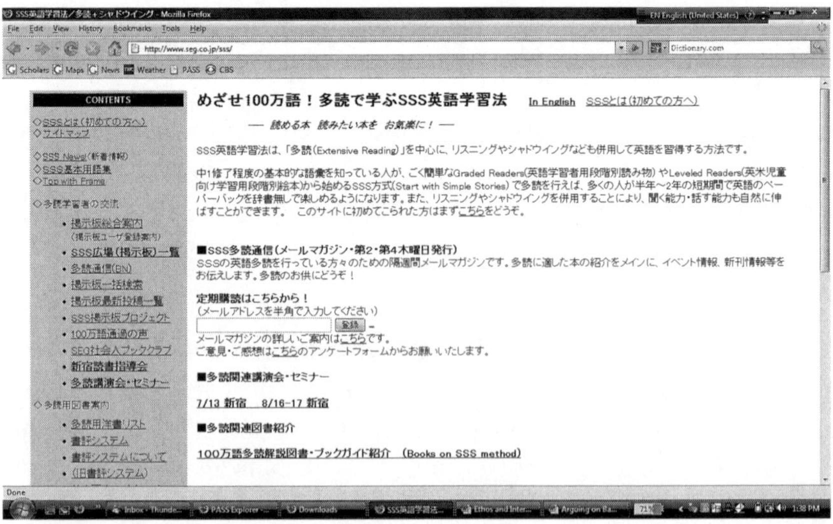

Figure 2.1. Index page of the SSS website, including a two-frame structure and navigation links, two examples of universal design features.

language, that page's features and layout tend to closely mirror those of the original language index page. However, the SSS English index page deviates from this common practice. It adopts one frame rather than the two apparent on the Japanese page, and it features a more elaborate introduction to the SSS method than does its counterpart. The introduction explains the Japanese context that necessitates the SSS method and the SSS study group's ways of promoting it. While the Japanese index page features a dozen navigation links, there is only one on the English index page labeled "To Bulletin Board in English." These design features indicate that in addition to Japanese users of the site, the study group has international English-speaking users in mind. Such users, if unable to read Japanese, would gain a basic understanding of the SSS method by visiting the English index page.

The ambience of the English index page and board is created through the superordinate network, the structure, and constitutive elements. It includes feelings of exoticness, support, and control. For example, suppose a Japanese person has heard about the SSS method, the study group, or the website. Upon entering the Japanese index page, she is surrounded by familiar linguistic and cultural symbols. She browses various pages in Japanese, becomes more interested, and then clicks "In English" in the top right corner of the Japanese index page. She opens the English index page and then clicks "To Bulletin Board in English" in the right corner. Once she enters the English board, she again meets with Japanese tabs at the top of the page (figure 2.2), which provide her pathways to return to the Japanese space anytime she feels uncomfortable or bored in the English space. Thus, the English board becomes like a Starbucks built adjacent to an Ippodo tea shop in Kyoto. While distinct, both shops employ Japanese linguistic and cultural symbols. The general ambience of the website entices the members to step in, while simultaneously allowing them to disengage whenever they are so inclined. Shuttling between the Japanese and English boards, the members inhabit an in-between space constructed of both local and translocal symbols.

Nevertheless, the Japanese and English spaces are not clear-cut due to transliteration. At least five linguistic symbol systems, including English, are used on the Japanese pages and boards. Take the Japanese index page as an example. English writing is blended in using expressions like "extensive reading," "graded readers," and "leveled readers." Three Japanese symbol systems appear: hiragana and kanji, or adopted Chinese characters, are used for native or naturalized Japanese words or to represent Japanese grammatical elements such as "併用して英語を習得する方法です"; katakana is used for foreign words

Figure 2.2. English bulletin board, featuring Japanese tabs to create a comfortable space of both local and translocal symbols for the website user.

and names, loanwords, onomatopoeia, scientific names, and sometimes to replace kanji or hiragana for emphasis, as with "リスニングやシャドウイング," "メールマガジン," and "メールアドレス." These katakana expressions are in fact onomatopoeia mimicking the phonetics of English expressions like "listening and shadowing," "e-mail magazine" and "e-mail address." And of course web design language anchors the superordinate system, shaping all other symbols and communication. The percolation of English symbols through English writing, katakana, and web-authoring codes have transformed these Japanese pages into multilingual spaces.

These spaces are cultural statements, too, providing some of the first instances of cosmopolitanism in the making in the SSS community. These spaces are sedimented discourses drawn from local and translocal histories. The so-called Japanese writing system, involving kanji, hiragana, and katakana, already marks the connections and commitments that Japanese people have historically had with other East Asian communities, regional polities, and Western nations. The English expressions and the web-authoring codes index their contemporary and ongoing engagement with discourses of English in Japan through the institutionalized teaching and learning of the language as well as Japanese people's encounter with modern technologies. When these symbol systems appear simultaneously in these spaces, they make powerful cultural statements, inviting communications of a boundary-crossing nature.

Establishing Adaptive Controls

Without adaptive controls, a network of information flows may lose balance. The adaptive controls can be divided into two types: nonverbal posting structures built by web designers and verbal instructions developed by the SSS study group to regulate members' online behaviors. Blending common practices of BBS and Japanese societal values, these two control mechanisms direct information flow and broadly define the nature of online interaction.

Like bulletin board postings in other virtual communities, the posting mechanism perpetuates both hierarchy and equality at the same time. As figure 2.2 shows, each thread is identified by indentation. Posts are lined up one below the other, with the lower one indented a few spaces, inexplicitly honoring the authors of higher-level (earlier) posts. Such a hierarchy ensures that information flows top-down as messages are posted chronologically. Such a structure also allows for equality. While posters can follow a certain thread, they can also start a new one on a different topic. As figure 2.2 shows, post number 1094 started a thread on the topic "Dead Until Dark," followed by post numbers 1098, 1101, and 1110. However, post number 1099 started a new thread with the topic "Why kids repeat the same phrase three times?" Members who entered the forum later can come back and post under either of the two threads. Thus, although each thread is organized hierarchically and linearly to facilitate information flows, posters also have the freedom to direct the information flow in multiple directions, posting under whichever threads they choose.

The hierarchical posting design has influenced the information structure of many posts. Within a particular post, members tend to copy previous posters' messages and type theirs underneath for clarity and focus. While the hierarchical posting structure is universally applied across electronic bulletin boards, the hierarchical information structure is local (cf. examples of BBS postings in You, 2008). The information structure suggests respect and courtesy among many posters, which can be confirmed by the polite language they use (see examples in the next section, "Building Individual Ethos").

In addition to posting structure, controls adapted through verbal means are equally crucial in constructing ethos. As with other virtual communities, the study group developed guidelines for regulating information flow and online behaviors. When someone wants to post a new message, he or she is reminded to read the "basic information about the BBS," "guidelines for BBS contributions," and "privacy of participants" at the top of the screen. Like netiquette rules, these informational pages, all written in Japanese, define for members the site's ethic, or virtue. By articulating the virtue, the study group in effect established a communal ethos.

Virtue is first reflected in the members' language. The propriety of discursive acts is succinctly described in the three principles of online contribution: 楽しく・優しく・思いやりを (pleasantly, kindly, and thoughtfully). Specifically, the study group suggests the subject matter to be addressed, the kinds of language to be used, and the ways to carry out constructive discussions. According to the "guidelines for BBS contributions," the group wants to see exchanges among users of the SSS method, reports on their reading amounts, and the struggles they experienced in reading. In terms of language use, members are advised to avoid speeches that would hurt, marginalize, or disrespect others. They are asked not to post emotional messages or use emotional words for argumentation. To produce constructive discussions, one is advised "to speak slowly, to choose her words carefully, and to use appropriate methods" ("Guidelines," section 3).

Virtue is also reflected in online behavior related to privacy. As the number of BBS participants increased and as offline meetings also began to increase, the study group decided to regulate online activities to protect participants' privacy. Therefore, it is now suggested that BBS participants not reveal certain information about themselves and others, including their real name, age, gender, and address. As a general rule, BBS participants are also advised either to avoid sharing photographs in which individuals could be identified or to obtain consent from photographed individuals before sharing their photographs online.

Virtue, therefore, is not abstract for this community. It is articulated and perpetuated in explicit, stated precepts about appropriate verbal and nonverbal online behaviors. It combines both local (Japanese) and translocal (Internet) values related to social propriety. As the study group stated, "掲示板も、一般社会も同じです" (the BBS is the same as the general society) ("Guidelines," section 2). Without making a distinction between Japanese and English, prescribed virtuous practices are equally applied to the latter. That means when Japanese members communicate in an allegedly foreign language, they need to act in a gentlemanly manner as Zixia had advised Sima Niu to do millennia ago. The group has defined virtue for this particular "society" using adaptive controls. However, just like in any society, the prescribed virtuous practices only represent the values and interests of a certain group in power; the prescriptions will be followed by some and actively negotiated or even altogether ignored by others.

Building Individual Ethos

Although the network afforded members a seemingly coherent CyberEthos, giving them a sense of order, control, and respect, members negotiated and appropriated the collective ethos to construct an individualized, multifaceted, and fluid ethos. Despite their attempts at adhering to the subject matter and language styles suggested by the study group, sometimes members deviated from these prescriptions. After examining my coding of the 270 threads, I identified narratives about reading experience and poetic engagement with the readings as two primary modes of discursive interaction, as well as numerous instances of code-meshing (Canagarajah, 2006, 2011; V. A. Young, 2004) as a strategy for indexing cultural conflicts and synthesis.

Narratives about Reading Experiences

Narratives about reading experiences and wordage progress (the number of words read) constitute a major discursive mode. As the study group suggested in the "guideline for BBS contribution," members were to share their reading experiences, to report and celebrate each other's wordage progress, and to help "those who are troubled" in their English reading. These suggestions defined the thematic boundaries of the community discourse and, to some extent, prescribed the discursive modes. Each narrative on reading experiences is a snapshot of cultural encounters, in which members engaged stories, ideas, and images from other places.

Such a typical approach to constructing ethos can be demonstrated in a thread starting with post 188. A poster, けん (Kenn), first announced that he and his wife had celebrated their achievements in SSS reading. Next, he provided a detailed account of his step-by-step achievements in vocabulary attainment. In post 189, モーリン (Moring) quoted and then commented on the first part of Kenn's message. Then he commented on a detail ("2 books—Traci Lords 'Underneath It All'") in the second part of Kenn's message:

> Hi, Kenn-san.
> This is Moring.
>
> 〉Yesterday, my wife and I celebrated my 1-year anniversary in SSS Extensive Reading.
> 〉We drank wine to the anniversary. I would like to report a little.
> Congraturation for your 1-year anniversary and your good wife.

> 〉I started SSS-E.R. at October 12th, 2002. And I got totally 3,425,256 words now.
> 〉In addition, what another good thing is my wife has gotten nearly 1,750,000 words.
> Wow! Your wife is also Tadoku-reader?
> You might buy many books and cost many money.
> But if your wife read same books, the cost comes half. That's good.
>
> I think you have good pace. It's almost 3-monthes for 1 million words?
> I want to do Tadoku-Reading on same pace as you.
> I hope you continue to read and keep your pace.
> Also I ask you to advice other Tadoku-reader for helping.
> Because you had read over 3 millions words and I guess the number of persons who had read over 3 millions words is not so many.
>
> 〉2 books——Traci Lords "Underneath It All," [Ocean's 11]
> I remember my promiss.
> But, I'm sorry, I had not read this book still now.
> I will read it before when I finish up 1 million words.
> Any way how many words does this book have?
>
> 〉I enjoyed E.R., and I really appreciate SSS-method.
> I feel same, too.
> Happy reading you at all !

The two members followed the study group's suggestions: supporting each other's reading and generating community knowledge. First, a member reported his (as well as his wife's) experience and achievements in reading extensively. Second, another member congratulated him and applauded his achievements. Third, they generated new knowledge by commenting on a particular book and contributing information about books appropriate for the reading program. Finally, the members agreed on the effectiveness of the SSS method, and one ended his post with the encouraging words "Happy reading." By behaving exactly as the study group had suggested, both members acquired ethos by conforming to the prescribed community virtue.

This exchange also marks a cosmopolitan ethos in the making. Moring singled out Traci Lords's book as one he also desired to read. Traci Lords is an American film actress, producer, film director, and writer. Born in Ohio, she first achieved notoriety for her underage appearances in pornographic videos and adult magazines in the mid-1980s. When authorities discovered that porn producers were taking advantage of her as a minor in making films, they arrested her and the owners of her movie and video agencies. The ensuing prosecution against the agencies forced the pornographic film and distribution industry to remove hundreds of thousands of films in which she had been exploited from store shelves to avoid the risk of prosecution for trafficking in child pornography. Twenty years later, Lords (2004) offers her own account of this sensational event. Reading this and many other fictional and nonfictional texts in English, as revealed in the long list of books that Kenn provided in a previous post, the community interacted with diverse cultures, peoples, and histories. The members' thoughts and imaginings went beyond their contingent groupings, be they the SSS community, their family, their city, or Japan. In the case of the Traci Lords book, they came to feel human pain inflicted by exploitive institutions beyond their own communities.

Poetic Engagement with the Readings

Another mode of discursive interaction is poetic engagement with readings. Sometimes the members responded to a book with short creative pieces of their own, creating imaginary dialogues with the Anglophone author. They remixed their readings and used them as starting points for their own creations. They wrote rhymes, poems, short stories, and scripts for talk shows. These pieces were remarkable for building ethos because, first, they engaged the members in sharing reading experiences as the study group had recommended and, second, they helped the members form a "writerly" as well as a "readerly" identity while experiencing the power of reading. More significantly, their writerly identities were constructed through a mixture of Japanese and non-Japanese cultural materials, again adding a cosmopolitan dimension to their ethos.

The formation of writerly and readerly identities can be illustrated in a thread starting with post 78. Kian revealed that he had written a rhyme for a picture book, *Miffy's Dream* (Bruna, 1984), which originally had not included written lines. Although his teacher offered some help, Kian still found composing a rhyme difficult. Then メイ (May) joined the conversation and shared her work, which encouraged Kian to share his in post 86:

〉Hello, Kian-san. May is speaking.
Hello, May-san! This is Kian.
Thank you for answering me!!

〉I walk with Sancho, my little lovely dog.
〉Rain or shine; even in the fog.
〉We walk through woods in the frosty park.
〉We walk with stars at night so dark.
〉When I throw his ball in the field,
〉He runs and jumps at it never to yield.
〉He often puts his head on my laps at ease.
〉I feel his warmness, patting him to please.

I like it very very much!!
You are a poet!

Here are my lines.
It is not so good but will you read it, please?

Miffy's Dream

Miffy is on a cloud.
It is a nice cloud.
She is floating in the sky.
She has a wonderful sight.
Where dees the cloud take Miffy?
Miffy meets Taffy.
They are facing each other.
They are floating together.
They are floating to the stars.
Now, they are playing with the stars.
Miffy and Taffy find shooting-stars.
They ride on the shooting-stars.
Oh, there is the moon.
We are coming soon.
The cresent is a slide.
They are happy and sigh.
It is getting colder.
They hold their shoulders,
Miffy and Taffy sleep happily together.

My teacer's one is much better, of course.
But he needed much time to correct mine.
So making a rhyme is very very difficult!

〉Happy holidays!!
You, too!!

A close examination of the exchange reveals a cosmopolitan edge to Kian's creation. His imaginative composition came from the picture book, one of the Miffy series created by the Dutch artist Dick Bruna. Typically, the Miffy books each contain sixteen pages of story. Each page has one illustration and four lines of Dutch verse; the last word of the second line rhymes with the last of the fourth. When the verse is translated into other languages, the original rhyming patterns tend to get lost or altered. In *Miffy's Dream*, one of the few wordless Miffy books, the little bunny and her friend float on clouds, catch stars, and sit on the moon. Kian was inspired to fill the voiceless pictorial space, possibly with verses found in other Miffy books. Using alliteration, repetition, and rhyme, however, he rhymed in a pattern different from the one typically found in the Dutch verses or translated English verses. In a sense, he used his own aesthetic taste to translate the picture book. By appropriating images and poetic conventions from outside his communities, Kian joined other Miffy translators in "inventing" the story, making his rhyme a local-global product.

Code-Meshing Indexing Cultural Conflicts

My thematic coding revealed numerous instances of cultural conflicts and resolution in the community discourse. One of them concerns the ownership of English. Members often discussed challenges with English writing. In the thread on Kenn's and his wife's reading achievements, for example, Kenn and Moring commented on Kenn's English. One praises the other's masterly use of English; the other responds with humility and modesty, stressing that English is not easy for him at all. Historically, humility and modesty have certainly been valued and practiced in almost all corners of Japanese society, so it follows that, as a communal practice, commenting on each other's English is also a way in which members engage the history of English in Japan and the dominant language ideologies in Japanese society. Kubota (1998) and A. Matsuda (2003) have indicated that, in Japan, people widely conceive of English as a language owned by Anglo-Americans. Most SSS members were conscious of each other's English use and appreciated each other's efforts to express themselves in a foreign tongue.

Even while viewing English as foreign, members displayed increasing confidence in using it. Some even held that since they were using English to express their ideas and culture, they could use it in their own style, explicitly challenging traditional Japanese views on the ownership issue. One thread discussed embedding Japanese in English posts. Professor Sakai, the head of the study group, had said at a seminar that the English board should not be constrained by English-only writing and that members could mix it with Japanese expressions. Member バナナ (Banana) brought up this assertion in post 217, which a few respondents applauded. For example, K子 (K-ko) expressed her support in post 222:

> 〉So, how about this ?
> 〉この掲示板も無理して英文を書くよりは、
> 〉日本語交じり ＯＫ にしましょう。 (酒井)
> 〉ね、そうしましょう。 [Let's make it ok to mix Japanese in English writing rather than forcing us to write in English (Sakai). Let's do in this way.]
> バナナさん、 I そんなわけで agree with you too! [So Ms. Banana, I agree with you too!]
> For example, it is accepted to write 虫食いのように in Japanese if I am not sure what I should say it in English . . . でしょ ? ちょっと見づらいかな? (^^;) [For example, it is accepted to write in Japanese that which looks like a hole a worm makes, if I am not sure what I should say it in English, isn't it? It is a bit hard to read, maybe?]
> Anyway, the most important for you is to write a lot in English even though you are not sure, so if you can mix some Japanese in your writing, it makes you easy!
> ということで、 Happy writing in 日本語まじりの English! [So, Happy writing in Japanese-mixed English!]

In this post K-ko welcomed the idea of mixing Japanese and English by actually performing it. What is even more significant about this thread is that, previous to it, only one other had mixed Japanese and English, yet many followed suit thereafter. Blending languages in these later threads suggests that a new discursive norm, as well as a subtle shift in ethos, emerged in the community. Their blending practice overthrew the historic and hegemonic imposition of Anglo-American standards of English on Japanese society; it demonstrated individualistic and subversive purposes to some members' discourse, adding nuanced meanings to their collective ethos.

Another conflict arose over the societal norms and the community virtue. The study group stipulated that members should avoid speech that would hurt, marginalize, or disrespect others. They should choose words carefully. However, there are places where these expectations were violated. For example, in a thread starting with post 411, two members discussed the most ridiculous ("OBAKA") scenes in the graphic novel *The Adventures of Super Diaper Baby* (Beard & Hutchins, 2002). Narrating the story in the tone of fourth graders, the American coauthors adopt features of typical fourth grade writing, including colloquialisms, vulgar terms, and spellings deviating from standard orthographic conventions. In post 420, ako, inspired by the playful English used in the novel, described her response to the scenes:

> Dwa———hahahahaha!!!!!
> (This is a new way of laughing in English invented by ako tonight!!)
> I, ako the frog, loves these kinds of OBAKA-English,
> POOP, POOPS, POOPing that I do every day !!!!!!
> Uuuuuuuuuuummmm. . . . . (ー ー ; ; ; ;) u
> I can't say these kinds of things in Japanese. . . . . . .
> Never!! Impossile!!!!
> But. . . . . English!!
> I am afraid of writing English more. . . . . . .
> Actually, recently I read "Nate the Great."
> I, ako the frog, hope that
> you understand my own way of writing English!!
> I, ako the frog, want to take any case of Tadoku problems !! (;-)
> (OH, NO!! Impossible dream !!)

In a self-deprecating manner, ako, or "ako the frog," names her own vulgar English—her laughter sounds and pooping sounds—"OBAKA English" (idiot English). However, her carnivalesque style clearly defied the study group stipulations on language use. Yet, given the context of discussing a book that the posters had read, such language use was not discouraged, criticized, or forbidden by the establishment or any members. Instead, it illustrated the liberating power of English, by not only entertaining the posters but also by providing them opportunities to say what they otherwise could not say in Japanese. English enabled them to transcend and shape, simultaneously, the local cultural and linguistic conventions. And the posters, by extension, came together because they jointly shared that liberating power. The liberating and uniting power of English in Japanese society has been similarly observed by Stanlaw (2004): the language enabled Japanese women to address issues in art that were difficult to discuss in Japanese. Deviating from the stylistic prescription for the board, ako established her ethos by offering the members a sense of liberty and lightheartedness. The liberating power of English in these instances forms an intriguing contrast with its constraining effects felt by some members introduced earlier. They found it difficult to express themselves entirely in English; therefore they decided to mix in Japanese expressions in their bulletin board messages.

Code-Meshing Indexing Cultural Synthesis

From moments of cultural encounter and conflict arose cultural synthesis. This can first be observed in the community members' styles of English. The members became more confident in using their own styles of English to express their emotions, thoughts, and imaginations. As the above quotes have illustrated, most participants used simple vocabulary and structures. Many sentences are fraught with "errors" when viewed from the prescriptive grammarian's perspective. In addition, members incorporated some transliterated Japanese expressions in their posts. For example, they customarily addressed each other by adding polite endings such as "san" and "sensei," as in "Furukawa-san," "Kian-san," and "Sakai-sensei." Some also used self-deprecating expressions commonly used in Japanese: "I feel [like] a complete fool"; "I sweat with shame." These expressions could generate a sense of cultural familiarity and comfort among members.

Some participants created a playful ethos by fusing Japanese literary, rhetorical, and cultural practices in their English-dominant discourse. For example, in a thread starting with post 320, a few members composed five-line poems for an English textbook exercise. After たこ焼 (Takoyaki) wrote one poem playing on his screen name, participant チクワ (Chikuwa) commented on the poem's stylistic and aesthetic achievements:

〉Takoyaki
〉Tako Tako
〉KORO KORO KORO
〉Where is he going?
〉Hole

〉Uuuuummmmm
〉"Hole" is not "まとめ."

Super! I can feel the enjoyable rhythm.
I also feel the Japanese style of “Happening, Continuing, Changing, and Ending” (起承転結).
I can imagine your moving and the stop.
The 1st line and the 2nd line <TAKOyaki – TAKO,>
and the 2nd line and the 3rd line <taKO – Koro>
They make a chain of rhythm, and the phrase “Where is he going?” makes the poem flow.
And with the last line “Hole” I feel sudden stop and “falling.” “Falling” is OCHI.
Too perfect . . .
Putting aside the reasons (リクツ), it’s simply funny!
Gyahahahahahahhahahah
. . . . geho, geho, geho

In the poem, Takoyaki successfully infused transliterated Japanese, making his piece a linguistic and cultural mix. Within the Anglo-American poetic frame prescribed in the textbook, he described the process of making octopus dumplings (takoyaki). When the dumplings are made, they end up in the holes (hemispherical molds) of a frying pan. “Tako” means octopus and “KORO” is an onomatopoeia, which signifies that something is rolling over. Chikuwa contributed to the mixing by unwittingly adding the html code “&#8211” in his response. He also noted in the poem the traditional Japanese writing style of “Happening, Continuing, Changing, and Ending.” The word “hole” probably created in Chikuwa’s mind an image of dumplings falling into holes. Thus, he called the last line (“Hole,” or the feel of “falling”) the punch line (“OCHI”) of the poem. “Ochi,” written as “落ち” in kanji, meaning “falling,” has two meanings here: punch line and falling. Whether Takoyaki consciously modeled the traditional Japanese style remains unknown, but Chikuwa’s adoption of the style as an interpretative frame suggests the cohesive power of Japanese literary heritage for the members. In addition, the entire discussion was framed in a comic book fashion. Both takoyaki and chikuwa are local food items. Chikuwa (竹輪, or “bamboo ring”) is a tube-like food product made of fish surimi and other ingredients, wrapped around a rod of either bamboo or metal before being steamed or broiled. The dialogue takes place around a dinner table where two food characters (octopus dumplings and bamboo rings) are chatting about cooking food/meanings. Chikuwa, while laughing loudly, chokes (“Gyahahahahahahhahahah. . . . geho, geho, geho”) in a manner commonly represented in comic books. Although the SSS members communicate in English, Japanese literary, comic book, and food cultures furnished important ethos-building "materials" to these individuals.

The dialogue didn't stay within the SSS community. As it circulated online and offline, it cooked new meanings. In addition to my readings are two interpretations of this dialogue offered by Yumi Matsumoto, a Japanese scholar in the United States. First, she viewed the nickname たこ焼 (Takoyaki) as marking a regional identity because the food was initially popular in Kansai (関西), the southern-central region of Japan's main island Honshū (本州), before it spread to other parts of the country. Second, understanding that the story line of Takoyaki rolling into a hole resonates with Japanese people not necessarily from Kansai, Yumi recognized the story line as coming from a well-known folktale, "mice and rice balls" (老鼠與飯糰 or おむすびころりん). The story goes that one day an old man went to a hill to gather firewood. He carried a big rice ball that his wife had made. After working hard all morning, he felt hungry. He sat on a stump nearby and grabbed the big rice ball to eat. When he was about to eat, the rice ball slipped out of his hands and fell down to the ground. It started rolling down along the slope and kept rolling so fast that the old man could not catch it. Then it fell into a big hole at the end of the slope, which was the home of a family of mice, setting off a series of fantastic events. Thus, Takoyaki said at the end of the poem that "'Hole' is not 'まとめ.'" It is not the conclusion, not the end of the story. Juxtaposed with my reading, Yumi's underscores the intertwining of regional and national identities in this English-dominant dialogue.

This dialogue showcases how, along with other symbol systems, English helps to engender a form of cosmopolitanism. First, used in local cultural practice, English creates translingual and transcultural interlocutors. In the dialogue both Takoyaki and Chikuwa drew from different linguistic and cultural sources to encode and decode meanings. Resorting to their knowledge of codes traditionally affiliated with a particular nation could not help them to do so. Second, with conscientious efforts of the audience, meaning making/cooking moved from personal and community levels to a global level. To communicate effectively, or in this case to create and appreciate humor, one must be sensitive to the diverse symbols involved, being able to gauge their indexed meanings and subtleties in context. Being a non-Japanese person, I resorted to my knowledge of Japanese language and culture as well as to information on Japanese food culture available on the Internet. As a Japanese person from outside the SSS community, Yumi added new and valuable readings of the dialogue. Third, English is interwoven with other linguistic and cultural symbols so that its boundaries are often blurred. While English and Japanese are marked by orthographic conventions in the exchange, metacognitively they might be code-meshed sounds and symbols for the two members. Fixing the production and interpretation of the dialogue to a particular location, language, or single cultural frame is futile.

Arts of the Dwelling Place Online

Ethos on the English board was constructed at the technological, group, and individual levels. At the technological level, the Japanese index page with the English pages embedded underneath it created a sense of freedom and control for the members. They could move freely between these multilingual spaces. Also at the technological level, hierarchical yet equal relationships between posts gave the members a sense of order. At the group level, the study group postulated rules on subject matter, language style, and personal privacy protection. These rules constitute a communal virtue, which blends the values of the study group leaders, the Internet, and Japanese society at large. However, life on the board is not exclusively defined by these rules. At the individual level, most members adhered to the rules by sharing reading experiences and poetic responses. A relative few subtly resisted and modified that communal virtue by introducing alternative subject matter and new language styles. Some from this latter group constructed unique ethoi by drawing on resources from local and translocal languages, literary traditions, and subcultures. Thus, since the opening of the English board, the members have constantly negotiated and appropriated virtue, engendering ever-evolving ethoi.

In the case of the SSS community, English has deeply percolated local practices, mediating the construction of a virtual dwelling place. In building their ethoi, the members accorded English new meanings and exercised control over this allegedly foreign tongue. They read books in English avidly; however, they were not always accepting of the authors' intended meanings. They aggressively interpreted the readings using local cultural references and personal sensibilities. They cooked novel meanings by creatively engaging these books. In their discussions of English and their actual use of it, they were unafraid to challenge and bend established norms by infusing local expressions and cultural meanings. Embedding English in their communal practice, members made it part of their linguistic repertoire, thus furthering their collective ethos.

The members' uses of English paralleled their ancestors' appropriation of classical Chinese centuries ago. Through Chinese and Korean immigrants, classical Chinese was introduced into Japan in the fifth century and became its first major writing system. In the early years, writing in Japan strictly adhered to the syntactic rules of classical Chinese. As the local literacy level improved, Chinese became available to Japanese elites. In the seventh century, they started composing kanji (Chinese character) texts using vernacular Japanese syntax and vernacular texts using kanji as phonograms. When the oldest extant chronicle in Japan, 古事記 (Kojiki), was composed in the eighth century, the practice of writing with Japanese syntax while using kanji, partially as phonograms, was firmly established (Seeley, 1991). The costs as well as the gains of a language being cosmopolitan are thus apparent: when a language is used by a new community, the phonologic, morphologic, syntactic, and pragmatic conventions will be modified and new meanings gained.

English along with other symbol systems lies deep underneath the arts of the dwelling place. This significant revelation comes, at least in part, from the fact that at present English hardly functions as a discrete code. Instead, it is often interwoven with other linguistic symbol systems and the digital codes of new media. The arts of the dwelling place therefore must be transliterate. The arts critical to the SSS community include multilingual and multicultural network infrastructure, personal narratives, poetic engagement, CE, and willingness to speak to strangers; they partly overlap with the arts of the contact zone, such as transculturation, bilingualism, imaginary dialogue, and vernacular expression. The website was constructed using multiple symbol systems, giving the participants a sense of both familiarity and exoticness, or comfort and attraction. The members were inclined to share personal stories, not only about their reading experiences, but also about significant events that had happened in their lives. These narratives created a web of connections, fortifying communal identification and solidarity. The members produced creative pieces as a means of sharing emotions, feelings, and imaginings arising from their reading experiences. They playfully and artfully mixed Japanese expressions with elements from multiple cultural sources into their English-dominant communications. Their concerted efforts to use English in community-accepted styles helped them to identify with one another. Japanese linguistic and cultural references mediated as yet another set of rhetorical resources for constructing the dwelling place. Above all of these arts of the dwelling place was members' willingness to engage strangers, near or distant, national or international, real or imagined.

When discussing cosmopolitan practice in communication, scholars typically define it based on target audience. They view textual practices intended for audiences outside one's finite, bounded communities as cosmopolitan (Pollock 2002; Schoene, 2010). For example, Pollock (2002), focusing on audience, makes the distinction between cosmopolitan and vernacular literary practices:

> *Cosmopolitan* and *vernacular* can be taken as modes of literary (and intellectual, and political) communication directed towards two different audiences, whom lay actors know full well to be different. The one is unbounded and potentially infinite in extension; the other is practically finite and bounded by other finite audiences, with whom, through the very dynamic of vernacularization, relations of ever-increasing in-communication come into being. (p. 18, emphasis in original)

According to the terms set by Pollock, the SSS community's discursive practices fall quite nicely into the vernacular realm. Most of the members are Japanese nationals residing in Japan. While recognizing the vernacular dimension, I argue that the symbolic resources used, particularly English, have effectively turned the members' communication into a cosmopolitan practice. Reading and writing in English, a language that was foreign, metropolitan, and international to most of the members, generated imagined and infinite audiences of other locations, races, and nationalities. In addition, there were a few instances in which the members invited Anglophone authors from outside Japan to join the BBS discussions of their books. In conversation with the imagined and real Other in English, the members were able to challenge conventional wisdom about Japanese linguistic and cultural values, demonstrating that their national identity was not fixed in a particular language or cultural practice.

As English penetrates different regions and social sectors, the scholarly approach to the intercultural discourse thus far developed needs to be reassessed and reoriented. Theoretical constructs, such as "contrastive rhetoric," "contact zone," "borderland," and "rhetorical encounter," invariably focus on differences, tensions, and conflicts as English enters local cultural practice (Lunsford & Ouzgane, 2004; Mao, 2006; Wolff, 2004). Their proponents tend to overlook the fact that English is able to bring people of different cultures, ethnicities, genders, and classes together to achieve shared goals. And, of course, when different people come together, conflicts will inevitably arise.

However, the SSS community reminds us of English's power not only to bring people together, but also to enable them to develop new identities and attachments, and ultimately new cultures. Their identities may not be fixed to their natural or contingent groupings, be they race, gender, class, or nation. By relating personal experiences, trading imaginings, and sharing dynamic emotions and feelings, a boundary-crossing community takes shape. It is a result of language's potential to construct such dwelling places that English has become cosmopolitan.

In enabling a cosmopolitan ethos, English has worked in conjunction with another globalizing medium—the Internet. The web and other information technologies seem to have speedily torn down national, geographic, and cultural boundaries, which used to hinder communication. And the most significant part is that with these new media, individuals practice electronic literacy rather than print literacy. Ulmer (2012) advances an analogy when describing identity arising from such practice: "Avatar is to electracy what 'self' is to literacy, or 'spirit' to orality." In the Vedic tradition, avatars are the manifestations of the divine in various aspects of human life and in the natural world. In the electronic world, avatars are the mysterious, multifaceted, and mutable identities that an individual can create, which not only transcend the conscious and the unconscious but also often emerge in the identities of the Other. The felt freedom to create different faces and voices prompted some SSS members to act out, taking on the roles of the Other. For example, some members chose screen names that they probably did not want to associate with in real life, such as the food names "takoyaki" and "chikuwa" and the racialized and derogatory name "Banana"; ako relocated to the fictional world of the super diaper baby by speaking OBAKA-English, which she would not be able to do in Japanese society. The avatar/ethos that electronic literacy afforded members prompted them to imagine objects and rhetorical acts beyond their everyday lives, beyond their own people, and to transform into citizens of a broader community.

The ability of English to bring a group of Japanese nationals together and foster a cosmopolitan consciousness compels us to reassess ethos theories. Historically, these theories were developed in specific cultures or communities and for effective communications within them. Isocrates and Aristotle articulated such theories in their writings concerning Greek city-state politics. Whether defined as the inherent ability to speak ethically or as moral character construed through speech, ethos was purposed to influence audiences at political assemblies, law courts, or public ceremonies. Confucius perceived ethos as arising from one's ritualistic behaviors rooted in Chinese sociopolitical traditions. Heidegger and Fleckenstein neither focused on any specific culture or community, nor did they recognize the potential of ethos for bringing together brothers and sisters from the Four Seas. The SSS community illustrates that ethos can be enacted across traditional, contingent groupings thanks to shared systems of communication and technologies. A reformulation of ethos has to consider the rhetorical potential resulting from the recent and profound mingling of peoples, of languages, and of cultures, as well as from the increasing number of symbolic resources available to individuals. A new theory of ethos ought to account for the strategies and consequences existent when dwelling places are built across contingent groupings.

In this chapter I have demonstrated English's ability to build a new culture in a social context where, traditionally, languages other than English dominate. We have also glimpsed some of the characteristics of English as a cosmopolitan language (entering local practice; interwoven with other linguistic, cultural, and technological symbols; conjuring up transliterate interlocutors; and fostering boundary-crossing consciousness and practices). Until now, scholars studying English from noncosmopolitan perspectives have often labeled English with ethnic, national, or geographical tags, such as African American English, Japanese English, or Hong Kong English, treating English as a local, vernacular, or national practice. Viewing English as a discrete linguistic system, some of these scholars have endeavored to identify key features of these so-called varieties of English. But when English is practiced in a community or a nation, to what extent can we confine its linguistic features to an ethnic, national, or regional category? In the next chapter, I will problematize these preceding scholarly efforts by examining CE in a national context.

3

Linguistic Creativity in the Diaspora

> I have grown up in the city with a large population of black people & comparatively I was really a minority in the schools I went to, with African American being the majority. So I am very familiar with the "African American vernacular." . . . I admit that with friends I know are from the city I feel more comfortable to speak like this vernacular because I am so familiar with it. —Jarinil, "Notes"

In writing studies it's common to hear the term "Englishes," plural form. When one sticks to the singular, he or she projects the idea that there is just one linguistic norm based on the speech of "native speakers" and the Anglo-American literary canon. To acknowledge the multiplicity of cultures, peoples, and contexts in which the language has been used both historically and at present, English needs to break from its traditional definitions marked by nation and nativity. Instead of a singular English, one currently hears multiple Englishes on American university campuses, including what scholars have identified as British English, Indian English, Chinese English, African American English, academic English, or business English. The first four of these varieties are associated with a nation, a location, or an ethnicity.

When scholars strive to pluralize English, there is a tendency to essentialize its varieties. Located firmly in the discourses of postcolonialism and multiculturalism, one can hardly avoid attributing to ethnic groups and cultures some constitutional characteristics. This essentializing practice often strategically provides a basis for political power, identity formation, conversation, and negotiation. As illustrated by the early work of contrastive rhetoric (Kaplan, 1966; Connor, 1996), with the intent of advancing intercultural education, researchers sought to identify the features of written English as produced by students of particular cultural backgrounds. Also, a large number of studies in sociolinguistics have been devoted to African American Vernacular English (AAVE) (Dillard, 1973; Gilyard, 1996; Green, 2002; Labov, 1972; Rickford

& Rickford, 2000; Smitherman, 1985, 2000). These studies demonstrate that this variety is different from mainstream American English, with AAVE possessing distinct pronunciations, lexicon, sentence structures, and language practices that mark African American history, identities, voices, and alliances. For furthering the intellectual conversation and effecting positive political action, this body of research deserves to be applauded. In the context of education, these efforts helped move forward discussions and enact policies concerning literacy education for minority students, such as the publication of "Students' Right to Their Own Language" by the Conference on College Composition and Communication in 1974. Again using AAVE as an example, should we teach African American students about this variety, help them acquire Standard English using AAVE as a bridge, or teach them to artfully mix AAVE and Standard English in their speaking and writing? These are among the varied positions currently held concerning the education of African American students (Ball & Lardner, 1998; Campbell, 2005; Elbow, 2000, 2006; Gilyard, 1991, 2011; Richardson, 2003; Young, 2007).

If we take a step back, temporarily setting aside postcolonial and multicultural discourses, some assumptions that supported the study of English varieties seem empirically questionable. With AAVE still as an example, a series of questions can be raised: How does one define the categorization "African American"? Do all African Americans speak AAVE in their home communities? Do only African Americans speak AAVE? Is AAVE defined by a relatively stable set of linguistic features? These are not new questions for scholars of AAVE and African American studies (Gilroy, 1993; Rickford & Rickford, 2000; Wolfram, 2003; Kendall & Wolfram, 2009). The epigraph to this chapter provides additional answers. Written as a class note by Jarinil, a Puerto Rican American student, her testimony shows that non–African American inner-city students are conversant in AAVE and speak like their African American peers when hanging out with other kids from the city (Philadelphia). What these questions point to instead is the fact that AAVE as well as other ethnic and national varieties of English are fluid language practices in an unstable, unfixed relationship with ethnicity and nation, and that their theoretical constructs are useful rhetorical contrivances in specific historical moments.

Questioning these Englishes as constructs draws our attention to the modernist thinking still lingering in language studies, including writing studies. When we establish and celebrate these varieties, in effect we reinforce imagined cultural and ethnic boundaries. We treat them like political entities and afford them sovereignty like nation-states. We perpetuate the dangers manifested in nationalism—the essentializing of cultures and peoples, the reifying of differences and divides, and the privileging of linguistic and literary norms that represent our politico-economic interests at the cost of those who are unlike us. Pollock, Bhabha, Breckenridge, and Chakrabarty (2002) were wary of the consequences of multiculturalism in the academy: "What we are calling a minoritarian modernity (as a source for contemporary cosmopolitan thinking) is visible in the new forms of transdisciplinary knowledge that we initiate in the 'multicultural' academy, where once we attempted to teach difference by emphasizing areal locality and specificity, today we try to struggle free from the self-fulfilling dialectics of the general and the particular" (p. 6). When we study and teach national or ethnic varieties of English, we largely continue to recognize people within national frames, a defining feature of the modernist project. In writing studies, as lamented by Royster (1996), we lack the notion of hybrid people, or "people who either have the capacity by right of history and development, or people who might have created the capacity by right of history and development, to move with dexterity across cultural boundaries, to make themselves comfortable, and to make sense amid the chaos of difference" (p. 37). We sometimes assume teleologically that people of a cultural category will use language in certain predictable ways. In reality, cultural synthesis takes place through the mediation of languages and dialects, giving rise to new cultural communities and practices. Further, people assume multiple identities, associations, and alliances as they interweave dialects and languages. Focusing on the cosmopolitan potential and responsibility of English in local contexts may enable us to break free from "the self-fulfilling dialectics of the general and the particular."

In this chapter I will examine the thinking behind Englishes and offer Cosmopolitan English as an alternative for understanding English use among cultural and ethnic groups. Instead of looking at a "variety" that has been much discussed in language studies, I will focus on one that is not as well known, variously called Chinglish, Chinese English, or China English. After reviewing the available conceptualizations of this nation-anchored variety, I will question some assumptions behind the Englishes construct. Then, adopting the notion of domestic diaspora, I will underscore the multiplicity and fluidity of associations (with nation, ethnicity, class, gender, location, and technologies) involved in the actual practice of this variety. While some assumptions behind the construct will prove to be empirically unfounded, the practice of China English, better called Cosmopolitan English, in various contexts is tangible.

China English and Domestic Diaspora

Scholars have thus far adopted an inference model for studying China English. A derivative of contrastive analysis in language-learning research, this model explains or predicts discursive features of China English based on Chinese discourse and cultural preferences. For example, in a study of 180 English expository essays written by Chinese students, Wang and Li (1993) found that 66.11 percent of them employ an "indirect" pattern, 6.11 percent use a "general/particular" pattern, and the rest use a mixed pattern. They attribute the predominant use of the "indirect" pattern to the circularity and indirection present in traditional Chinese essay writing. Similarly, Kirkpatrick and Xu (2002) and Xu (2010) suggest that because English is widely used in China, millions of English speakers will inevitably create a variety of English that bears Chinese syntactic and pragmatic norms. Such norms include subjectless sentences, "frame-body" sentence and discourse patterns, and face-saving rhetorical moves. In her analysis of Chinese American writer Ha Jin's novel *In the Pond*, Zhang (2002) identifies a series of "nativized" discourse patterns, rhetorical strategies, and speech acts, and she argues that they are located in the "texture of Chinese ideological, political and socio-cultural representations" (p. 305). Resorting to Chinese discourse features and cultural traditions for reference, these scholars have discovered a range of features in the English used by Chinese speakers.

The inference model falls short in uncovering China English's linguistic and rhetorical potential due to its three assumptions characteristic of modernist thinking. First, it essentializes both Chinese people and China English. It assumes that Chinese discourse strategies are static regardless of the language being used in any mode or dialect, by any speaker or writer, and for any audience at any time; by the same token, the inference model assumes that a collection of easily generalizable Chinese characteristics also exists in China English. Second, the model only considers the interactions between Standard English and Standard Chinese, two highly formalized social dialects, and it fails to account for a multilingual, English-speaking Chinese society. Third, by treating Chinese language and culture as a singular and the main variable, the model neglects the context and the speaker/writer in fashioning specific discursive strategies of China English. If we cease focusing exclusively on Chinese characteristics in lexicon, syntax, and discourse and start examining China English as used in particular contexts and for particular audiences, we may unveil a wider scope of its linguistic and rhetorical potential.

Indeed, Chinese users of English are multilingual. According to the official count, there are fifty-six ethnicities within the country, and many claim languages of their own. A sampling includes Chinese, Kazakh, Korean, Manchu, Mongolian, Tibetan, Uyghur, and Zhuang. The national majority group, the Han people, speak Chinese, which is represented by seven major regional dialects: Mandarin, Wu, Cantonese, Min, Hakka, Gan, and Xiang. These dialects are so distinct and mutually unintelligible that some linguists, including Leonard Bloomfield, consider them different languages (DeFrancis, 1984). Even within a major dialect, some regional variants can be mutually unintelligible. For example, I grew up speaking Hakka in South China but couldn't understand Hakka speakers in some neighboring counties. As a standardized version of Mandarin is mandated in schools, educated Han normally have Standard Mandarin and a regional Chinese dialect at their disposal. Educated ethnic minorities usually speak both Standard Mandarin and their ethnic language. Together with English, most educated Chinese people have at least three linguistic systems in their communicative repertoires.

Despite the prevailing assumption of a unitary Chinese culture, like any modern nation China has always been a multicultural society. When culture is defined in anthropological terms, the nation claims the cultures of at least fifty-six ethnicities. Major Chinese cities have become internationalized, attracting millions of foreign migrants and workers, so major national cultures, such as American, British, French, German, Korean, and Japanese, are well represented there. When culture is defined by social production, China embraces both traditional farming and industrial cultures. When defined by personal income, Chinese culture consists of a low-income class, a middle class, and a high-income class. Regional variations in food, clothing, architecture, and dialects define regional cultures. The rise of new media also enriches contemporary Chinese political and literary cultures (Yang, 2010). All these variegated cultural norms and codes constitute a trove of resources for Chinese users of English.

College-educated white collar workers, or "white collars" as they are called in China, make up the main body of English users in the country. The number of college graduates rose from 0.61 million in 1990 to 1.69 million in 2008 (Department of Comprehensive Statistics, 2005; Department of Education, 2009). From 1980 to 2008, China graduated more than 30 million college students.[1] Since English became a compulsory course for secondary and tertiary Chinese education in the late 1970s, statistics indicate that as of 2008 more than 30 million Chinese students had studied English as a school subject for at least eight years (six years in secondary school and two years in college). After passing the required College English Test, students reach an intermediate English proficiency in reading, writing, and listening comprehension, a level similarly required by Anglo-American universities for international students seeking higher education degrees. Instead of preparing students to study abroad, Chinese colleges focus on making sure they can work competently in their fields. As the key users and shapers of China English, these white collars need to be better understood.

Most white collars share a domestic diasporic identity. Being first-generation college goers, they usually leave their hometowns to study and work in other cities. In fact, many leave their rural birthplaces to work in metropolitan centers such as Beijing, Shanghai, and Guangzhou. Inevitably they encounter an array of challenges as they adapt to an urban lifestyle. In the big cities they form various communities and organizations to network with and support their fellow provincials or townsmen. The cultural and economic shifts they experience in the massive migration from city to city and from rural to urban areas in some ways resemble the transnational experiences of various diasporas. *Diaspora* is commonly used to describe any population considered "deterritorialized" or "transnational" or to describe any population originating from a land other than that in which it currently resides and whose social, economic, and political networks cross the borders of nation-states. Granted, the movements of Chinese white collars happen largely within national borders, but considering the vastness of the country and the fact that the white collars' social, economic, and political networks cross various regions, they can be called a "domestic diaspora." The term has been used by scholars to describe similar movements of populations elsewhere. For example, Page (2007) calls people who used to live in small towns in Cameroon but who left to work elsewhere a domestic diaspora, and both Thomas (1990) and Shapiro (2001) describe, as a domestic diaspora, the movement of African Americans from the South and Southwest to cities of the North and Midwest in the twentieth-century United States.

By focusing on the white collars' diasporic identity, I want to emphasize their cosmopolitan connections. When they move, they form new associations while maintaining old ones. However, they can hardly be locked into a single category, be it cultural, ethnic, or geographic. Labeling the white collars as a diaspora certainly accords them victimized status, a status of having become alienated and deserted by their original communities. "Cosmopolitans today are often the victims of modernity, failed by capitalism's upward mobility, and bereft of those comforts and customs of national belonging. Refugees, peoples of the diaspora, and migrants and exiles represent the spirit of the cosmopolitical community," write Pollock, Bhabha, Breckenridge, and Chakrabarty (2002, p. 6). While some may also view Chinese white collars as victims of global capitalism and China's fast industrialization, they do not represent the typical diaspora in the modernist sense. In fact, the modernist sense perpetuates the old, imperializing, essentializing form of ethnicity. Instead, the Chinese white collars' diaspora experience should be defined, using Hall's (1996) words, "not by essence or purity, but by the recognition of a necessary heterogeneity and diversity; by a conception of 'identity' which lives with and through, not despite, differences; by hybridity" (pp. 119–120). Highlighting diaspora as an everyday and everywhere phenomenon reminds us of our multiple cultural roots and shifting social connections whether we physically inhabit Cameroon, China, Japan, or the United States.

After reviewing literature in anthropology, sociology, and cultural studies, Vertovec (1997) has identified three meanings of diaspora. First, diaspora has been conceived as a "social form," involving specific social relationships, political orientations, economic strategies, and collective ties with certain history and geography. Second, diaspora can also be viewed as a "type of consciousness." We can understand diasporic consciousness by examining people's experience, their state of mind, and their sense of identity. Third, diaspora can be viewed as a "mode of cultural production." In the context of globalization, cultural objects, images, and meanings flow across national borders resulting in a "variegated process of creolisation, back-and-forth transferences, mutual influences, new contestations, negotiations and constant transformations" (p. 278). Domestic diaspora can be similarly viewed as a social form, a type of consciousness, and a mode of cultural production. The term highlights the ubiquitous movements of people, shifting social relations, and constant cultural crossings even in a national context. Adopting these three meanings, we can then look at how English along with other local languages mediates Chinese white collars' social relations and their articulation of diasporic consciousness as a mode of cultural production.

To accomplish this, I will focus on English-dominant white collar discourse on Internet forums. There are several reasons for making this choice. First, online forums are home to diverse modes of discourse such as announcements; short exchanges; and digital stories, poems, and essays, which offer a broad view of English as a local practice. In contrast, messages transmitted via other platforms, such as e-mails, personal blogs, instant messaging, and cell phones, tend to be private, transient, and limited in the modes of discourse. Second, online forums often entice a larger number of participants than do other platforms. For example, the Hujiang bulletin board system (BBS) (沪江论坛 http://www.hjbbs.com/), the most popular English BBS in China, claims 2.6 million registered members. Other popular sites include the 21st Century Community (21 世纪社区 http://forum.21stcentury.com.cn/) and the 24En BBS (爱思英语论坛 http://bbs.24en.com/). To meet the needs and interests of participants with various English proficiencies, these BBSs host forums with assorted focuses.

The data to be examined come from a 21st Century Community forum. The community is an online platform offered by 21st Century Newspapers, a popular English-learning newspaper group targeting students at all levels in China. Thanks to the popularity of its newspapers, the group attracts a good number of students and white collars to its online spaces. The community had hosted over 303,300 registered members by the end of 2009. Participation in the community is on a voluntary basis with no access restriction for nonregistered participants; however, only registered members can post messages. In the community, there are thirty-three forums for different types of participants (teachers, college students, teens senior, teens junior, kids, etc.) with varying interests (language pedagogy, language skills, opinions, Q&A, etc.). I will focus on a forum called "English Writing 英语原创: 原创英语小文章." The Chinese title emphasizes original creations in English. According to what was revealed in the forum discussions, most participants were Chinese college students and white collars. Sometimes internationals, such as English-language teachers and professionals, would drop in as well. I chose to study this forum due to the numerous instances of linguistic and cultural crossings taking place therein. I started following their discussions in 2005, and by the end of 2010, the forum featured over three thousand threads of discussion. With a shared interest to circulate their English creations, the participants have effectively constructed a CyberEthos (Fleckenstein, 1999), a "dwelling place" where they deliberate on issues of migration, family, work, friendship, and politics.

I studied threads initiated by white collars or individuals with white collar personas. I determined white collar identity based on what these individuals revealed in their initial and subsequent posts. For example, some active members tended to attract those of similar backgrounds, eliciting a string of follow-up posts. For manageability, only threads that attracted more than fifty follow-up posts were examined. Twenty threads, totaling 2063 posts, met these requirements by the end of 2010. Among the white collars who started these threads, a woman nicknamed "Sunshine" claimed the greatest popularity. Of the twenty threads that I examined, she initiated nine. Five additional threads were also started by females. Due to the strong presence of female voices, as we will soon see, the overall sample tilts toward a distinct femininity in persona, sentiment, and language style. Since the data come from a self-selected English-learning community who exchanged posts online, the sample also bears clear features of Internet English and English used by language learners.

Thematic analysis was combined with linguistic and rhetorical analysis to understand white collar English. In the thematic analysis, I sifted through every post in the twenty threads and identified themes that reflected the white collars' major concerns. Some of these themes are migration, friendship, family, romantic relations, workplace, English writing, and international politics. Then I grouped them roughly according to the three meanings of diaspora. For example, diasporic consciousness tended to emerge when members discussed their experiences as migrant workers; diasporic relations could be seen when members talked about friendship, family, and workplace. And certainly, conversations under any of these themes may reflect the three meanings of diaspora.

Under these themes I searched for moments indicative of linguistic creativity, or moments in which the white collars had drawn on diverse languages, modalities, and cultures to construct their identities and connections as participants in a diaspora. Linguistic creativity is defined here as discursive choices made strategically to achieve a certain rhetorical purpose. These choices may manifest in lexical items, idiomatic expressions, figures of speech, and discourse patterns and strategies. Both linguistic and rhetorical analyses are employed to examine linguistic creativity. Linguistic analysis focused on the choices a member made at the lexical, syntactic, and discoursal levels. Rhetorical analysis focused on how a member made a discursive choice in relation to audience, communicative intent, and an intended CyberEthos. I will present a rhetorical and linguistic analysis of some of those moments with the end of highlighting the cosmopolitan dimensions of the white collars' diasporic lives.

Domestic Diaspora Consciousness

The diasporic consciousness emerges conspicuously when white collars describe their movements between cities. This consciousness is marked by an individual's awareness of decentered attachments, of being simultaneously "home (and) away from home" or "here and there." A sense of instability and fluidity of life permeates narratives and reflections posted on the forum. Sunshine, the most popular member, describes her arrival in Shanghai from South China, constructing an ethos of a migrant worker:

> Sitting in front of the newly-bought desk by my host, I hoped to tackle everything with the new Korean ballpoint pen every day in Shanghai.
>
> Shanghai is the most attractive city in China, different from Guangzhou. When walking along the neat street against the cool autumn wind, I felt good: It is Shanghai; I'm here now. She is like an elegant lady, peaceful but open minded which is opposite to Guangzhou, an impetuous boy, energetic but impolite.
>
> However, there still many interesting things happened since the day I stepped out of the train and on the land that Annbaby, a pop writer in China, described.
>
> At 5:20 A.M., August 28, 2002, I arrived. ("流年 [Fleeting years]" post no. 2.)

Sunshine's English depicts her feelings upon arrival in Shanghai. Her use of similes ("elegant lady" versus "an impetuous boy") vividly captures two cities' characters in the eyes of a young migrant worker. Permeating the text are outpourings of delight ("I felt good"), excitement ("I hope to tackle everything . . ."), and enchantment ("many interesting things" and the pop writer "Annbaby"). Having just arrived in a new city, Sunshine hopes to "tackle everything" with her "Korean ballpoint pen," which signifies both her multilingual repertoire and writing's pivotal role in her diasporic life.

As time went on, her CyberEthos evolved. Despite her excitement and joy, her mention of Annbaby's (安妮宝贝) literary description of Shanghai indicates the darker side of Shanghai living. In the short story 上海冬天 (Winter of Shanghai), the net writer Annbaby describes men and women living restlessly in this cold metropolitan center, indulging in net love and sex. Similarly, in a diary entry dated "May 2003" (eight months after her arrival), Sunshine comes to discover this "cold" city through workplace language practice. She contrasts how her former students and her current coworkers address her:

> How I missed my big babies!
>
> "Silly Sunshine!" "Our Shineshine!" "Silly Baby!" How I hope to hear their calling me again. They made me warm and comfortable. "Sunshine" "Sunshine" and "Sunshine" are around me plus with their candies and smiles.

> But now, only "Miss Wang" or something like that. Polite means distance actually.
>
> "Ms Wang" is polite.
>
> "Ms Wang" is distance, too.
>
> So how can I feel there is friendship in "Ms Wang."
>
> And what's difference between friends and collegues?
>
> COLD POLITE.
>
> Could a BF change all these? I'm far from the good old days with my big boys and can't go back to it even if I back to Nanning or Guilin because we can't stay in the same place. My Silly is in Guilin; Land Nanning and Fatty and Mosquito.
>
> Cold polite is somewhat worse than SARS. Can I manage to live in the city around the cold polite for the rest of my life? ("流年" post no. 3)

Once Sunshine immerses herself in city life, she becomes devastated by feelings of alienation. She uses a parallelism to underscore the ubiquitous use of formal terms of address in the new place ("Those who said they are my friends called me 'Ms Wang.' Those who worked with me addressed me 'Ms Wang.'"). She uses short sentences to metonymically show the coldness she experienced among her colleagues ("Polite means distance actually. 'Ms Wang' is polite. 'Ms Wang' is distance, too." "COLD POLITE."). She transliterated expressions from local dialects or Standard Chinese: "Silly Sunshine," "Our Shineshine," "Silly Baby," "Miss Wang," "Ms Wang," "Fatty," and "Mosquito." Names index social relations. Confucius (1989) admonishes in the *Analects* that to effect social change, names need be applied correctly. The narrator's yearning for intimate names used by her former students indicates her desire for closer human relationships in Shanghai. This evocation of intimate names signifies a paradoxical dualism: her experiences of alienation in Shanghai, on one hand, and her identification with old places and individuals, on the other—or in the words of Clifford (1994), "the empowering paradox of diaspora is that dwelling here assumes a solidarity and connection there. . . . [It is] the connection (elsewhere) that makes a difference (here)" (p. 322).

While Sunshine responded to alienation with narratives filled with local cultural references, some others resorted to translocal references to fashion a collective ethos of support. Several times Sunshine casts doubt on the meaningfulness of her new life. She wants to escape her harsh reality: "It seems that there's no way to escape from the world where now I have to stay. Like a long lost child in the dark forest, I find no one near me and no way out, either. 'What am I gonna do?' Many a time I questioned myself, and God, as well. Still, no answer" ("Lost in the Forest," post no. 1). Her loss of direction in life elicited 169 sympathetic and encouraging responses, representing diverse worldviews and arguments. One response, titled "Life," is a mixture of Anglo-American cultural values and Christian thoughts:

> human is different from anything else, for he has thought.
> but it is the same with others for he has his limit.
> life is so fraguil, sometimes even a falling leave can take it away. life is so strong, it donnot fall down even before death.
> "no pain, no gain," but how about pain without gain.
> someone can enjoy happiness just from his or her born.
> for someone live in city is just a dream.
> you can do nothing before God.
> but i believe every dog has its day. (Allen002, "Lost in the Forest," post no. 21)

Adopting several antitheses, Allen002 demonstrates his dialectical thinking. In this poetic and humorous statement, he sees both the fragility and strength of life. Despite his despair over the disparity between the haves and have-nots and over living a hopeless city life, he still wants to live with dignity. In his statement he uses two Anglo-American expressions—"no pain, no gain" and "every dog has its day"—expressions probably acquired from his English textbook. He also evokes some Christian thoughts, such as the unique nature of humans, the fragility of life, and God as an omnipotent being.[2] In the exchange, it is worth noting that both Sunshine and Allen002 appeal to God as a global cultural reference. Their evocations of Christian deity are not isolated instances in the white collars' discourse, but rather they are pervasive. Regardless of whether they are Christians or not, this phenomenon reaffirms a century-long effect of English education in China. My study of English writing history in Chinese schools (You, 2010) unveils that students have always consciously or unconsciously negotiated with Christian values in their English discourse.

In addition to rhetorical choices, linguistic choices also assist in constructing diasporic consciousness and identities. The online discourse quoted so far reveals a wide spectrum of deviations from Standard English, which is taught in Chinese schools. White collar English styles help these individuals stake a symbolic claim to uniqueness as college-educated individuals. The most prominent deviation is the frequent omission of articles preceding nouns, as in the following sentences: "And that's [the] difference between friends and collegues?" "[A] human is different from anything else, for he has thought." "for someone live in [the] city is just a dream." The members also treat some verbs and adjectives as nouns. For example, Sunshine repeatedly uses "polite" to mean "politeness," and Allen002 uses "born" to mean "birth" in the sentence: "someone can enjoy happiness just from his or her born." The front-loading of adverbial phrases, a feature of Standard Mandarin (Kirkpatrick 1991, 1993), is also noticeable as Sunshine says, "When walking along the neat street against the cool autumn wind, I felt good" and "However, there still many interesting things happened . . ." Orthographic deviations—misspellings and nonstandard uses of punctuation—also abound. These deviations can be explained either by the carefree nature of online discourse or by the members' underdeveloped competencies with Standard English. However, to attribute these deviations to the influence of Chinese languages and cultures seems simplistic and far-fetched. Regardless of origination, as scholars of English as a lingua franca have claimed, such deviations seldom cause miscommunications (Kaur, 2011; Mauranen, 2006; Seidlhofer, 2004). Almost everyone deviates from Standard English, and most of the time nobody cares.

Diasporic Social Relations

Online discourse also mediates the making of diasporic social relations. As we have already seen in Sunshine's posts, she consciously recalls the "good old days" with her former students in South China as a strategy for dealing with her hollow human relationships in Shanghai. Other forum members also evoke the notion of "home." They regularly share experiences of returning home to visit parents and relatives, observe traditional festivals, or participate in hometown celebrations. Such topics reveal not simply homesickness but, more importantly, their efforts at maintaining relationships with their old homes. In one post, for example, lile1111 describes her brother's wedding that was held in her hometown:

> The bride wore a brand-new white wedding gown and wore beautiful make-up, sitting in the wedding car together with the bridegroom. After they arrived the new house, the bride bend over on the groom's back, others from the groom's family will rob the bride's shoes and kept them out of the door, trying to ask for red bag or gifts for change. Don't consider this a really robbing, they are just for fun. Finally the bride and groom went into the house, the children will surrender water

> to them for washing hands and also the bride will give them red bag. After they changed an other suit, all the people went to the restaurant for lunch, it was a big feast. There also are games for the new couple, songs given by the relatives, everyone was enjoying their time at the moment. ("Everyday Writing," post no. 123)

Evoking local and translocal references, lile1111 detailed a modern-day wedding. The groom carrying the bride on his back into the house, friends and relatives robbing the bride's shoes, and the couple handing out little red envelopes containing cash are all local practices. Wearing white wedding gowns and driving a decorated wedding car are imported practices. Thus, the wedding delineated by lile1111 is a cultural synthesis, as is her English. The wedding ceremony is an important ritual that embodies a wide spectrum of social norms, customs, and mores, involving complicated relationships and institutions. By performing rituals or participating in their performances, as I argue elsewhere (You, 2006), one will identify both with community values and community members. Articulating the ritualistic practices at a wedding as a strategy for reconnecting with her cultural roots must have resonated with the audience as dozens of responses followed.

Discussions of workplace relations and economic strategies abound on the forum, strengthening the collective CyberEthos of support. As a way to foster new relations in their present "home," members share stories about bosses, workmates, and roommates. They share strategies for navigating the labyrinth of corporate culture, a relatively new culture emerging after both global capital and a market economy reentered China in the late 1970s. The following is an exchange between two individuals—Greenfield and sky song—on how to bargain for a salary increase:

> on one hand try your best to finish the work
> the other hand fight with your boss for more reasonable reward
> yes, i mean "money"~~~maybe it's superficial but also realistic~.
> (Greenfield, "流年" post no. 62)

> My boss told me just now that my salary will have a big rise at the end of this year. However, I also received an interview call offering me double my current salary. Hope that I can fail in the interview so that I can stay in this company because i really want stability. I may also succeed in the interview and give my boss a paper and let him make decision. (sky song, post no. 63)

> i'm glad to hear that you will get both higher salary and a better job. It's favorable for you to lead a better life. maybe it's not very easy to make a decision but i think you will choose the right way ~~congratulation!!~~and treat me a big meal~~i like eating. . . . . . . mouth-watering~~hahaha^-^. (Greenfield, post no. 66)

By sharing economic strategies, the two interlocutors foster new relationships, which are partly based on work ethics and market rules. The exchange is rhetorically significant: both translocal market and local secular values are appealed to. While Greenfield's first two suggestions (working hard and requesting a salary raise) and sky song's response to these suggestions are all based on market logic, Greenfield makes his last suggestion (treating him to a big meal) according to local custom. Asking someone who has achieved success to treat his or her friends to a meal is a common practice in part of Chinese society. The meal is an important ritual for sharing feelings and building bonds. The way Greenfield writes his last sentence—combining short phrases and a smiley—shows his excitement, happiness, and humor.

As we continue to observe white collar English, it is important to note its idiosyncratic and fluid nature. It continues to exhibit article omission preceding nouns, the use of adjectives and verbs as nouns, misspellings, and nonstandard uses of punctuation. There are also numerous instances of ungrammatical uses of present participles, gerunds, and tense markers. However, nobody deviates from Standard English in wholly consistent, systematic ways. For example, Greenfield uses the indefinite article "a" inconsistently: "I am glad to hear that you will get both [a] higher salary and a better job. It's favorable for you to lead a better life." And he uses the preposition "on" in one sentence but not in another: "on one hand try your best to finish the work. [On] the other hand fight with your boss for more reasonable reward." What these fluid deviations suggest is a worry-free, casual mood, a mood probably derived from the rather informal social relations developed in the virtual space among the white collars.

Cultural Production of the Diaspora

As white collars shuttle between physical spaces and between cultural spaces, they produce artifacts that juxtapose elements characteristic of these spaces. Several examples I have quoted so far offer us a glimpse of this process of cultural production, such as Sunshine's account of her changing sensibilities while living in Shanghai and the transcultural exchange between Greenfield and sky song concerning how to navigate the corporate reward system. These cultural artifacts have captured personal and local responses to diasporic life experiences.

As an example of creativity, artful English goes beyond the personal, helping create local-global connections in meaning making. Although swamped by daily chores, the forum participants remain attentive to what is happening inside and outside the country. They discuss news and issues of great public interest, creating what Bhabha (2004) has described as "an 'in-between' temporality that takes the measure of dwelling at home, while producing an image of the world of history" (p. 19). Through reporting and debating news items, forum members recast and circulate nonlocal ideas, images, and icons, perpetuating a cosmopolitan ethos. For example, a forum member was deeply concerned about the U.S. invasion of Iraq in 2003. Adopting the innocent voice of an Iraqi child, she chose to compose a poem in reaction to news coverage of that war:

> A poem of an iraqi child
>
> Dad, where did u go
> Mum and i needed u so
> I heard the terrible sound & smelled the smoke
> but what happed, i don't know
>
> Dad, where did u go
> Mum and i missed u so
> Mum is tearing
> I am scaring from heart to soul
> but what had happened,
> people say that i am too young to know
>
> Dad, come back
> Mum and i love u so
> She says you will be back
> With good news and hope.
> (Joyce, "A poem of an Iraqi child" post no. 1)

The poet uses short first-person rhymed lines to imitate the voice of a child. The poet's screen name "Joyce," etymologically connected to the concept of "joy," forms a contrast with the child's sadness, which constitutes a stark irony. Dotted with casual Internet spellings, such as "i," "u," and "&," the poem takes on a hint of net culture. In a later post, the poet explains her state of mind by echoing German philosopher Kant's cosmopolitan, antiwar sentiment: "When i wrote this poem, my tears were full of my eyes. I really felt heart-braking when the war began" (post no. 39). In defense of his cosmopolitan outlook, Kant argued that war is an evil in itself and that reason therefore "absolutely condemns war" and sees the achievement of peace as an "immediate duty" (Reiss, 1970, p. 104). The poet's empathy appealed to other forum members: some composed sequel poems by adopting the voice of the father; others made comments on the poems and the Iraq War. One of the sequel poems reads,

> You ask me when I will come back,
> I don't know, and I can't be sure.
> Maybe when the rainbow appears,
> when the sun begins shining,
> or when the serious typhoon stops,
> I will come home.
>
> Forgive me for leaving you alone,
> take care of yourself.
>
> I miss you and mom deeply.
>
> You ask me when I will come back,
> I ask myself as well,
> Maybe when the catastrophe stops,
> when the hateness dispears,
> or when the misunderstanding is resoloved.
>
> Forgive me fo leaving you alone,
> Don't be anxious about dad, I will take care myself.
>
> I miss you and mom deeply.
>
> You ask me when I will back,
> Who will tell me the answer?
> And Who can?
> But I think it's the coming future.

> Even though we are separated temporarily,
> we will get together.
>
> Belive dad, I promise it.
>
> I miss you and mom deeply.
> (smallsmall, "A poem of an Iraqi child" post no. 2)

Together with the first poem, this piece creates a grave dialogue between a loving father and an innocent child, and symbolically between the white collars concerned about world peace. The poets convey their sympathy and support for the Iraqi people and their implicit condemnation of the U.S. war machine. Similar to the first poem, the narrator paints a depressing picture of the war ("I don't know, and I can't be sure"), but her optimism for the future permeates the discourse. However, if the poet intends to speak like an Iraqi, her use of the typhoon metaphor seems a cultural oddity. Typhoons only form in East and Northeast Asia and are commonly used in Chinese literary works. The set metaphors—"rainbow," "sun," and "typhoon"—are more reflective of local life experiences. However, considering that the poem is composed by a Chinese multilingual, her "error" can be appreciated as an artistic maneuver. In a multilingual and multicultural online space, the meshing of a Chinese symbolic device in a fictional Iraqi discourse is meaningful.

In this artful thread, English enabled these individuals to express critical views toward war, turning the thread into an international tribunal. Joyce composed her poem in English probably because she wants to share her sadness and indignation, not only with Chinese audiences, but also with international ones. Most forum members follow suit and use English to write sequel poems or comments. And these messages do reach audiences beyond their authors' immediate national borders. MikeG, living in Philadelphia, responds to Joyce's poem:

> Please know that Americans are also touched by this poem and the horrors of the war in Iraq. We never want to see the innocent people hurt. Many of us are lovers of peace. Our government always tells us that we must fight to preserve peace. But our hearts know that peace does not come from violence. I pray that the war will end. (post no. 55)

MikeG's response not only confirms the deliberative and judicial nature of this artful thread but also suggests that this online community, or more broadly this domestic diaspora, is both open and fluid.

Moving from Englishes to Cosmopolitan English

The construction of diaspora, an emergent culture in China, is performed predominantly in English in this particular online space. Mediated by linguistic and nonlinguistic symbols, white collars represent themselves as individuals who work away from their old homes but manage to retain some connection to it. They strive to survive in their new homes by developing translingual and economic strategies and forging a variety of social relations. They develop their diasporic consciousness by constantly contrasting here and there, the present and the past. The wide use of English on this forum, as well as the other forums on the same digital platform involving more than half a million individuals, indicates that English has deeply entered local cultural practices. The popularity of English-based BBSs, personal blogs, and e-mails has ushered English into the average Chinese person's interpersonal communication, fostering an increasingly expanding English-literate public. As my analysis of the forum discourse shows, English usages in local contexts are becoming increasingly creative.

How do we characterize the white collars' creativity on this forum? If we conceive of these individuals as literary beings who share diasporic experiences, then these twenty threads can be viewed as one multivocal white collar narrative. In this narrative, writers strive to depict their diasporic consciousness, identity, and social relations and to share economic and cultural strategies for surviving in the here and now. From this perspective, the white collars' creativity can be understood as a kind of literary creativity. After examining multilingual writer Han Jin's novels, Zhang (2002) identifies linguistic creativity in areas such as lexical items, metaphors and proverbs, and discourse patterns and strategies. With the ostensible mediation of the Internet, which is missing in Han Jin's novels, creativity also abounds in the twenty analyzed threads.

At the lexical level, English terms are invented exhibiting local color. First and most noticeably, the forum members create screen names by translating local expressions or mixing English with Chinese family names. For example, "Sunshine," "Chinazero," "Green field," "soundtoy," "Raintear," "smallsmall," and "Blue stripe" are probably Chinese translations or spontaneous contrivances. "Michael.qin," "sky song," "Lacey gu," "SallyHsieh," and "Jayson_liu" are created by blending English first names with Chinese family names. Naming, a salient act of identity, marks alternative identifications for these members, identifications that stretch beyond their local cultural and linguistic lines. Second, terms with local cultural meanings are translated or created. For example, Sunshine talks about "Annbaby" (安妮宝贝) when describing her first impression of Shanghai, and lile1111 describes newlyweds giving out "red bags" (红包) as part of a local wedding ritual. On the second day of the wedding, the couple will "go back home" (回娘家) to visit the maternal family.

Creativity also has materialized in the members' uses of figures of speech, most of which can hardly be pinned down to a specific cultural, linguistic, or ethnic origin. Sunshine is a master of similes. She compares Shanghai to "an elegant lady" and Guangzhou to "an impetuous boy," forming an intriguing antithesis. She uses "my big babies" to describe her former students, signifying her parent-like relationship with them. When her life is filled with uncertainty, she feels like "a long lost child in the dark forest," and she uses writing to awaken "sleepy love in heart." In the thread "A poem of an Iraqi child," members prefer metaphors. Joyce never mentions the Iraq War but uses "the terrible sound" and "the smoke" to insinuate it. In her response poem, smallsmall uses three metaphors—"sun," "rainbow," and "typhoon"—to express an Iraqi father's optimism. The thread also contains figures such as intermittent repetition, antithesis, parallelism, rhyming, and the use of rhetorical questions.

Appropriation of local and translocal discourse strategies constitutes another creative dimension. For example, when advising Sunshine on how to survive life challenges, Allen002 borrows Christian and secular Anglo-American expressions. In the conversation between Greenfield and sky song, Greenfield blends market and capitalist discourses with local folk discourse. He advises sky song on how he should demand a salary raise and later congratulates him for receiving it by asking him to treat, a typical and culturally appropriate demand among friends on such occasions.

Addressing multilingual audiences, forum members blend multiple linguistic and cultural symbol systems, defying any attempts at fixing their identities to a particular culture, language, or location. The two aforementioned poems are examples of linguistic and cultural mixing. The poets mix linguistic strategies from literary Chinese, Standard English, and Internet language, and they blend in translocal cultural traits resulting in a cosmopolitan, humanistic appeal. Mixing symbols from multiple languages is commonly seen in other threads as well. For example, in a thread titled "Fading," two women continuously offer emotional support to each other. One of them, qiaozi, mixes Standard English, Standard Mandarin, Chinese regional dialects, and Internet language in the following two messages:

> raintear, my beloved girl, i cannot often surf online now. we will together become birds and trees next life! we are peace-lover-birds-and-trees!

> during the period i disappear from internet, i hope you and a la will still enjoy your life and share your feelings with us! 不要牵挂我, 我很快乐的, 就是希望你们也都很愉快很健康 [Don't worry about me. I am very happy and I hope you are both happy and healthy.] (post no. 17)
>
> raintear, i miss you friends so much! now I'm in Shijiazhuang! how great the life is! i was living in 太行山 [Taihang Mountain] for twenty days. 哦, 多想跟你们讲讲农村的元宵节啊! [Oh, how eagerly I want to share with you about the Lantern Festival celebrated in the countryside] raintear, be happy, 囡囡 [your little sister] will be companying with you! :p 唠唠嗑, 说说话, 夸夸俺们可爱的 raintear! [We will chitchat and praise our lovely raintear!] (post no. 84)

In these messages qiaozi not only uses English and Standard Mandarin, but also uses three terms from Chinese regional dialects—*a la* (阿拉, meaning I or we) from Shanghai and Ningbo dialects (regional variants of Wu), 囡囡 (*nan'nan*) from Wu, and 俺们 (*an'men*, meaning we or our) from Mandarin. The predominant use of lowercase spellings and a smiley (":p") are typical of Internet language. What is fascinating about qiaozi's translingual practice is the fact that, as she reveals in one of her posts, she actually grew up in the North, speaking Mandarin. However, she uses two address terms from the southern dialects to signify intimacy with her net friend Raintear, who grew up as a southerner. As people and language practice are not fixed to geographic locations, their migrations allow individuals like qiaozi to appropriate linguistic features from other peoples and other regions in their communications.

The white collars' creativity challenges a fundamental assumption in the China English construct. Scholars have consistently conceived China English as a discrete formal linguistic system (Li, 1993; Kirkpatrick & Xu, 2002; Xu, 2010). However, white collar language defies this conceptualization. Years of stringent standardized testing and training have instilled Standard English in the white collars, but, as their online discourse illustrates, and with each possessing different proficiencies and exigencies, their English deviates spectrally from the standard code. In fact, each white collar helps to develop and then adhere to an individualized, variable style. This style consists of Chinese borrowings, reduced or altered English forms, and creative new constructions inspired by a variety of representational systems. This form of English is negotiated by participants in every context as they construct intended meanings. Without a formal, uniform code like Standard English in sight, China English does not seem so different from either Lingua Franca English or plurilingual English used in South Asia, all of which Canagarajah (2009) describes as "highly fluid and variable form[s] of language practice" (p. 7). A major difference, though, lies in the fact that in English as a lingua franca forums, or in business or online gaming contexts, people use English out of necessity rather than choice. Using English as a willfully selected lingua franca offers English a symbolic value distinct from that of a traditional lingua franca: Chinese users create an educated, cosmopolitan persona in the translocal context.

The analysis of white collar discourse confirms some features of Cosmopolitan English and simultaneously reveals new ones. The white collar community illustrates that English, interwoven with other linguistic, cultural, and technological symbols, has profoundly entered local cultural practice (at least in the English-learning community). It conjures multilinguals as moving between and meshing linguistic symbol systems, and English communication enables the rise of a cosmopolitan disposition. Further, white collar English shows that English is so deeply intertwined with other linguistic and digital symbols that viewing China English as a discrete, self-sustaining linguistic system could only be arrived at a priori. Instead, in light of Canagarajah (2009), Higgins (2009), and Pennycook (2010), varieties of English categorized based on nation, ethnicity, and location are best viewed as a fluid, situated language practice. As a fluid, variable form of language practice, white collar English reveals the creative potential of Cosmopolitan English. Using the inference model and resorting to Chinese discursive and cultural features to understand China English veils its translingual and transcultural character. The model overshadows the meaning potential of English as a cosmopolitan language.

Domestic diaspora offers a unique perspective for understanding English. Used by diverse Chinese peoples with various proficiencies, China English can hardly be described as a system with stable lexical, syntactic, and pragmatic features.[3] Neither has it shown a stable affiliation with the Chinese nation or with Chinese culture. Although China English has been examined in relation to white collar and domestic diaspora identities, I do not suggest that China English maintains a categorical relationship with white collar culture. Domestic diaspora functions as a heuristic, forcing us to step out of national, ethnic, or class frames in our studies of English.

My student Jarinil reminds us of blurring linguistic and cultural boundaries. One year after she had taken my English course, I wrote her an e-mail asking her whether she could show me examples in which she had used her knowledge of Chinese language, Chinese culture, and other cultures in her coursework, especially in writing assignments. Without a permanent home of her own, she had lived in Philadelphia with a Chinese family for a while and had taken a few years of Chinese in college. She responded with the following e-mail message:

> I wish that I was of better help to you in fulfilling your interest, however, even though I had thought about it very hard and for a while I am not too aware of these issues in my life. I am sure that they exist, however, perhaps I have become too familiar with the presence of these cultures in my life. Thus, the boundaries between one and the other have been blurred as I perhaps seemlessly cross-incorporate my knowledge of these cultures, as you stated, but it is so natural that I do not know I'm doing it.

Her response suggests that while scholars have worked conscientiously to demarcate English practice along national, ethnic, and regional lines, that is not the way ordinary multilinguals experience language on a daily basis. English does not exist as a discrete system but is instead, in practice, meshed with symbols of other languages and diverse cultures.

In this book I place African American English on a par with other ethnic and cultural varieties, treating each as a language practice of a different diaspora. From the Englishes perspective, this move would probably be criticized. With a keen interest to uncover systems underlying language acts, the Englishes perspective views AAVE as a variety developed in English-dominant contexts where AAVE is spoken as a first language marked by a long history of racial injustice—slavery, segregation, oppression, and now mass incarceration. In contrast, English in Japan or China does not enjoy first-language status or stability of grammatical features; their users do not share the same social positioning as African Americans. From a cosmopolitan perspective, however, these so-called varieties are invariably connected with the diasporic experiences of their speakers. AAVE originated with Africans who were forced to leave their homelands and then dispersed across the Atlantic and North America, and they continue to move within and across national, ethnic, and class boundaries. Removed from their traditional cultural designations, speakers of English in Japan and China live in an in-between space. As illustrated by the Start with Simple Stories study group, in chapter 2, and the 21st Century Community forum, in this chapter, participants have to negotiate with personal and collective histories connected with English in the local context. They appropriate historical elements to construct meanings for an indeterminate future, or in the words of Bhabha (2004), their art of English use "renews the past, refiguring it as a contingent 'in-between' space, that innovates and interrupts the performance of the present" (p. 7). English used in these diasporas is a way of being and a practice in the making.

Although we have focused on a Chinese diaspora thus far, the diasporic perspective on culture, language, and nation can also enable English users in the United States to decenter themselves. The example of Jarinil taking on features of AAVE and Chinese cultural elements in her English use can be a starting point. It calls for other U.S.-centered English users to examine their language and cultural relations. Are they, their families, and their friends geographically or imaginatively fixed in one location? Do the communities that they identify with have a history of dealing with languages other than English and cultures other than that of the United States? While some may embrace the English-only ideology, are all Americans monolingual speakers of English? When these English users compare the Chinese and Japanese online communities' transliterate practices with their own in social media, they probably will be amazed by the numerous similarities they perceive. Like their Asian counterparts, so often they forge relations with strangers by sharing their thoughts and life experiences online. They use words, images, and video clips to construct a particular CyberEthos, which, again, so often spans across borders of nation, geographic region, ethnicity, class, gender, and language. By doing so, they can no longer define themselves by a fixed relation to any of these categories.

In this chapter I have challenged some assumptions behind the Englishes construct, underscoring the problems of fixing a variety of English to a nation, ethnicity, cultural group, or location. While recognizing the vivacious use of English within various communities, I don't see English as practiced in these communities as a linguistic system with stable and easily identifiable features at the lexical, syntactic, and pragmatic levels. Viewing these English-using communities as diasporas highlights the mobility of people with unstable, fluid linguistic and cultural associations. At the center of English use in these communities is transliterate creativity, the ability of constituent members to mobilize and blend linguistic, digital, and cultural symbol systems to forge border-crossing relations. Transliterate creativity relative to English has been amply demonstrated by creative writers (Kellman, 2000), many of whom have a keen sense of the available means of expression rendered by their lingual and cultural resources. In the next chapters, I will use these writers' creative works to further explore the possibilities of Cosmopolitan English.

4

Transliterate Creativity in the Literature of Globalization

Though much scholarly attention has been given in the past few decades to how multilingual writers use English in literary contexts, this has not been the case in writing studies. Research efforts have largely come from comparative literature, linguistics, language pedagogy, psychology, and history (Kellman & Lvovich, 2015). Predominantly, scholars have adopted either a postcolonial or a multiculturalist perspective for understanding the work of these literary writers. Scholars adopting a postcolonial perspective have generated insights on how such texts evidence the intricate relationships evolving between local political, economic, and cultural entities and the British Empire (Ashcroft, 2009; Bhabha, 2004; Kachru, 1990; Liu, 1995). Those adopting a multiculturalist perspective have focused on how these writers draw on multiple languages and English dialects to construct multicultural identities and voices in contexts where ethnic groups and individuals struggle against white political, economic, and cultural hegemony (e.g., Cortes-Conde & Boxer, 2002; Giaimo, 2010; Lambert, 2008, 2011; Li, 2004; Yao, 2010). Recently, distancing themselves from both the postcolonial and multiculturalist perspectives, some scholars including Beaujour (1989), Besemeres (2002), Ch'ien (2004), Hess (1996), Kellman (2000), Lennon (2010), Skinner (1998), and Yildiz (2012) examined writers from both former colonial and noncolonial contexts, focusing on the political and literary affordances of the various languages that these writers chose to compose their work.

Among these explorations into the literary work of multilingual writers, Braj B. Kachru's theorization of bilingual creativity has remained the most insightful.[1] His study of contact literature reveals that at lexical, syntactic, and discoursal levels, "non-native" English writers proactively draw from multiple languages and dialects. They adopt nativized thought processes that neither conform to canonical discourse types, text designs, or stylistic conventions nor stay within the traditional thematic range of Anglo-American English

(Kachru, 1982, 1987, 1990, 1995). Kachru's mapping of bilingual creative strategies has served as a powerful construct, helping other scholars explore the ways in which English has been appropriated by multilingual creative writers such as Albakry and Hancock (2008) on Anglo-Egyptian novelist Ahdaf Soueif; Cruz (2011) on Philippine writer Gregorio Brillantes; Mercanti (2009) on Indian writer Raja Rao; Zhang (2002) on Chinese American writer Han Jin; and Watkhaolarm (2005) on two Thai novelists, Kumut Chandruang and Pongpol Adireksarn.

Kachru's study of bilingual creativity largely focused on writers from former colonial countries where English is spoken in local communities. These writers have often been perceived as contributors to the literature of their respective nations. However, as English now percolates through almost all parts of the world and has often become a near-universal requirement in formal education, it is used for increasingly diverse creative purposes (Lee, 2004; Moody, 2006; Stanlaw, 2004; You, 2010). In countries and regions where English is not commonly used in local speech communities, writers with material resources may still publish what is traditionally called "high literature" in English. They compose not necessarily for local communities but for a larger readership beyond regional and national borders. In Anglo-American nations, where English is the default national language, many creative writers are multilingual/multidialectal. The expansion of translingual creativity, the mobility of writers, and the increasingly blurred boundaries between languages and between cultures warrant a reexamination of Kachru's theory of bilingual creativity.

This chapter explores multilingual writers' creativity from a cosmopolitan perspective. I will first critique Kachru's theory of bilingual creativity and offer a reformulation by taking a less-bounded perspective on language, nation, and culture. Adopting this perspective begs several questions: How does English, when mediated by languages, dialects, and media, acquire its meanings in literature? How do multilingual writers draw on fluid cultural forms and processes? And how do writers shape English in specific literary contexts and make it part of their communicative repertoires rather than simply nativize it as a second or foreign language? Adopting this less-bounded perspective, I will then analyze the works of three multilingual/multidialectal authors, focusing on their strategies of making meaning together with a global audience. Taking a cosmopolitan perspective will enable us in writing studies to further appreciate the creativity that English, along with other languages, affords multilingual writers.

Moving from Bilingual to Transliterate Creativity

In Kachru's formulation of bilingual creativity, a bounded perspective on nation and culture is prominent. Writing about multilingual writers in former colonial countries, he points out the inadequacy of using monolingualism as the norm for describing and analyzing linguistic interactions in traditional multilingual societies. He suggests that models proposed for discourse and textual analysis of monolinguals' linguistic interactions are inadequate for the analysis of bilinguals' language use (1990, p. 159). The distinction Kachru makes between the monolingualism of ideal "native speakers" in Anglo-American nations and the multilingualism of "non-native speakers" from former British colonies is valuable in underscoring the latter's multilingual repertoire. However, this strategic distinction also creates a binary of literate cultures not reflective of facts on the ground. So-called native English speakers may not always practice monolingualism. Their monolingual practices are almost always a result of nation-state mandates as perpetuated through language policy, formal schooling, and the publishing industry. It is almost impossible to single out an Anglo-American author, past or present, who exclusively uses Standard English in his or her work. Most practice translingualism by drawing diverse resources from their repertoires, which are constituted by regional dialects, professional jargon, and other language resources. In fact, Standard English is itself a historical product of translingualism, formed through individuals constantly drawing words and expressions from other languages and non-Anglo cultures.

The binary of literate cultures is also reflected in Kachru's definition of contact literature. He defines it as English writing by English as a second language, or ESL, authors "to delineate contexts which generally do not form part of what may be labeled the traditions of English literature (African, Malaysian, and Indian and so on)" (1990, p. 161). He goes on to explain that contact literatures have "both a national identity and a linguistic distinctiveness" (p. 161). The linguistic realization of such identities is achieved in several ways, making contact literatures a blend of two or more linguistic textures and literary traditions, with extended situational contexts within which they may be interpreted and understood. Thus, the definition of contact literature is closely connected to the "context of situation," localities beyond what Kachru terms the inner-circle countries. Contact literature represents literate translingualism in contexts that generally are not accepted as part of the traditions of English literature. The emphasis on localities could be understood as part of the postcolonial discourse of nation building, but this emphasis also unwittingly overshadows the importance of translingualism as having always been practiced in the traditions of English literature (Artiano, 2015; Hale, 2005; Rosenwald, 2008; Schendl & Wright, 2011). While the notion of contact literature promotes and celebrates the national and regional literatures written in English in former colonial contexts, it has also perpetuated a static and monolithic view of Anglo-American nations, cultures, and literatures.

Locality is again central to the notion of nativization, or the linguistic realization of literary distinctiveness. Kachru (1990) identifies three primary ways in which English is nativized in the literatures of former colonial nations—the nativization of context, of cohesion and cohesiveness, and of rhetorical strategies. In the case of contextual nativization, "[local] cultural presuppositions overload a text and demand a serious cultural interpretation" (p. 165). In postcolonial nations, the native speaker's concept of cohesion and cohesiveness is redefined in each institutionalized language variety via various types of lexicalization, collocational extension, and uses of grammatical forms. A writer provides authenticity to speech acts or discourse types in his or her work by employing various rhetorical strategies, such as using native similes and metaphors, translating proverbs and idioms, and producing culturally dependent speech styles and syntactic devices. Nativization can be viewed as a postcolonial perspective on English use. This perspective promotes the secular and modernist distinction between "us" and "them" or "native" and "foreign." Historically, English was indeed not part of the local communicative repertoire before Anglo-American colonization; the distinction made between foreign and native emerged as a discursive strategy, adopted from former colonialists, to underscore this historical process of cultural colonization and adaption. But if English has already become part of the communicative repertoire of the local, as it indeed has, one has to question whether nativization remains a useful construct for understanding English in multilingual writing.

In his discussion Kachru tends to reify English either as a medium or as a code of communication. He states that "when we call English a global medium, it means that those who use English across cultures have a shared code of communication. . . . We have one language with many voices" (1995, p. 7). Taking a structuralist view toward media, he emphasizes English as a discrete system of its own. In reality, English is always interwoven with and mediated by other linguistic and nonlinguistic symbol systems, forming a communicative ecology. The coding and decoding of meaning cannot depend solely upon English; meaning is always co-generated. In contemporary literature written in English, new media increasingly penetrate writing and reading processes, turning writers and readers into "prosumers" rather than consumers. Visual novels, Twitter fictions, and electronic poetry are just a few examples (Lennon, 2000; Raguseo, 2010; Strickland, 2006). Visual and audio effects, human-machine interaction, and textual circulation all combine to give meaning to a text.

Also indicative of Kachru's bounded approach to nation and language is his reticence about code-switching in bilingual creativity. Literary critics have referred to the cultural and literary strategy of using two (or more) languages or dialects simultaneously in a literary text as code-switching, interlingualism, or translingualism (Sánchez, 1986; Kellman, 2000). According to Sánchez (1986), "in an interlingual experience, the tensions in syntax, the connotations, the ironies, and the reverberations of words and images interlock, pulling in two different directions at once" (p. 86). A writer may throw in a few words from a different language to spice up the text; he or she may switch between languages or between dialects at inter- and intra-sentential levels. In the United States, code-switching, or translingualism to use a more apposite term, has been practiced by both mainstream canonical and minority writers (Montes-Alcala, 2012).

In the age of globalization, the creative work of multilingual writers could be studied using a less-bounded perspective to nation, culture, and language. Globalization here is first understood as people, images, technologies, ideologies, and capital spilling over traditional political boundaries and creating novel "uncertain landscapes" through their complex interaction (Appadurai, 1996, p. 43). Globalization is also understood, in the context of literate practice, as individuals moving out of local reading and writing scenes and forming networks of interactions (Brandt & Clinton, 2002). Contemporary works by multilingual writers in English can be termed the literature of globalization. Literary works written in this globalizing medium have the potential for global circulation, consumption, and adaptation. Because of the worldwide circulation, market, and readership, a writer not only adopts discourse features, thought processes, and cultural elements of local speech communities, however elusive or idealized these communities may be, but also those of other communities already in circulation. However, to maximize the impact (often economic) of their work, writers are frequently pressured by their literary agents and the publishing industry to translate, to be translated, and to adopt Standard English. These pressures can sometimes cripple writers' abilities to effectively represent their distinctive voices (Anzaldúa, 2007; Anzaldúa & Moraga, 1984; Anzaldúa & Keating, 2000, 2002; Lennon, 2010; Moraga, 1983, 1993, 1997; Stavans, 2001).

To distance myself from the view that languages are discrete systems, I call the creative work of multilingual writers "transliterate creativity." *Transliterate* is used here to emphasize the fluid, unstable, and blurred boundaries between languages, between dialects, and between cultures in these writers' communicative repertoires and the writers' ability to defy and transcend these boundaries in their work. Used by literary critics, the term "translingual," in contrast, has often referred to writers crossing linguistic boundaries rather than to their language practice as an integrative and dynamic use of semiotic resources (Liu, 1995; Kellman, 2000). This different use of terms can be illustrated by Kellman's (2000) explanation of code-switching: "Code-switching is common among bilingual speakers, and authors who would represent speech as it is actually spoken create internally translingual texts, often between colloquial and formal or between regional and standard forms of the same language. Any writer of any scope is always ranging between registers" (p. 15). Clearly, he focuses on crossing linguistic boundaries (levels of formality and regional and standard forms) in everyday language practice rather than on the fluidity of language boundaries in writers' repertoires. A less-bounded perspective to language and culture entails the following orientations in studying the literature of globalization:

- Instead of examining how writers blend elements from national, regional, or ethnic cultures, we study how they draw from fluid cultural forms and processes.
- In addition to studying how writers draw lexical, syntactic, and discoursal resources from English and other languages, we also examine how a text derives multiple meanings from its symbolic ecology, including from linguistic and nonlinguistic dimensions, and how English is mediated by other languages, dialects, and media in the text and in the contexts of production, circulation, and consumption.
- Instead of studying the nativization of English, we pay attention to how writers adapt English in its literary contexts and make it a part of their communicative repertoires.

This less-bounded perspective refuses to view national, regional, or ethnic cultures as monolithic and static or as easily generalizable; instead they are fluid and shaped by diverse intra- and transnational cultural forms and processes. This less-bounded perspective also refuses to view languages, dialects, and media as discrete systems ripe for structuralist analysis. English is always entangled with other languages, dialects, and modes of communication, for example, print, digital, and oral, in practice. It needs to be examined in relation to other languages and media. This less-bounded perspective refuses to view writers' uses of English as nativization of that language. While English does take on local colors in specific literary contexts, equally meaningful to consider is how it has come to serve and empower individual writers by appealing to audiences and performing identities.

Taking the less-bounded perspective, I will examine Raja Rao's *Kanthapura*, Xiaolu Guo's *A Concise Chinese-English Dictionary for Lovers*, and Sapphire's *Push*, all tours de force in the literature of globalization. Aligned with the type of analysis used in comparative literature, I read through these works and identified themes, scenes, and language strategies that might resonate with a global audience possessing diverse linguistic and cultural experiences. With cosmopolitanism and transliteracy being the themes of this book, I will focus, in the sections to follow, on the fictive scenes that foreground issues of language, power, education, and access. These scenes provide rich sociohistorical contexts for understanding certain language practice in the fictional world. In addition, these scenes help to illustrate the affordances of taking a less-bounded, cosmopolitan perspective to understand these multilingual writers' creativity. With these scenes, specifically, I will examine how local or global cultural forms and processes are appropriated, how local language practice is represented, and how cosmopolitan identification may be forged among the readers. I will start with Raja Rao's *Kanthapura* (1938/1967), which has been studied by scholars, including Kachru (1990, 2005), predominantly from nationalist and multiculturalist perspectives.

Reading *Kanthapura* as Literature of Globalization

Celebrated for their Indianness, Raja Rao's works have long been canonized in Indian English literature. However, scholars still disagree on how exactly one defines Indianness. In both Western and Indian canonical formulations of Indianness, the idea of "unity by diversity" has been favored. Differences resulting from diverse cultural and linguistic traditions and realities on the Indian subcontinent have had to conform and submit to a dominant class or a nationalist agenda. In contrast, Mercanti (2009) recently suggested "diversity in unity" as an alternative for reconfiguring Indianness. For him, unity refers to "both common humanist values shared by all and India's ever-increasing heterodoxy and assertive multiculturalism—cross-cultural and cross-linguistic contexts capable of coexisting with the old and the new, the indigenous and the 'imported,' in a creative fusion of different cultures that gives rise to singular results and new permutations" (p. xxx). Such reconfigured Indianness calls for and celebrates a cohesiveness of multiple negotiations across cultural and linguistic traditions and contexts.

Scholars, including Kachru, have aptly demonstrated how in *Kanthapura* Rao reconciles Indian mythologies, legends, and customs with Western literary conventions. To illustrate the contextual nativization in Rao's novel, Kachru (1990) cites a narrative in which a storyteller intermingles the birth and deeds of Mahatma Gandhi with the narratives of a multitude of the pantheon of Hindu gods. Gandhi rallied people from village to village and led them to "slay the serpent of the foreign rule," as did Krishna the flute player in Hindu mythology (Rao, 1967, p. 12). In reality, sensitive to Indian religious and political traditions, Gandhi developed a series of nonviolent strategies for effecting social change in colonial India. Kachru uses this example to illustrate the interpretative difficulties inherent in texts written by multilingual writers for monolingual English readers: the presupposition of the discourse interpretation "extends the cultural load of English lexis from conventional Greek and Roman allusions to Asian and African myths, folklore, and traditions" (p. 166). It is the extension of the cultural load of the English lexis, or the cultural differences indexed by the English lexis, that could cause interpretative difficulties for the hypothetically monolingual reader.

The attention given to how Rao blends Indian and Western literary traditions using particular themes and styles, however, often leaves the novel's transnational connections much less attended to. These connections give Rao's work the potential to appeal to a broader readership than just Indians and monolingual English readers. In the end, his work appeals to readers not only in the East and the West but also to those in the industrialized North and in the developing South. For example, the narrator describes the Soviet Union in the beginning of the novel in a narrative that shows how Soviet society provides the local villagers an alternative vision of the world:

> But there was one thing she spoke of again and again—and, to tell you the truth, it was after the day the sandal merchant of the North came to sell us his wares and had slept on her veranda and

> had told her of the great country across the mountains, the country beyond Kabul and Bukhara and Lahore, the country of the hammer and sickle and electricity [. . .] and there in that country there were women who worked night and day, and when they felt tired, they went and spent their holiday in a palace—no money for the railway, no money for the palace—and when the women were going to have a child, they had two months' and three months' holiday, and when the children were still young they were given milk by the government, and when they were grown up they were sent free to school, and when they grew older still they went to the Universities free, too [. . .] (Rao, 1967, p. 29)

The narrator, an aged widow, becomes excited when talking about this remote country, and the long sentence drags on for several additional lines. What is significant here is that this passage reveals the way the villagers are exposed to revolutionary ideals. The ideals are related by a female villager who has learned them from a guest, a "sandal merchant of the North." This remote country "beyond Kabul and Bukhara and Lahore," in the North rather than in the West, instills transnational imaginings in local villagers. The ideals of this country are represented and put into circulation using cultural symbols, such as "the hammer and sickle and electricity," which are evoked repeatedly in the later parts of the novel (Rao, 1967, p. 143).

If Indian myths, folklore, and traditions indexed in English cause interpretative difficulties for the monolingual reader, the lexis coded with ideas, images, and symbols from the international communist movement, a form of cosmopolitanism, engage a world readership and effectively elevate *Kanthapura* from a local literary tour de force to literature of global significance. The novel reveals that Indians were faced with several competing options for achieving national independence in the 1930s, including both Gandhi's nonviolent resistance and a violent alternative adopted during the Russian Revolution against the Tsarist autocracy. The step-by-step strategies laid out by the Gandhists in the novel provide not only Indians, but also interested readers in other countries, tools to effect social change or even national independence. With a global readership interested in decolonization and national independence, Rao's English is both Indian and cosmopolitan.

Rao also consciously blurs lingual and dialectal boundaries. Scholars have recognized his adroitness in this regard. In an interview with Rao, Jussawalla and Dasenbrock (1992) remarked that "much of *Kanthapura* reads as if it were translated from Kannada; the syntactic patterns are those of Kannada," Rao's native language (p. 154). Rao concurred but added that he actually heard English in his head when writing much of the novel. In the North American edition of *Kanthapura* first published in 1963, there are fifty-seven pages of glossary originally drawn from Arabic, Persian, Sanskrit, and modern regional languages. Flipping through the novel, one can easily note italicized expressions from the classical texts of Hinduism originally written in Sanskrit, such as "Veda Sastra Pravina Krishna Sastri," "Sankara Jayanthi," and "Sankara Vijaya." Some local expressions of various origins are not translated, such as bodicecloth, bandicoot, dharmawar sari, coolie, dhoti, khadi, thothi, and toddy. Some of these words have now entered the English vocabulary. The mixed use of these transliterated and nontransliterated expressions reminds readers of the multilingual and multicultural realities in which the narrator of the novel lives.

Intriguingly, this multilingual reality is contrasted with a narrative about establishing Hindi as a national language. Considering the fact that Rao was an adherent to Gandhist nationalism, the narrative captures not only tensions between, but also authorial negotiations with, that nationalism and the multilingual landscape. It is important to note that even an aged widow in a remote village (the narrator) draws from multiple languages and cultures in her speech. However, some Gandhists feel strongly the strategic need for a national language as part of a movement toward decolonization and independence:

> He [Sankar] said Hindi would be the national language of India, and though Kannada is good enough for our province, Hindi must become the national tongue, and whenever he met a man in the street he did not say "How are you?" in Kannada, but took to the northern manner and said "Ram-Ram." But what was shameful was the way he began to talk Hindi to his mother, who understood not a word of it, but he said she would learn it one day; and he spoke nothing but Hindi to his daughter, and if by chance he used an English word, as they do in the city, he had a little closed pot, with a slit in the lid, into which he dropped a coin, and every month he opened it and gave it to the Congress fund. (Rao, 1967, pp. 98–99)

The passage, on one hand, reveals the multilingual contexts in which Sankar, a Gandhist, lives. He possesses competence in English, Hindi, and Kannada.

He is, on the other hand, willing to give up his provincial tongue, probably his first language, to pursue Hindi, either his second or third language. The contrast between the narrator's applied multilingual repertoire and Sankar's determination to establish Hindi as the national language calls the reader's attention to the language issues connected to India's pursuit of nationhood. Historically, establishing national languages has been considered indispensable for modern nation building, and as a strategy it was adopted by Indian nationalists for negotiating differences within multilingual and multiethnic India. Contrasted with the narrator's translingual practice, this particular episode reveals a critical linguistic strategy in nation building, commonly found in new nations rising from the ashes of colonialism. Choosing to write his first and later novels in English, an official language of India, instead of Kannada, his mother tongue, Rao metonymically declares an alignment with the nationalist movement.

Canonizing Raja Rao's works as Indian literature is part of the nation-building endeavor, but as demonstrated thus far, his *Kanthapura* embodies tendencies of globalization. A study of Rao's literary creativity additionally needs to account for the cosmopolitan nature of his English. To the end of addressing issues that transcend local contexts and in addition to focusing on the nativization of English, scholars must attend to the ways Rao shapes his English to engage his diverse audiences. In the two passages I quote from *Kanthapura*, his English indexes the circulating ideas, images, and symbols of the international communist movement of his time. It draws the reader to the nearly universal tension among multilingual, multicultural, and multiethnic realities and the need for linguistic and cultural unity in newly independent nations. It is through this adapted English that Rao has appealed to audiences both inside and outside of India.

If Rao depended on local communities for discourse patterns and features in his writing, such influences are less salient in *A Concise Chinese-English Dictionary for Lovers* by Xiaolu Guo (2007). Both a film director and writer, Guo divides her time between London and Beijing. After writing several Chinese books, she published this English-dominant novel with a major international press. Written and read by individuals unconfined to one geographic or cultural location, the book becomes a literary expression of globalization. In depicting a Chinese woman's cross-national experience, Guo, like Rao, could not rely on a single community for discourse features and patterns. Continuing with the less-bounded perspective, I examine next novelist Guo's strategies for making English both individual and cosmopolitan.

Writing across Borders

Guo's coming-of-age novel depicts a young Chinese woman's transnational travel, which gradually leads to her cosmopolitan disposition. In her early twenties and knowing little English, the protagonist (nicknamed Z) goes to study English in London. During her one-year stay, she is exposed to London's metropolitan culture. She falls in love and cohabits with a British man twenty years her senior. While living in England, she has the opportunity to travel to some European countries. Wherever she goes, she consults her Chinese-English dictionary and reflects upon her daily encounters. The story captures this unprivileged traveler's struggle for linguistic and sexual maturity. At the novel's conclusion, she ends her romantic relationship and returns to Beijing.

Cultural displacement is a major theme of the novel. To portray Z's sense of displacement, Guo draws on more than Chinese and British cultures; ideas, images, and symbols circulating through mass media are utilized regardless of origin. For example, on her flight from Beijing to London, Z questions her intent to study in England by groping for references from American TV shows. "What else I knowing about West? American TV series dubbing into Chinese, showing us big houses in suburb, wife by window cooking and car arriving in front house. Husband back work. Husband say Honey I home, then little childrens running to him, see if he bringing gift" (Guo, 2007, p. 4). Never having been to London before, Z recalls scenes from American TV episodes to help imagine the place that she is heading to. For her, there is no difference between London and the TV scenes because they all signify the foreign, the West. After she lands in London, American movies, such as *Alien*, *Austin Powers*, *Titanic*, and *Rush Hour*, provide her further references and strategies for wrestling with displacement and for making sense of her new life. It is important to note that Z draws these references not from her lived experience in the United States but from her life in China, where she had seen these films. The deep penetration of Hollywood movies into Chinese society makes their characters, plots, and symbols part of contemporary Chinese culture, specifically Chinese media culture. As a film director, Guo draws easily and abundantly from this part of Chinese transnational culture.

The protagonist further blurs national and cultural boundaries by citing authors and artists of different origins. These authors, from China, Mexico, Iran, France, and the United States, come to help Z make sense of her struggles while living with her boyfriend. For example, in the middle of the story, she flips through Mexican artist Frida Kahlo's paintings and compares this artist with her boyfriend. Near the end of the novel, she reads the work of American poet Walt Whitman and finds similarities between a man in one of his poems and her boyfriend. Then she reads French writer Gustave Flaubert, trying to figure out the multiple contradictions that her boyfriend embodies:

> In Hackney Town Hall Library we sit and look at books.
>
> Gustave Flaubert said, "In Pericles' time, the Greeks devoted themselves to art without knowing where the next day's bread might come from. Let us be Greeks!"
>
> I close the Flaubert book, looking at you. You are reading a book with the picture of sculptures. I keep thinking about Flaubert's words: artists should devote themselves to the art, like a priest devote to God. But what is so important about art? Why it should be like a devotion? (pp. 265–266)

Flaubert's words serve as a window through which the protagonist can inquire into her boyfriend's mind and soul. The quote provides a heuristic for inquiry. Because her boyfriend is a Westerner, she probably finds Western writers and artists conducive to understanding him. Together, these references help construct his Western otherness, a kind of reverse Orientalism for Z. While understanding her boyfriend is a cross-national and cross-cultural effort for Z, selecting book and art references of diverse origins to develop the story indicates the novelist's creativity.

Texts, symbols, and products of the women's health and sex industry also come to mediate the protagonist's growing maturity. The novel is centrally about Z seeking her identity through a series of sexual encounters. Handling a condom for the first time, she reads the instructions line by line and discusses them with her boyfriend (pp. 58–59). She visits a peepshow room in London to watch a live sexual performance (p. 108). One of her Japanese friends presents her a vibrator as a birthday gift. Never having seen one before, Z reads the instructions carefully (pp. 128–129). When she travels in Portugal, she buys a book on women's pleasure. After reading about masturbation skills from the book, Z comments,

> Masturbating, I never tried it before. Nobody Western would believe that I never try to masturbate as a twenty-four-year-old

> woman. Or maybe I did but I didn't know what I was doing. Sex in my understanding means something to do with a man, but not to do with myself. Having sex with oneself is like talking to oneself: bit mad. When I saw that Soho peepshop, I never thought to do with me. I also believed no love then no sex. Sex is an expression of love. But somehow this idea is changing. Now I feel tortured by the desire inside my body, and I feel strongly how much this desire wanting to be fulfilled. (p. 193)

The circulation of sexual identity discourse has tantalized and seduced this "innocent" Chinese woman, innocent because she has come from a different discourse community. She has a notion before coming to Europe that sex is an expression of love. What she has encountered in the above examples can hardly be categorized as the culture of a particular nation. Instead it would be appropriate to call it a transnational culture of women's health and sexuality, a form of cosmopolitanism. Products, ideas, and practices of this culture, including condom and vibrator instructions, women's health books, and sex services, all come to mediate Z's sexuality. They are generative in the novelist's imagination.

When Kachru (1990) discusses the linguistic realization of distinctiveness in contact literature, he highlights presuppositions grounded in local histories and cultures. Different from what has been traditionally expected of the historical and cultural milieu of English literature, these presuppositions cause interpretative difficulties for the monolingual reader. But in the literature of globalization, when works are written about contemporary or fictional societies, the presuppositions are not always local. Even local events aren't divorced from the global circulation of cultural forms and processes. In both *Kanthapura* and *A Concise Chinese-English Dictionary for Lovers*, we have observed two writers' skilled uses of global flows of ideas, images, and symbols in developing their stories. In Guo's later novels such as *Twenty Fragments of a Ravenous Youth* (2008) and *UFO in Her Eyes* (2009), the stories all take place in contemporary China. However, transnational cultural elements continue to abound because imperialism, Westernization, and globalization have left Chinese society "in exile." The uncontaminated, premodern Chinese cultural tradition is nowhere to be found. While presuppositions based on local histories and cultures are important to consider in the literature of globalization, we also need to account for those that have transcended the local.

Writing Translingually

Linguistic creativity can be understood in almost diametrically opposing ways. On one hand, language use is always creative; it is always a design. One varies his or her words in response to different contexts and purposes. The words constitute a contingent nexus of social arrangements, the life experiences of the interlocutors, and the interactional order between them (Scollon & Scollon, 2004). On the other hand, creativity in literary studies often means writing in a manner different from one's quotidian speech by employing figures of speech, genre features, and patterned structures uncommon to that speech. The language of *A Concise Chinese-English Dictionary for Lovers* perfectly combines these two opposing perspectives of creativity. As a multilingual speaker, the protagonist's every utterance is a blending of several languages and dialects, either explicitly or implicitly. It becomes language play for both the protagonist and the writer. In addition, the novel's design presents two faces—public and private—by adopting the aesthetics of both a diary and an annotated dictionary.

The most striking aspect of the protagonist's language probably comes at the morpho-syntactic level. Z narrates her story using what I have called Cosmopolitan English (CE). Patient readers will recognize her language patterns after a few pages and come to understand her better, which is an instance of negotiating with CE in context. Z habitually drops the verb *be* and auxiliary verb *do* in her utterances in the beginning of the story. She also tends to add *–ing* to active verbs. In the following passage, she uses diverse verb forms, some conforming to Standard English and some not.

> As I far away from China, I asking me why I coming to West. Why I must to study English like parents wish? Why I must to get diploma from West? I not knowing what I needing. Sometimes I not even caring what I needing. I not caring if I speaking English or not. Mother only speaking in village dialect and even not speaking official Mandarin, but she becoming rich with my father, from making shoes in our little town. Life OK. Why they want changing my life? (p. 4)

Due to her Chinese background, one may reasonably suspect that Chinese syntax has been blended in her English expressions. In this short passage, three sentences come very close to the structure of Standard Chinese, or what Z calls "official Mandarin":

Why I must to study English like parents wish?
为什么 我 必须 去 学 英语

Why I must to get diploma from West?
为什么 我 必须 去 拿 学位

Why they want changing my life?
为什么 他们 要 改变 我的 生活

Beyond these sentences one may argue that Standard Chinese has affected the rest of her English. In the passage Z also comments on her parents' linguistic abilities. There is little doubt that Z also speaks her hometown's dialect(s), most probably one (or more) of the Wu dialects in Zhejiang Province. Therefore her home dialect(s), indeed, may have affected her English. Z, or more accurately the novelist, has worked with at least three distinct linguistic symbol systems in her narrative—her home dialect(s) (probably one, or more, of the Wu dialects), Standard Chinese, and English.

The trajectory of Z's English development marks another aspect of the novelist's creativity. At the end of the story, a year after moving to London, Z's English has changed significantly. While it continues to exhibit minor deviations from the orthographic conventions of Standard English, the most conspicuous nonstandard features of her English have disappeared. In an interview with BBC China, Guo revealed that she spent half a year working on the first few pages of Z's voice.[2] Conceivably, much of that time was devoted to tweaking Z's fledgling English, making it resemble that of a language learner from China. As the story progresses, Z uses diverse and complex sentence structures. Thanks to her own translingual experience, Guo metonymically captures how a language learner works with several languages and dialects while developing competence in English.

Z's English shares major characteristics with that of educated contemporary Chinese society. Due to her interaction with diverse speakers of English, Z gradually moves from a highly idiosyncratic, nonstandard style to one closer to Standard English. Though not disappearing, Standard Chinese and Chinese regional dialects become more cognitively latent. In chapter 3 I showed that educated Chinese individuals demonstrate different levels of English proficiency and that they often blend Standard Chinese and regional dialects, explicitly or implicitly, in their written English. While Standard English rules linger in the back of their minds, their English often refuses to conform to these rules. And English usages among Chinese speakers are never stable; they are always evolving like Z's. In her novel Guo manages to portray in Z the coalescent and evolutionary nature of CE.

Chinese languages not only scaffold Z's English cognitively, but they also creep into her narrative explicitly, at both syntactic and discoursal levels. Z tends to use Chinese phrases intra-sententially when she compares a phenomenon or a topic cross-culturally. For example, she describes the vagina of a prostitute from the peepshow: "Now she lays her back on the stage, raising her two legs high above. 阴道—Yin Dao: the tunnel of darkness, that is Chinese word to say vagina. Her tunnel of darkness is right in front of me. Her secret tunnel, winding and curved, is like a maze" (p. 109). Seeing another women's vagina for the first time, Z is both curious and excited. The Chinese expression, both its ideograms and its sound, provide Z a visual cue—"tunnel of darkness"—to observe, to describe, and to understand: "Her secret tunnel, winding and curved, is like a maze."

Chinese also enters the discoursal design. In two instances where Z does not feel like speaking or writing English, as she confesses in the novel, she uses Chinese. Guo uses several dictionary entries per chapter, and she titles each chapter using the name of a particular month. Under each dictionary entry, Z shares an event that is related to the entry or that has prompted her to consult the entry in her Collins dictionary. One of her entries (figure 4.1) is on freedom (p. 154). In this entry Z lays out her take on the notion of freedom after her boyfriend demands freedom in their relationship. She deliberates about the relationship between love and freedom using Standard Chinese. She deliberates within her own world, protected by her Chinese, with no intention of communicating with her boyfriend. Guo compensates for Z's refusal to translate by offering an English translation on the opposite page, another translingual act.

Writing as a Citizen of the World

What does Guo's transliterate creativity suggest about her identity and her sense of audience? Does she view herself as a Chinese writer writing for a Chinese audience or for monolingual English speakers? If we consider Z to be Guo's alter ego, then we gain a glimpse of the evolution of her identity in the following reflection:

> The day when I arrived to the West, I suddenly realised I am a Chinese. As long as one has black eyes and black hair, obsessed

freedom ('fri:dəm) *n.* **1.** being free; **2.** exemption or immunity, e.g. freedom from hunger; **3.** the right or privilege of unlimited access.

freedom

我说我爱你,你说你要自由。

为什么自由比爱更重用?没有爱,自由是赤裸裸的一片世界,为什么爱情不能是自由的? 难道爱情是自由的监狱?那么多人活在监狱里头吗?

Figure 4.1. Page from Xiaolu Guo's novel A *Concise Chinese-English Dictionary for Lovers*, featuring Z's perception of freedom and how it relates to her understanding of relationships and language.

> by rice, and cannot swallow any Western food, and cannot pronounce the differences between "r" and "l," and request people without using *please*—then he or she is a typical Chinese: an ill-legal immigrant, badly treat Tibetans and Taiwanese, good on food but put MSG to poison people, eat dog's meat and drink snakes' guts.
>
> "I want to be a citizen of the world." Recently I learned to say this. I *would* become a citizen of the world, *if* I have a more useful passport. Ah Mrs. Margaret, that conditional again! (p. 148, italics in original)

Z's Chinese identity is defined by surface features and shaped by the circulating British stereotypes about Chinese immigrants. While affirming her identity as Chinese, she begins to be attracted to the idea of becoming a citizen of the world. She wants to be a cosmopolite but recognizes the constraints caused by her physical features and her citizenship. The tension between her cosmopolitan desire and her national identity again surfaces when she reveals one of her dreams a few months later. In the dream Z has written a best seller, a cookbook of three hundred noodle recipes for British housewives. She explains how noodles can be cooked: "It's also about two-way-cooking, meaning either it can be prepared as Chinese food or it can become Italian spaghetti. For example, one can just change ginger into basil, or replace chilli to rosemary with a bit cheese, then noodles will get totally different *identity*" (p. 234, italics in original). Z's way of preparing the noodles can be read allegorically as a concern over how to construct/cook her identity. One can turn Chinese noodles into Italian spaghetti by replacing the taste-defining sauces. Similarly, a new identity can be cooked by substituting some elements of an old identity. Or one can cooked up multiple identities depending on which identifying elements he or she chooses to exhibit at a particular moment. But one thing is certain: after staying in London for a year, Z has changed, and her identity has transformed. In the epilogue, on an airplane heading back to Beijing she observes her reflection in the window: "I look at the window and it reflects a stranger's face. It's not the same 'Z' as one year ago. She will never look at the world in the same way. Her heart is wounded, wounded, wounded, like the nightingale bleeding on the red rose" (p. 279). Her diasporic experiences have transformed her as taste-defining sauces do to noodles.

Shuttling between London and Beijing, like Z, Guo will probably not claim a single identity, an identity fixed to a nation-state. She in fact has taken on Z's dreamed identity—a world citizen who could travel without being constrained by her passport. That perhaps explains why Guo, a published novelist in Chinese, chose to write this novel predominantly in English and to publish it with an international press. By writing in English, Guo more fully represents Z's cultural and linguistic struggles in Britain. More importantly, the choice aligns better with Z's new acquired identity, a citizen of the world, and so with Guo's identity as an author of the world. English enables Guo to communicate with a wide audience without being translated, technically anyway. Whereas Gloria Anzaldúa (1987) challenges North American Anglos to meet her halfway in Spanish, here Guo takes on the challenge of meeting the rest of the world in English, but in her own style of English.

If we no longer view Guo fixedly as a Chinese writer, but as a writer of both China and the world, we should not entertain unidirectional or nation-bound views of her use of English. In attempting to expand Chinese literature or to build a Chinese literature in English, one could view her writing as Chinese. This is the nationalist perspective commonly used for understanding Raja Rao's *Kanthapura*. But in the age of globalization, where people, cultural products, information, and capital increasingly flow across and blur national boundaries, we need to seriously attend to a less-bounded perspective on literature and language, treating them as an integral part of transnational flows. Guo's use of English should not be viewed solely as a nativizing practice.

Instead, while negotiating Anglo-American national linguistic standards, she adapts English by fusing languages, dialects, genres, and media. As a writer of the world, it is more important for Guo to tailor her English to suit particular purposes in each of her works.

In the two novels examined thus far, translingualism has involved the writer writing predominantly in a second language, adroitly mingling fluid cultural forms and engaging, as a cosmopolite, with critical social issues arising from globalization. However, transliterate practices are not solely the property of writers from former colonial nations. Anglo-American writers also perform them, by crossing or transcending linguistic, cultural, and national boundaries. They foreground the dynamics of languages across styles, genres, and registers. To illustrate their creativity, I will briefly examine Sapphire's much acclaimed novel, *Push* (1997), which was adapted into an award-winning motion picture in 2009.

Sapphire's *Push* as a Cosmopolitan Novel

The story focuses on a young African American woman named Claireece Precious Jones. Repeatedly raped by her father, Jones gives birth to a baby at age twelve and a second one at sixteen. Failing in the public school system of Harlem, New York, Jones is referred to a special school sponsored by the welfare system. There she meets a language arts teacher named Blue Rain, who engages her students by asking them to keep journals that she responds to in private. In class discussions and with her journal responses, the teacher challenges her students' deep-seated prejudices. This unique approach to literacy education has also a therapeutic function, bringing students of different languages, sexes, races, and nations together. Within two years Jones improves from a second-grade level of English proficiency to an eighth-grade one, gaining confidence and pride in her life as she does so.

To portray Jones's struggles in public schools and society at large, Sapphire mingles multiple languages and writing styles. The narrator, Jones, uses the street language of New York City to tell her story. Many of Jones's dialectal features fall within the realm of African American Vernacular English, including the use of double/triple negatives, the absence of the third-person-singular present-tense marker s, the invariant *be*, the zero copula rule, and the use of *done* to indicate a complete action. Sapphire often represents Jones's speech by deviating from the orthographic standards, as in the spellings "fahver," "nuffin,'" "git," "borned," "wif," and "chile." By contrast, Blue Rain, cautious and thoughtful in her speech, uses Standard English most of the time. The following conversation illustrates various aspects of translingualism in the novel. Jones is telling Blue Rain that she has stolen her file from a social worker:

> "Ms Rain, I didn't steal that file I wouldn't know what my difficulties was!"
>
> "You read the whole thing by yourself?" Ms Rain ask.
>
> "Yeah, basically," I say, then, "Am I gonna hafta go be home attendant?"
>
> "No!" Ms Rain say. "So stop worrying about it. We cross that bridge when we come to it. Trust me," she says, then "No, trust *yourself*. But what I'm worried about right now is, if this Ms Weiss is someone they have you talking to to try to work out your history with and you can't trust her, you're not getting the help you need." (Sapphire, 1997, p. 123, emphasis in original)

The two social dialects, one street and the other prestige, illustrate the author's acute awareness of the importance of multidialectal practices in literary creativity. As the story unfolds, the students, as a class, produce a book of life stories that reveal their distinct cultural and linguistic experiences. In one of the stories, the narrator switches from English to Spanish at both discoursal and sentential levels to capture a Puerto Rican mother and daughter's struggle to survive in the United States.

However, we can't fully appreciate Sapphire's transliterate creativity without also considering social factors in the construction, circulation, and consumption of her work. Some critics, as well as the author herself, have pigeonholed the novel as African American literature, and for good reasons.[3] Sapphire is an African American, and the story deals with an African American woman's struggle for survival. The novel has adopted one of the archetypical African American literary tropes, that is, witnessing/testifying (Atkinson, 2000). Using African American vernacular, the narrator shares her experience of being suppressed and abused in an unjust social system. She repeatedly appeals to African American artists and religious leaders such as Alice Walker, Langston Hughes, and Louis Farrakhan. The story line strongly resembles Alice Walker's *The Color Purple* (1982)—the main character is raped by her father in the beginning of the story; the story is narrated almost entirely in African American vernacular; and writing provides the central means of testifying, protest, and survival for victims of racial oppression and sexual abuse. *Push* once again captures the sufferings of African American women.

In spite of these connections to the African American community, it is beneficial to adopt a less-bounded perspective in reading *Push*. In the story Jones communicates with communities, defined by race, sexuality, and nationality, that are larger than her own. In the beginning of the story, Jones shows hatred for the people around her—her parents, crack addicts, homosexuals, white people, and immigrants. After she is identified by social workers as a rape victim and as HIV positive, she joins support groups in addition to the literacy class. Through friendships with other women who also have been sexually assaulted by family members, Jones is gradually liberated from both homophobia and xenophobia. She describes her transformation after a Survivors of Incest Anonymous meeting:

> Afterwards we go out for coffee. I have never been "out for coffee" before. Rita put her arm around my shoulder, I order hot chocolate 'cause that's what I like. Blond girl who is airline stewardess say, "Precious! That's a beautiful name!"
>
> I'm alive inside. A bird is my heart. Mama and Daddy is not win. I'm winning. I'm drinking hot chocolate in the Village wif girls—all kind who love me. How that is so I don't know. How Mama and Daddy know me sixteen years and hate me, how a stranger meet me and love me. Must be what they already had in their pocket. (pp. 130–131)

One of her support group members, Rita, comes from a broken Puerto Rican family, and the airline stewardess is white. The appreciation and love that Jones's parents failed to show her eventually come from strangers whom she used to blindly hate. Jones comes to realize that virtues like appreciation and love for others are part of human nature—something that the strangers "already had in their pocket." In an interview with TV anchor Katie Couric, Sapphire underscored her intent to use Jones and other characters to transcend racial, sexual, and national biases present in American society:

> There is a Hispanic girl; there is a Jamaican. And all these people are people she has been taught to hate. She's been taught that what little she has, which is next to nothing, is being taken away from her by foreigners. She's been taught that the moral underground of her community is being destroyed by homosexuals and prostitutes. So all of that I wanted to challenge by creating characters that she has to. . . . She has to question her all prejudices before she can become a human being. (Couric, 2009)

If Jones represents failed inner-city African American youth, then Sapphire's imaginative and incremental enlightening of Jones's soul only suggests that open dialogue is a viable way to the salvation of an individual, race, or nation. As also revealed in the interview, Blue Rain's approach to literacy education, which encourages open dialogues across differences, has been adopted by some literacy programs in New York City.[4]

The novel, in fact, contributes to an African American cultural tradition through its cosmopolitan emphasis. Every literary tradition has its cosmopolitan dimension, or its humanist connections. African American intellectuals and writers have always looked beyond their own community for the salvation of their race. For example, Frederick Douglass, Martin Luther King Jr., and Alan Lee Keyes repeatedly appealed to the Jeremiad model from the Judeo-Christian tradition to argue that African Americans are a chosen people. If the social injustices they faced were not corrected, they warned that godly wrath would descend upon America (Howard-Pitney, 2005). In the twentieth century, African American intellectuals actively participated in the worldwide decolonization and independence movement. W. E. B. Du Bois looked to Japan, India, and later the Soviet Union as exemplary models for the salvation of his race. During the civil rights era, much of the cultural work produced during the Black Arts movement in Detroit was generally inspired by Mao Zedong's thoughts on the politics of art and the Chinese Cultural Revolution (Mullen, 2004). In putting Jones in dialogue with people outside her race, Sapphire has joined historical figures who maintain cosmopolitanism in the African American cultural tradition.

Amidst all these achievements by both Jones and Sapphire, the street languages of New York City, especially vernacular English, are placed at the forefront of the story. Nonstandard English provides Jones and her classmates a tool for expressing their feelings, creating a climate in which they can begin to trust each other. In their class book stories, vernacular enables the students to better represent their true selves and true voices. While evolving tensions between Standard English and vernacular parallel the frictions between the suburban middle class and the street, it is vernacular that effectively breaks down prejudices and connects individuals of different cultures, languages, and nationalities. It is this English practice that eventually enables Jones to come to a cosmopolitan understanding of humanity. When she learns that her son is HIV negative, she starts to ponder about God appreciatively: "God ain't white, he ain' no Jew or Muslim, maybe he ain' even black, maybe he ain' even a 'he.' Even now I go downtown and seen the rich shit they got, I see what we got too. I see those men in vacant lot share one hot dog and they homeless, that's good as Jesus with his fish" (pp. 138–139). In this monologue, both God and her vernacular English mediate Jones's pondering on the human condition, as God is now seen to provide livelihood to all human beings regardless of their skin color or social status. Jones identifies with homeless people in vacant lots and humans in general; as God provides life for his children, they provide livelihood to each other. The novel testifies once again to the ability of certain language practices to foster a cosmopolitan ethic.

Cosmopolitan English and Worlding Contradictions

Clearly, writing studies has a lot to learn about multilingual creative writers, and creative writers in general. Thanks to disciplinary divisions, the field has largely neglected these writers, relegating their work to scholars in literature and linguistics. Remarkably, my analysis of three such writers reveals that their strategies for meaning making as well as for negotiating with linguistic nationalism and literary sponsors closely resemble those found among nonliterary writers. Even while taking significant creative license, these writers still need to wrestle with national language standards as well as their sociohistorical contingencies to develop their styles. Like writing studies, literary studies has long been shaped by nationalistic impulses, a situation that marginalized multilingual writing and writing in "foreign languages" in the process of canon formation. By giving attention to multilingual writers, literary studies has embraced a critical stance to nation, culture, ethnicity, and language. It is imperative that we in writing studies become familiar with the existent scholarship on multilingual creative writing and participate in this ever-growing area of study. Ultimately we also need to shake loose the confines of the bounded perspective to nation, culture, and language.

As the English-literate population continues to expand globally, more individuals are adding English to their creative repertoires. How is one to understand literature created on the world scene by these writers? Lennon (2010) suggests that world literature is best defined by antinomies, or "insoluble, and precisely in their insolubility, *useful* paradoxes and problems . . . [world literature] is an act of and an encounter with worlding contradictions: of privacy by publicity, silence by speech, locality by globality (or transnationality, or transregionality)" (p. xvii, italics in original). Every writer has to wrestle with these universal contradictions in his or her creative process. As my examination has revealed, Raja Rao, Xiaolu Guo, and Sapphire manage to capitalize on English's affordances; they were able to give voice to their protagonists' private and public selves in multilingual and multicultural contexts, to transcend locality, and to engage audiences beyond the authors' natural groupings. But to publish in English, the national language of Anglophone states, these writers had to submit to the conventions of the publishing industry, thus devoicing their protagonists in some instances.

Scholars, in turn, also have to wrestle with these ever-present, universal contradictions in their readings of multilingual writers. Writing in a period of nation building and multiculturalism, Kachru has aptly demonstrated how multilingual writers from postcolonial contexts are able to nativize English through their creative processes. The contact literature they produce effectively breaks away from the discourse features, patterns, and conventions commonly associated with Western literary traditions. In an age of globalization, this nationalist and structuralist perspective can be complemented by a cosmopolitan perspective on nation, culture, and language. This alternative reminds us of the "worlding contradictions" that multilingual writers must work through: on one hand, such writers try to capture the fluid and unstable linguistic and cultural forms and give voice to their protagonists' private and public lives; on the other hand, they have to negotiate the linguistic standards reinforced by national and international publishing houses. Considering the bounded perspective as well as the less-bounded one will enable us to better account for the contradictions inherent in the works of multilingual/multidialectal writers.

The three novels all point to another worlding contradiction caused by social systems in creating and maintaining certain forms of language and language practice. To work toward an imagined Indian nation, for example, multilingual speaker Sankar decides not to use his mother tongue and instead switches to Hindi; he even goes so far as to educate people around him about the nationalist language ideology. However, both Z and Jones feel embarrassed, insecure, and marginalized when interacting with characters speaking Standard English, the reified linguistic standard. They are victimized by the imposing social systems of their respective contexts. CE is the everyday lived experience of English users. In an imperfect world, they have to wrestle and negotiate with the standards or norms imposed by a daunting system of state apparatuses, schools, and (for authors) publishing houses, all of which are propped up by ideology. Sapphire gives us hope for elements of that system by constructing a tearful and cheerful literacy education story. However, cheerful stories are not found everywhere, as literacy practice is neither universal nor egalitarian, but it is instead stratified along national, ethnic, class, and gender lines. According to Blommaert (2008, 2010), “literacy regimes” function hegemonically to perpetuate the ideologies of those in power with little regard for the experiences of individuals. When CE speakers cross national or ethnic borders or the borders between home and school, they have to find ways to make CE matter in their educations. They will be victimized if they are not highly sensitive to these literacy regimes. In the following chapters we will explore strategies for helping CE speakers shuttle between literacy regimes.

5

Crossing Literacy Regimes

Globalization both accelerates and amplifies the migration of texts and literacy practices, but not without roadblocks (Blommaert, 2008, 2010; Blommaert, Collins, & Slembrouck, 2005; Leonard, 2013, 2014; Marko, 2012; Mihut, 2014; Pandey, 2015; Prendergast, 2008; Vieira, 2013). To illustrate, in *Grassroots Literacy* Blommaert (2008) offers two fascinating sets of documents. In the first set, an itinerant farmer in Zaire (now the Democratic Republic of the Congo) produced three versions of his autobiography for a Dutch woman as repayment for her patronage. Though the first version was written only in Shaba Swahili, the second and third were written in Shaba Swahili and French. Similarly in Blommaert's second set of documents, a Congolese artist composed, at the request of his European patrons, a brief history of Zaire in French to contextualize his political paintings. After analyzing these handwritten documents, Blommaert identifies an array of textual and material characteristics that constitute what he calls "grassroots literacy." While both individuals tried to compose in standard genres for the consumption of specific European audiences, according to Blommaert, their nonelite forms of writing prevented them from conveying intended meanings in translocal contexts.

Some characteristics of grassroots literacy resemble those we have observed in some styles of Cosmopolitan English (CE). For example, the two Congolese writers deployed graphic symbols in ways that defy orthographic norms, applying nonstandard spellings, "erratic" punctuation, and unsystematic uses of uppercase and lowercase. They moved between languages and adopted local language varieties, colloquialisms, and other "impurities" in their texts. They wrote in genres that employ locally available textual resources and knowledge economies. Because such texts are often only locally meaningful, Blommaert suggests that they lose "voice" when they travel to other geographical or social spaces. Similarly, Brandt and Clinton (2002) warned that "when groups are really left to devise their own literacy practices out of local resources, that is not necessarily a sign of empowerment but rather, potentially, a sign of isolation, a lack of political or economic incorporation" (p. 355). The dangers of devoicing when texts travel across space and time are significant, which lends naturally to questions about the value of CE in translocal contexts. In previous chapters I emphasized the ethical, social, and literary meanings that CE helps to create in local communities and national contexts. However, if the use of CE only entails meaningful voice in local contexts, then it is questionable as to whether it is truly cosmopolitan.

In this chapter I will first review Blommaert's notions of literacy regimes and scales in understanding the travel of texts and literacy practices. I want to suggest that by emphasizing the rigidity and normality of literacy structures, he fails to give adequate account to the agency of all parties involved in grassroots literacy practices. Canagarajah (2013a) will be useful in illustrating the point as he shows the ability of sub-Saharan African workers to cross scales in English-dominant nations. In higher education it is imperative that students and scholars with diverse literacy practices be socialized into communities of knowledge production and dissemination. Drawing on a study that a colleague and I conducted at an American-style summer school in Shanghai, I will show that subject teachers, representing elite literacy regimes, can appreciate the meanings and voices in student texts that exhibit features of grassroots literacy. Further, some of these teachers developed adaptive strategies for helping students expand their communicative repertoires, enabling them to move between literacy regimes. Years of transliterate practices had prepared these teachers to cross literacy regimes to the end of meeting their students halfway.

Literacy Regimes, Scales, and Negotiations

When studying local-global connections in literacy practice, Blommaert (2008) underscores hierarchical social structures' facilitating and impeding the global flow of texts. Drawing on multiliteracy theories, he points out that literacy is not unitary but instead comprises diverse forms and practices. An individual draws from a particular set of resources in his or her repertoire when performing a literacy activity. For example, handwriting a letter and composing an e-mail require two different sets of resources, both material and nonmaterial. One involves the ability to hold a pen, write legibly, spell words orthographically, and understand the genre features of a letter; the other requires access to a networked computer, typing skills, and genre knowledge of e-mails. However, due to power differentials and inequality, literacy resources are not evenly distributed. According to Blommaert (2008), repertoires are stratified and often locked within certain literacy regimes: "Repertoires are internally and externally stratified, with all kinds of internal distinctions marking differences between 'better' and 'worse' resources, and external distinctions defining the resources from one repertoire as 'superior' or 'inferior' to those of other. Literacy is organized in *literacy regimes*, in structures of distribution, access, value and use that are closely tied to the general make-up of societies" (p. 6, emphasis in original). A text is produced in a certain literacy regime with its own system of use, values, and functions. In an age of globalization, Blommaert contends that while texts travel, their own system of use, values, and functions often does not travel along with them. By composing documents in Zaire and utilizing locally available linguistic and cultural resources, the two Congolese writers separated themselves from their better educated, material-rich European audiences by occupying a different literacy regime.

To account for the difficulty that local meanings and voices have accompanying texts in translocal movements, Blommaert (2010) introduces the notion of sociolinguistic scales, or semiotized space-times. He explains, "Social events and processes move and develop on a continuum of layered scales, with the strictly local (micro) and the global (macro) as its extremes and several intermediary scales (e.g. the level of the state) in between" (p. 32). In this stratified, hierarchical scale system, texts of lower scales tend to index locally situated, personal, contextualized, subjective, and specific meanings; in contrast, texts of higher scales index timeless, translocal, impersonal, decontextualized, objective, and general meanings. Individuals with power or professional training are able to move from lower to higher scales, known as "scale-jumping" (Uitermark, 2002, p. 750), while the less powerful and less educated tend to stay at lower scale levels.

Scale-jumping sometimes happens along with a change of register (Blommaert, 2007), but it often can take place within one register. In sociolinguistics a register is a variety of a language used for a particular purpose or in a particular setting. Working within the register of academic writing, for instance, in the previous three chapters of this book, I identified specific instances of English use in a variety of contexts and described them. When performing these acts, my writing stayed at a low scale level. Then taking a step further, I performed analysis, offered interpretation, and connected my observations of these instances of English use to a critical issue in writing studies (i.e., there is an ethical imperative for the field to understand new cultural formations and transliterate creativity in globalization). I made the move by drawing on theoretical concepts and published scholarship. Moving from locally situated, personal, subjective meanings to translocal, impersonal, and general meanings, my writing shifted from a low scale level to a higher one.

Even when one travels with high multilingual fluency, including that of English, literacy regimes and scales may still be tangible. For instance, in her ethnography of several Slovakian professionals, Prendergast (2008) notes that "no amount of English fluency would allow" them to completely transcend the stereotypical designations the "global economy had assigned them" (p. 4). As they moved across regions inside and outside Slovakia, the English-language knowledge that they had worked so hard to gain in order to become socially and geographically mobile "was no longer the knowledge that counted" (p. 53), rendering these individuals stuck as they attempted to move. Similarly, Leonard (2013) underscores the "slippery," unreliable nature of literacy practices/resources among four immigrant women in the United States (p. 21). Her interview-based research reveals that these individuals' literacy knowledge and skills either retain or lose value when they travel across national borders and that social, political, and financial factors can block access to spaces where multilingual practices can be used. Literacy regimes and scales are constituted not only by certain literacy practices and resources but also by sociopolitical factors.

To underscore the social structures underlying literacy practices, however, Blommaert has portrayed literacy regimes and scales as rigid and static without giving adequate consideration to human agency. The notion of scale has been critiqued by sociologists, sociolinguists, and literacy scholars (Blommaert, Westinen, & Leppänen, 2015; Canagarajah, 2013a; Marston, Jones, & Woodward, 2005; Moore, 2008; Kell, 2013).[1] In sociolinguistics Canagarajah (2013a) views the scale metaphor as too normative, unable to accommodate the possibility that norms at different scale levels are open for renegotiation, resistance, and reconstruction. The scale metaphor also shows insufficient sensitivity to the ways "people negotiate spaces, bring them into being, or modify them in their favor" (p. 158). To illustrate the agency of those less privileged in negotiating norms and reconstructing space-times, Canagarajah presented an interview study involving sixty-five professional workers from sub-Saharan Africa who had settled in English-dominant nations including Australia, South Africa, the United Kingdom, and the United States. One of the questions he asked his participants dealt with how they handled the tensions between the variety of English they spoke and the other varieties spoken in the host community. The interviews reveal that these migrant workers accommodate their interlocutors' codes while retaining their own; they view their most valuable skill as the ability to shuttle across norms to co-construct indexicalities. Thus, Canagarajah characterizes the translocal scale as diverse and plural instead of homogenous or uniform: "The language norms in this scale level are polyaccented, multilingual, and plural. This scale level accommodates diverse local norms. It is in this sense that it is translocal: i.e., it goes beyond local norms and indexical orders, and accommodates the norms of diverse localities" (p. 163).

Blommaert, Prendergast, Leonard, and Canagarajah have all focused on the challenges of unprivileged travelers, the first three scholars highlighting their inability to move their literacy practice to a higher scale level, the last scholar underscoring their ability to negotiate norms and spaces at higher scales. To add to Canagarajah's argument that the translocal scale is characterized by diverse and plural norms, I want to shift our focus to the privileged who, occupying elite literacy regimes, may rescale or move to lower scales to understand the unprivileged. I want to suggest that when a language is shared, it creates a sense of mutuality among the privileged and the unprivileged and may encourage the former to use their rescaling skills to accommodate and help the latter move to higher scale levels to the end of enabling local meanings, voices, and values to travel across contexts. For example, Mihut's (2014) ethnographic work reveals how four Romanian Americans cultivated their multilingual and multicultural competence through years of migration experiences and later helped Romanian immigrants prepare legal documents for settling in the United States. In Blommaert (2008) the two Congolese writers created documents in local literacy regimes. However, their European audiences exhibited no incomprehension or misunderstanding of these texts, thanks partly to Blommaert's mediation, that is, his translations, interpretations, and explications. Certainly, audiences (including Blommaert himself), from their own contexts and literacy regimes, can extract new meanings from the Congolese texts; these meanings sometimes can run counter to the Congolese writers' original intentions.

To illustrate the multiple roles that the privileged can play in facilitating (and/or impeding) the circulation of texts and their local meanings in translocal spaces, I will draw on a study that a colleague and I conducted (You & You, 2013). In the study we examined the kinds of accommodations that American content teachers made when using writing to facilitate learning at an English-medium summer school in Shanghai, China. Our analysis unveiled several strategies adopted by these professors for valuing and accommodating the students' English styles and other literacy resources. The professors created a space for grassroots practices in the academic literacy regime, which has been traditionally viewed as monolingual and as maintaining rigid norms.

The professors' strategies suggest that with skills to move between scales, the privileged can help the unprivileged cross literacy regimes in translocal spaces. The professors are in a sense privileged and students are not in a context where English is dominant and disciplinary knowledge is valued, but the privilege is qualified, not absolute. Mediating actions, texts, and meanings oriented both to the universal and the particular, or rather the global and the local, English became cosmopolitan in a transformed pedagogical setting.

Meeting in a Translocal Space

The summer school in Shanghai epitomizes the push and pull of China's drive for internationalizing its higher education. Over the last three decades, fueled by economic growth and a desire for better education, a large number of Chinese students have traveled to English-dominant nations for university study, leading to an economic loss and brain drain. At the dawn of the new millennium, to counter this human capital flight, like their peers in some Asian and European nations, Chinese universities started offering English-taught courses in the humanities, business, and medicine to both domestic and international students (Hayhoe, Li, Lin, & Zha, 2011; Kirkpatrick, 2011). Meanwhile, Anglo-American universities have established offshore programs or campuses in China. Internationalization of higher education has meant, for China, not only the global exchange of ideas, technologies, and educational practices, but also a fight for a share of the highly lucrative education market. The summer school was conceived as a for-profit institution in response to these economic forces in Chinese higher education. Established by a group of U.S.-educated Chinese nationals in 2009 and joining hands with prestigious Chinese universities, the school offers entry-level courses typically found in American universities. It targets primarily Chinese international students returning from North America for the summer, promising them that they would be able to transfer credits gained to their universities. Serving as an extension of American higher education, the school found a business opportunity in Chinese universities' relentless efforts for internationalization.

All professors, either tenured or tenure track, came from well-ranked American universities, unequivocally making them representatives of elite literacy regimes. Most courses offered in the school were general education courses typically taken by students in their freshman and sophomore years in the United States. Each professor was provided a Chinese undergraduate teaching assistant from the same or a related area of study. These assistants had studied at least one year in an American university. They were expected to help the professors prepare for daily teaching, answer student questions, and grade papers and exams. In the study we focused on nine professors (and their teaching assistants) in the humanities and social sciences. Among them, two were of an ethnic minority and were multilingual speakers: Professor Chang originally came from Taiwan, and Professor Walker was African American.[2] The rest were Caucasians and primarily English speakers, except Professor Smith, who also spoke fluent Chinese.

The six-week program attracted Chinese students who had enrolled or planned to enroll at American universities. Like the 21st Century Community forum participants discussed in chapter 3, the summer program students were part of the Chinese diaspora. Most of them left home to study in a different city or overseas. They were multilingual, typically speaking English, Standard Chinese, and a local Chinese dialect (such as Mandarin, Wu, Min, Cantonese, or Hakka) or a minority language (such as Korean, Mongolian, or Tibetan). To ensure that the students had adequate Standard English proficiency, the school adopted admission standards in transnational education, standards compatible with those of American institutions: the students must have a valid Test of English as a Foreign Language (TOEFL) score higher than 80 (Internet-based test) or equivalent scores on other forms of TOEFL, have a valid International English Language Testing System (IELTS) score higher than 6.0, or have studied or graduated from an institution where English is the primary language of instruction. The summer program students, thus, had demonstrated adequate familiarity with Standard English, a CE style. Because they were able to transfer most, if not all, credits gained in the summer school to North American institutions, the school attracted more than a thousand students in the year the study was conducted.

The summer school became a translocal space where the deterritorialized students produced texts to be read by local and nonlocal audiences alike. The program participants occupied two distinct literacy regimes and scale levels. At a local-national scale, the students used locally available resources to complete writing assignments; these resources included paper, pens, computers, local newspapers and magazines, their local languages and dialects, their style of spoken and written English, handwriting and/or networked computer skills, subject knowledge, and knowledge of the genres required by the assignments. While locally available, some of these resources are of a globalizing nature, such as networked computers, English, the genres required by the assignments, and translocal cultural materials. Some of the American professors mobilized their rescaling skills to design assignments and read student texts. They were literacy sponsors and brokers. Brandt (2001) defines literacy sponsors as "any agents, local or distant, concrete or abstract, who enable, support, teach and model, as well as recruit, regulate, suppress, or withhold, literacy" (p. 19). Lillis and Curry (2006) view those who influence texts in important ways in academic knowledge production as literacy brokers. In helping their students acquire subject knowledge, the professors at the summer school not only assessed the students' locally produced texts but also assisted them in relocating these texts to a higher scale level.

Most scholarship available in English on how teachers broker multilingual students' academic literacy has focused on English for academic purposes in courses and writing center tutorials (such as Belcher & Braine, 1995; James, 2010; Janopoulos, 1992, 1995; Spack, 1997a; Tardy, 2009; Zamel, 1995) and recently on secondary-school subject courses (Chval & Khisty, 2009; Enright & Gilliland, 2011; Franquiz & Salina, 2011; Gorgorio & Planas, 2001; Kibler, 2010; 2011; Parks, Huot, Hamers, & H.-Lemonnier, 2005). Some studies have focused on university content courses in the United States (Casanave, 2002; Fishman & McCarthy, 2002; Leki, 2007; Prior, 1998; Zamel & Spack, 2004). Despite the widespread use of English as the medium of instruction in non-English-dominant contexts, only a few studies published in English have examined content teachers' literacy brokerage in higher education (Fortanet-Gómez, 2011; Harbord, 2010; Kam & Meinema, 2005).[3] Thus, in our study we were primarily concerned with two issues. First, what challenges do professors perceive in the Chinese students' use of written English specific to subject learning? These challenges evidence the gap between the two literacy regimes that the students struggle to cross. Second, what adaptive strategies do professors adopt to help their students meet the academic standards set forth in translocal contexts? The professors' mediation in the students' literacy activities can potentially offer us insights into what roles the privileged can play in the negotiation of norms and reconstruction of translocal spaces by the unprivileged.

The data reported here came from several sources including interviews (with professors, their teaching assistants, and their students), class observations, faculty meetings, course materials (syllabi and handouts), and students' written work. We interviewed the professors, asking about their use of writing tasks to facilitate student learning at the summer school and about their customary practices in the United States. We interviewed the teaching assistants to ask about their professor's use of writing in facilitating student learning and how the professor graded quizzes and exams. We also interviewed some students for their opinions on writing in content courses, their attitudes toward the professors' writing assignments, and their attitudes toward their own writing. The specific interview questions for the professors, teaching assistants, and students are available in You and You (2013). We collected student writing performed in and outside the summer school classes. We didn't collect the professors' U.S.-based assignment sheets, and we had to trust their own descriptions given in the interviews. We also collected course syllabi and handouts that professors used at the summer school. We observed each professor's classes at least twice during the semester. Additional observation was conducted at three faculty meetings and multiple informal faculty gatherings to understand further their concerns and strategies in teaching Chinese students.

To identify the professors' adaptations, we adopted the following procedure in our data analysis. First, we examined their claims about how they taught the courses and assessed student learning in both China and the United States. Second, we triangulated these claims with our class observations, interviews with their teaching assistants, course materials, and student writings; then we identified differences in their pedagogical practices across the two locations, anticipating the existence of differences in the professors' beliefs, perceptions of their students, pedagogical techniques, and assessment techniques. Third, we marked the differences with codes before grouping those codes by similar concepts to make them more workable. From these concepts, categories of pedagogical adaptations gradually emerged. Fourth, to understand better how these pedagogical adaptions might have enabled scale-jumping, I searched for instances in the interviews, class observations, and student writings where students were encouraged by these adaptions to move between local (personal, contextualized, subjective) and global (general, abstract, objective, decontextualized) scales in meaning making (Blommaert, 2010; Leander & Lovvorn, 2006).

The professors' adaptations could be viewed as part of a concerted effort to build a "dwelling place" where the summer school teachers and students worked together to foster learning. To build their ethos, both parties brought in their cultural experiences, values, and symbolic resources. To understand their ethos, it is worth examining their language styles and strategies. When I listened to the recordings of the interviews, classroom observations, and faculty meetings, I first noted the styles and strategies used by both parties. Then I more closely analyzed the linguistic features (such as words, syntax, formality, register) of their styles. These styles and strategies then shed light on CE at work in the summer school.

Literacy Challenges in Scale-Jumping

The professors noted multiple challenges in the students' use of English, particularly written English, most of which, however, are also found among American college students. Based on their students' class participation and written work, these professors unanimously recognized their students' low English proficiencies and their difficulties in organizing thoughts into coherent passages. Echoing previous research in writing in the disciplines (Agutter, 1979; Crank, 2012; Fulwiler, 1986; Zawacki & Habib, 2010; Zhu, 2004), they identified challenges specific to the subject areas as limited vocabulary knowledge, unfamiliarity with thinking and communication in particular disciplines, and lack of personal voice. Marking their unprivileged status, these challenges are obstacles for students wishing to jump scale levels or wanting to meet subject-area writing expectations.

All professors mentioned at one point or another that their students were not good at English; however, most did so without any degree of specificity. Not having been trained in language studies, they might lack the meta-language to specify their students' language challenges. Research in English as a second language (ESL) writing in the United States, despite the deficit model it has taken, can shed some light on these professors' perceptions. Compared to American-born students, or against monolingual norms, ESL students reportedly master less lexical, grammatical, and rhetorical knowledge as a result of having had less exposure to and less experience with various academic genres (Silva, 1993). They are likely to have worse intuitive textual knowledge, or to lack what Leki (2007) has described as a "backlog of experiences with English grammatical and rhetorical structure to fall back on" (p. 59). In addition, Kibler (2011) found that some adolescent ESL students "shared a frustration that they do not have a 'backlog' of vocabulary knowledge, saying they did not understand or know how to use the more 'formal,' 'good,' 'difficult,' or 'big' words they felt were expected in content area writing" (p. 223).

In our study the students' limited vocabulary knowledge stood out as the only area of English that caught the professors' attention. At a faculty meeting they concurred that a majority of the students lacked vocabulary knowledge, particularly that of special terms, which hindered not only their comprehension of lectures but also their production of written work. At the same time, some professors expressed the understanding that lacking knowledge of special terms was not an issue unique to these Chinese students but one common to undergraduates in American universities who are new to a subject area. A few not only recognized the issue but also took every opportunity to enrich the students' lexical knowledge. For example, Professor Jones, an art history professor, shared at the meeting her efforts at integrating language lessons into her teaching:

> I put *a lot* of emphasis on language here. Like I put up a sculpture today of a dying soldier. Usually in the States I will talk about pathos and things like that. And here I said okay, what does pathos mean? We have sympathy, empathy, these kinds of. . . . What's the difference between sympathy and empathy? What's the difference between sympathy and finding something pathetic? And I feel like at the end of the language lesson, they've learned some subtleties of language but also they can apply these notions they identified to the work of art in the end. (July 21, 2011)

This is an instance of a professor modeling scale-jumping for her students. She juxtaposed global concepts (pathos, sympathy, empathy, and pathetic) with a local example of art appreciation (a sculpture of a dying solder). Without understanding those global concepts as marking various types of emotional identification in academic discourse, the students would have a difficult time comprehending Professor Jones's lectures, demonstrating art appreciation, or expressing criticisms in their writing tasks.

Another obstacle in the student's way as they attempted to produce quality work was their unfamiliarity with disciplinary thinking. As entrants to subject areas, they were strangers to the reasoning patterns expected therein. Thus they sometimes could not fully comprehend the writing assignments. Several professors shared this observation in our interviews. For example, Professor Smith, a history professor, noticed this transitional issue in a midterm exam. In his Chinese history course, the class studied a peasant rebellion in the late Ming Dynasty (1368 C.E.–1644 C.E.). In an interview Professor Smith noted his students' failure to grasp the historical significance of this event on an exam question: "A lot of them have learned this, but they have learned it in a high school way, in which it's black and white, it's good, bad, without looking at the social context or the historical context in which these developments happened" (July 30, 2011). Without understanding a specific discipline's reasoning patterns, the students tended to answer questions simplistically or by ignoring prompts altogether.

Held against an American academic standard, the students were also said to have lacked individual voice and personal reflection in their work. Several professors expressed this view in our interviews, noting that the students were good at imitating and memorizing materials but poor at staking out their own perspectives. For example, Professor Taylor, a political science professor, touched on this point when describing a research paper assignment in her world politics class. Walking hastily to her class, the professor spoke in a choppy style: "Take a problem in contemporary world politics, global warming, or, you know, nuclear weapons, anything they want to study. Take a problem and then research, find at least two articles on each side of a controversy, evaluate them and write a paper, giving those sides and then giving your side. Giving your side is something that they have trouble with" (August 4, 2011). The professor underscored the importance (at least in U.S. academic writing) of understanding an argument from multiple sides and then taking a personal stand. Like Professor Taylor, a few others characterized their students as being reluctant to state their perspectives on issues.

Thus, the challenges for the Chinese students attempting to migrate from one literacy regime to another fell into two interconnected areas: language and disciplinary conventions. Their English was considered to be lacking proficiency when compared with monolingual native speaker norms. They also lacked knowledge of special terms, understanding of disciplinary thinking patterns, and personal voice, all critical resources of the academic literacy regime. The professors didn't simply identify these challenges. Some of them developed strategies for accommodating the students' grassroots literacy practices, helping them cross literacy regimes. Some of these strategies may seem familiar to writing studies scholars. However, it is important to keep in mind that these strategies, which we will explore next, were developed by faculty teaching courses in areas outside writing and languages.

Making a Space for Grassroots Literacy

Adjusting the Writing Tasks

Partly due to the shorter length of the summer term, all professors adjusted the writing tasks used in their courses. Five professors managed to keep the term paper as the staple assignment, but even they modified expectations. Some dropped essay questions from exams, recognizing the students' inadequate training in essay writing. Like most entering first-year students in American universities (Crank, 2012; Kiuhara, Graham, & Hawken, 2009), the only academic genre the students had practiced was the five-paragraph essay required on standardized tests for university admission, such as the IELTS, SAT, and

TOEFL. However, this essay has been found to require interpersonal and textual strategies different from those found in most academic genres such as research articles and lab reports (Coffin & Hewings, 2004).[4] Professor Walker, a sociology professor, chose short-answer questions by tapping into the students' literacy resources. In the United States she typically gave two multiple-choice-question quizzes, one essay exam, and one final paper. At the summer school she instead opted for three quizzes, each consisting of multiple-choice and short-answer questions. She made the change because of her unsuccessful experience with essay exams in the summer school in the preceding year. In an interview she related that "too much of the weight was based on their writing . . . I didn't think it's fair" (July 27, 2011). She claimed that the students would find it easier just to transfer ideas from their memory to paper than to construct a coherent passage. She used a short-answer question from her first principles of sociology quiz to illuminate her students' strengths and weaknesses:

> One of the questions was—"Define the strengths and weaknesses of two of these research methods: experiments, survey, and participant observation." Most of the students who did not want to write an essay were able to create some configuration like this: survey, participants, advantages, and disadvantages, like bullet points. They knew the information. They did not write an essay. But they answered the questions. And many of them did well. But if you look at their writing in other areas, it's very bad. So through memorization they can do it. But through writing it as a narrative, they have difficulty in doing that. They can talk it, they did understand it, but they do not have the mechanics, and because I said you cannot use spelling machines . . . they cannot get their ideas out of their head. (July 27, 2011)

Professor Walker recognized that her students were able to present the required information orally and graphically but that they found it difficult to construct an essay coherently and orthographically, especially without the help of an electronic translator. In a short answer the professor showed us in the interview, the student created a table to organize information in his comparison of two research methods. He used short sentences and phrases without having to create a prose passage. After identifying her students' strengths, the professor began assessing their learning by tapping into those strengths, or as she put it, "They do very well in this kind of scenario. So I am trying to design the next quiz towards this strength because it is not fair to assume they don't know the information. It's just I've got to find more formula that they can bring information forward" (July 27, 2011). The interview indicates that while recognizing essay writing as her students' weakness, the professor sought to find strengths in their grassroots practices. "Find[ing] more formula" was her attempt to connect the students' local literacy practices to disciplinarily accepted ways or genres for assessing learning.

Providing Support for the Writing Assignments

Several professors provided explicit instruction for major writing assignments by helping students develop and structure their ideas. The professors' in-class activities included having workshops and group discussions, as well as introducing worksheets and providing detailed feedback on student writings. Training the students to reason and communicate within disciplines, these activities provided students with important resources for scale-jumping. For example, one of the philosophy professors, Professor Chang, designed worksheets to guide her students in their reading and writing processes. The purpose of these worksheets was to teach the students how to engage with arguments in philosophy. When reading a passage, the students needed to answer three heuristic questions in the reading worksheet:

- What is the thesis?
- What are the premises?
- Possible objections?

To answer these questions, the students were pushed to elevate the details of the passage from the local to a global conceptual level. When writing an essay responding to a philosophical passage, they were expected to be able to address similar questions. In the draft worksheet, they were asked to include the following sections in their essay:

- Introduction
- Summary of the author's argument
- My objection to this argument
- Response
- My reply

Clearly the second and the third bullet points in the draft worksheet, as a synthesis of the three bullet points in the reading worksheet, put the student writer in conversation with the author. The fourth and fifth bullet points encouraged the students to further their philosophical engagement with the author. To perform these five rhetorical moves, the students had to navigate between local, personal experiences and global, philosophical concepts. The draft worksheet enabled the students to transition from reading to writing; it also provided them an organizational frame for their philosophy essays, which deviated from the often linear and monological frame of the five-paragraph essay. Over the semester Professor Chang's students composed four short essays using these worksheets. If necessary, she would conference with them to improve both the substance and style of their essays.

Professor Chang attributed this regimental method to her students' literacy challenges. When she taught at a private university in California, she did not use these worksheets because she team-taught with a writing instructor who took care of the writing component. Later, when teaching independently at a California State University, where her students were not as strong in philosophical reasoning and writing, she designed these worksheets to help them. Speaking in a CE style that blended Chinese and English in an interview, she offered two reasons for adopting these worksheets in the Chinese context: First, philosophy papers are written differently from those in other disciplines in terms of reasoning pattern and style, or in her words, "Philosophy 的 paper 与其他的学科的 paper 不一样" [Philosophy paper is different from paper in other disciplines]. The students needed to receive special training to be able to think like Western philosophers. Second, the Chinese students' English proficiency was relatively low, and they typically did not value analysis and logical reasoning in their writing: "比较低 level, 不重视分析、逻辑、思考这样的东西" [relatively low level, don't value things like analysis, logic, and thinking] (July 25, 2011).

When responding to student writing, most of the professors did not feel comfortable discussing surface-level language issues. In our observations philosophy professors Grieco and Chang offered the most written feedback to student writing. For example, Professor Grieco commented extensively on his students' short essays for his introduction to philosophy midterm. He circled, underlined, and numbered various items in the essays. In the margins or at the end, he offered several numbered comments that corresponded to the numbered items in the essays. Seldom did the professor comment on surface-level language issues, either in grading the essays or when returning them in class. A student tried to answer the question: "In the lion's share of your essay, explain the argument discussed in class for why free will and determinism are incompatible." Professor Grieco commented on the essay as follows:

1. But this is not what the question asks for.
2. You need to explain this.
3. What do you mean by "choice"? Why not "many" instead of "none"?
4. Theoretically but not practically predictable. You are supposed to explain this.
5. Explaining this argument is what the question asked for. You stated it, but explained nothing.
6. All this is irrelevant to the question. It is as if you did not read the question that you were supposed to be answering.

These comments strongly indicate that the professor focused on how well the student had answered the essay question. The words used most in these comments are "question" and "explain." The student was urged to explain the argument, as required in the essay question. While it's praiseworthy that the professor was focused on content rather than form, the content response was telegraphic. The word "explain" itself doesn't make it clear to students what would constitute an explanation in philosophy. Offering detailed but not always clear comments on the students' midterm essays thus served as a type of instruction in philosophy writing. The students learned what the professor valued in their writing. Both philosophy professors seemed to value analysis and logical reasoning above all else, which matched our observations of their classroom teaching.

Valuing Students' Multilingual Resources

About half of the professors allowed, and a few even encouraged, their students to use Chinese, or a CE style with mainly Chinese syntax, in their written work and class discussions. They did not view Chinese as an obstacle or as interfering with subject learning. Instead, they created a space for it in the academic English literacy regime, a practice that encouraged students to mobilize local (personal, storied, and affective) knowledge in subject learning. Professor Taylor was one of them, by allowing Chinese in group discussions. For example, when she assigned a group paper in her American government course, she let the students sit in groups to discuss how they would carry out the project. The students were asked to trace the movement of the Affordable Health Care for America Act, passed in March 2010, through the American political system. In the political system chart the professor originally presented in a PowerPoint slide and later repeatedly referred to, four components were referenced—the inputs, the decision-making core, the outputs, and the feedback. In the group that we sat with, assignment sheet in hand, the students discussed the following items predominantly in Chinese with distinct regional accents:

1. The designation of responsibilities concerning the project
2. How to write up the sections suggested in the assignment sheet
3. The weight of the group essay in the final grade and the professor's practices in designing exams
4. The student preference for short essays over multiple-choice questions on the midterm
5. The meanings of some bullet points on the assignment sheet
6. The motivations for choosing this course and the unexpected challenges that arose during it
7. The structure and the length of the group essay

While much of the discussion involved group management, the list indicates that students stayed focused on the writing assignment throughout most of their time together, and Chinese enabled them to jump scales in multiple aspects. For example, Chinese allowed the students to develop affective knowledge by sharing personal narratives and feelings about this course, including the professor's assessment approach and the assignment. Chinese also mediated the on-task discussion, allowing students to easily connect local, personal perspectives with global, textbook knowledge (i.e., American political system). Take, as illustration, the follow dialogic exchange related to item 5 (the meaning of bullet points listed on the assignment sheet):

A: 后面的那个理论是, 利益集团、竞选、国会、 judicial 、还有那个, 还有那个官僚集团那些 . . . [The latter part of the theory involves interest groups, election, parliament, judicial, and that, and that bureaucracy and so forth . . .]

B: 官僚干吗啊? 它到底是什么? [Why bureaucracy? What is it?]

A: Bureaucracy 它其实就是 . . . . 就相当于代表政府的 Department of State. Bureaucracy 就是一个机构, 为了去 serve 某个 purpose。 [Bureaucracy actually is . . . actually equals to Department of State, which represents the government. Bureaucracy is an organization, designed to serve a certain purpose.]

B: 但是没有很大用途 . . . . [But it is not very useful . . .]

> A: 你要理解它的 . . . . 超三角关系, 其实就是帮政府服务的一个机构。就是把这些大的 concept 解开。 [You need to understand its . . . super triangular relationship. It is an organ to serve the government. We need to dissect these broad concepts.] (August 4, 2011)

In this brief exchange both students asserted their own perspectives on the American political system. Student B's perspective clearly stood out: "Why bureaucracy? What is it?" "But it is not very useful . . ." Using Chinese, student A first directed the group's attention to the components of the political system. Next, he clarified a difficult concept, bureaucracy, for student B. Finally, in the last sentence, he commented on how to write the group essay—to identify the major components of the political system and analyze how each worked in the movement of the bill. Chinese, or moving between Chinese and English, enabled the students to juxtapose local and global scales of knowledge; they delved deep into the political-system chart and the writing assignment.

Professor Taylor allowed Chinese in group discussions but not in class discussions. In a sit-down interview she claimed that if she had allowed Chinese in class discussions, then she would not be able to understand her students. In the United States, she taught at a liberal arts college where the majority of her students were American born. She did not ask them to use languages other than English in class, but she was aware of other professors in her college who used Spanish or allowed Spanish in content courses:

> We have had courses though in [college name] because some faculty who were bilingual in Spanish and English who worked with things like Introductory Economics in Spanish, and it was offered that way so students who were Spanish majors could get some credits towards their Spanish language. So it wasn't just heritage speakers who took this course but American students whose first language is English also took the course. And Latin American History too, I think, speaks the same language. (August 12, 2011)

Professor Taylor's remarks indicate that she had been exposed to the idea of using languages other than English in content courses. However, she viewed herself and her American students as monolingual and therefore had not used, nor had she allowed her students to use, other languages in class. She made the change in China because she found herself a minority in a multilingual classroom.

In addition to the American government group discussions, a psychology professor allowed students to use Chinese on in-class writing assignments.

On the quizzes he created for his two courses, the instructions stated, "If you cannot remember the English word for a concept, you may use the Chinese word." Apparently, he wanted to accommodate students who had limited knowledge of special terms. The professor usually asked his teaching assistant to grade the quizzes; therefore, multilingual answers did not pose an issue. However, while the instructions only allowed Chinese for concepts whose English equivalents the students did not remember, neither the professor nor the teaching assistant penalized the students for choosing to use Chinese for more than these concepts. For example, a question was asked on the second quiz in the principles of psychology course: "How is Life Expectancy defined?" The teaching assistant placed a check mark next to the following answers given by two students, allotting both full credits:

> Life Expectancy mean 平均寿命, or 预期寿命. Life expectancy is the expected number of years of life remaining at a given age, and from birth is a frequently utilized and analyzed component of demographic data for the countries of the world.
>
> Life expectancy means how long you can expect to live, when you live, which ~~life standard you have.~~ 根据测量之前人能活多长时间, 以你的健康状况衡量你能活到多少岁 [To estimate how many years you will live based on, first, measuring how long the older generations have lived and, second, your health condition.]

While the first answer uses a complete English sentence, the second one contains an incomplete one followed by a complete Chinese sentence. The incomplete English sentence offers an inaccurate and partial definition, which was then improved on by the Chinese sentence. In an interview the teaching assistant explained that in the United States short-answer questions were typically used in low-level psychology courses for nonmajors. When she graded them, she looked for main points and keywords: "几个 main points, 几个 keywords 我看到就算对 [When I spotted several main points, several keywords, I would mark the answer as correct]" (August 12, 2011). She might take a few points off if a student made errors in English spelling or syntax. Mixing English with Chinese was not an issue as long as the students could explain themselves clearly to her. The availability of the Chinese-speaking teaching assistant allowed the psychology professor to value and evaluate Chinese students' thoughts expressed in their native tongue, despite their limited English-language proficiency. However, it is intriguing and worth noting that the teaching assistant demonstrated standard language ideology but not monolingual ideology. That is to say she allowed some elements of CE (e.g., blending languages) but disallowed others (e.g., orthographic and syntactic deviations).

Connecting to Local Cultures

The professors also carved out a space for local cultural meanings in the academic regime. For example, the art history professors arranged a day trip to the Shanghai Museum. One of them asked her students to compare two pieces of Chinese artwork for their term paper. Professor Taylor, when assigning one of the papers in her American government class, asked students in the written instructions to "compare and contrast American and Chinese political systems by examining at least two of the following: political culture, political participations, political parties, legislatures, executives, rights, and the role of the media in the political system."

Efforts to usher local cultural meanings into the summer school courses expanded the students' literacy networks, enabling them to connect their out-of-school meaning-making practices with in-school ones. The extent to which a professor could bring local culture into his or her teaching depended on what the course was. A few courses focused on topics about China, such as Chinese History: Late Imperial China, Investment in China, and East Asian Economic Development. Among the courses that didn't deal with China directly, Professor Walker's Principles of Sociology used local cultural materials the most extensively. In our observations of her class, for nearly every concept and principle introduced, she encouraged her students to find examples in Chinese society, effectively bringing a global scale down to a local scale level. She assigned her students to collect materials published locally for class discussions, such as newspaper articles, picture books, and advertisements. She invited guest speakers from local communities to talk to them. She asked her class to design questionnaires on sexual harassment and to conduct a survey on the summer school campus. On her quizzes she would always ask one short-answer question related to China. In an interview she explained the China factor in enabling learning:

> Can you apply this to something? And there is a question, that's always like, about China. I explained that in the American context. Can they show me how this idea might fit China? . . . And more than half of the students will pick that one [question]. More

> than half of the students will pick something that they can then apply to China, which I appreciate. There's learning for me. But also I don't care if they have applied to Venezuela. Just show me that you have been applying with the ideas. (July 27, 2011)

The professor emphasized her students' ability to apply ideas discussed in class to actual social phenomena in China or elsewhere. Short-answer questions encouraged the students to evaluate and insert local cultural meanings into their texts rather than just reproduce information from the textbooks or the professor. The option of examining their own cultures was inspiring, as "more than half of the students" picked the China question.

Valuing local cultural meanings encouraged the students to make positive connections between their languages. When her introduction to sociology class discussed issues of education and human development, Professor Walker had her students watch a video online before attending a guest lecture delivered by a Chinese woman writer, also a former middle school teacher. She then asked her students to discuss, in writing, the connections between the video and the lecture. The video was an animated lecture given by British education and creativity expert Sir Ken Robinson (2010) on changing education paradigms. The guest lecturer discussed in Chinese her unique approach to teaching; instead of teaching to the standards set by educational authorities, she encouraged her students to find their true desires and to think about the value of life. Thus, the assignment effectively elevated a local literacy practice (attending a Chinese lecture and writing about it) to a higher, translocal, and academic scale level. One of the students described how the guest lecturer encouraged them to take hold of their lives:

> In response to the second and third questions she brought to us, she told us several traditional Chinese concepts and sent my classmates some of her calligraphy that could embody those concepts. By "处下" (Chu'xia, literally meaning stay in low position), she said that we should keep a low profile to get adapted to our (social) environments. Also, we need to treat the changing world with inner peace ("静," Jing). She then mentioned that we should "never say 'I am busy'" ("勿称忙") because the character 忙 is a combination of "忄 (meaning hear/mind) and 亡 (death/loss)," which means that if you always say busy, you will lose your mind. Besides she remind us to think about ourselves everyday and get an insight of anything we encounter from superficial level.

The guest lecturer used Chinese concepts as principles for dealing with the difficulties of everyday life. The above passage indicates that in this assignment the students' composing processes were translingual and transmodal. After watching an animation featuring British-accented English and attending a lecture in Chinese, they drew connections, in written English, between the two sources. This can be seen in the above passage as the student synthesized the lecturer's main points by translating and transcribing key Chinese concepts. When composing for Professor Walker, who knew little Chinese, each student had to adopt translation, interpretation, exposition, and transcription strategies. These students came to understand through experience the vitality of being able to function in and across multiple languages and modalities in academic disciplines.

Crossing Literacy Regimes as a System Project

Enabling the unprivileged (as previously defined) move between literacy regimes requires human agency, which is a system project. Canagarajah (2013a) has demonstrated the agency of migrant professional workers in negotiating norms and reconstructing translocal spaces in English-dominant nations. Studying the privileged provides insights into the other side of the story, that is, enabling the unprivileged to move between literacy regimes. The American professors recognized several challenges confronting the Chinese students attempting to construct texts for audiences of higher scale levels. The professors adopted a series of strategies to help them learn by completing writing assignments. The roles the professors played in enabling the students to move from one literacy regime to another remind us that valuing and guarding local meanings and voices in translocal contexts is a system project. It requires not only individual agency but also the concerted efforts of all parties in the context, including institutions that reify and maintain the systems of use, values, functions, and norms in a higher literacy regime.

First of all, it was critical that the professors recognized the students' challenges in writing English. However, their perceptions were typically limited to the idea that some students had a hard time constructing coherent passages and expressing personal voice, and they were unsure how to help them with their surface-level language issues. In addition to linguistic challenges, some professors recognized their students' unfamiliarity with the ways scholars reason and communicate in their specific disciplines. They felt more comfortable addressing disciplinary conventions in their students' writing than they did grammatical concerns. Roberts and Cimasko (2008) and Zhu (2004) similarly observed that business, social science, and engineering professors tend to edit semantic gaps as opposed to grammatical items in multilingual student writing. Previous studies have revealed that undergraduate students (especially nonmajors in general education courses, regardless of linguistic background) typically do not view academic writing as a disciplinary specialist would (Geisler, 1994; Haas, 1994; Russell & Yanez, 2003). Therefore, the Chinese students' difficulties in reasoning and communicating in specific courses may or may not be related to their multilingual status.

Most of the professors adjusted the writing load and adopted short essays and short-answer questions as their key assessment tools. They recognized that understanding student needs and pedagogical contexts was more important than assigning the same amount of writing as they had in the United States. The shorter length of the intensive summer program also prompted them to reduce the writing load, a practice commonly found in the United States. Using short-answer questions instead of essay questions deemphasizes the students' weak essay-writing abilities while allowing them to practice some basic written modes, such as narration, description, and comparison/contrast, before transitioning to more challenging modes such as argument and persuasion (Drury, 2001). These short-answer questions also allowed the students to use other meaning-making strategies developed in grassroots practice, such as short sentences, phrases, bullet points, charts, diagrams, and hand-drawn images.

One may question whether the professors, by adjusting the writing assignments, lowered the standards of learning. In their studies of writing in subject courses in English-medium high schools, Kong (2010) and Wilcox (2011) suggested that teachers and administrators lowering their expectations for multilingual students had detrimental effects on their learning, promoting simplification of writing goals and a focus on surface-level editing and mechanics. In one of the faculty meetings we observed, the professors discussed whether they should lower academic standards in view of the students' levels of English proficiency and essay-writing ability. They concurred that they shouldn't; otherwise, the students wouldn't be able to succeed in American universities. It was also impermissible because the students might later request to transfer credits to their American institutions, and it would be unfair to do so without equivalent performance standards and metrics for evaluation. Therefore most professors kept the term paper as the cardinal assignment and the short-answer questions in midterms and finals as the key assessment device. Additionally, some required other types of writing during the semester as they had in the United States. For example, Professor Walker assigned personal narratives, poetry, article summaries, lecture reports, and survey reports in her sociology classes. These assignments asked the students to make sense of reading materials, to connect them with their life experiences, and to reorganize their subject knowledge. The wide array of genres in which the students composed during the two or three courses they took at the summer school ensured that they were continually challenged as writers, avoiding the simplification of writing goals that sometimes occurs when standards are lowered. In principle, the students were assessed on how well they had accomplished learning typically expected in a university course.

Some professors capitalized on the students' multilingual and transcultural resources in facilitating learning. They were "teaching to their [students] strengths," as Professor Walker remarked in one interview (July 27, 2011). Some allowed Chinese in group discussions and quizzes, making it an important scaffolding tool for consolidating and constructing subject knowledge. In addition to recognizing the students' multilingual competence, some professors incorporated local cultures into their teaching, creating a positive and invitational learning environment for students. Even in courses that did not explicitly focus on China, the students were encouraged to bring Chinese publications into class discussions and to use those materials in their writing assignments, elevating local cultural meanings to a global, academic scale. This practice confirmed the importance of their home cultures and languages in academic literacy while helping to establish connections between students' multiple languages.

The ability to meet the students' literacy needs correlated positively with the professors' previous transliterate experiences. These experiences had furnished the professors with necessary rescaling skills. For example, Professor Walker, an African American, studied language, gender, and identity issues in her own scholarship. She was married to an African man, and she had traveled to and worked in multiple nations. Professor Chang received academic training in Taiwan before pursuing doctoral studies in the United States. She taught for seven years in multilingual university classrooms in California before coming to the summer school. Professor Taylor was familiar with colleagues who had taught content courses in Spanish at her college.

Central to the professors' accommodations was the CE they shared with their students. A linguistic analysis of the recorded data reveals different styles among the professors' English, and the same analysis evidences their variegated translingual skills. For example, in the "Literacy Challenges in

Scale-Jumping" section of this chapter, the professors' quoted comments about their students' literacy challenges seem informal, marked by pauses, colloquialisms, and fillers such as "like," "feel like," "things like that," "okay," and "you know." Professor Taylor exhibited these traits in her comment pointing out her students' difficulties in taking sides. On her way to class, she made the remark in an informal style. In contrast, in the section "Valuing Students' Multilingual Resources," intriguingly, Professor Taylor's comment on her colleagues' teaching in both English and Spanish seems formal, using multilayer subordinate clauses. She opted to speak formally probably because it was a sit-down interview. Knowing that I understand Chinese, both Professor Chang and the psychology professor's teaching assistant blended English and Chinese when addressing me. Once each of these English users' speech is transcribed, it can clearly be seen as having deviated tremendously from Standard English. Instead, their speech resembles that of students in Professor Taylor's class. Mihut (2014) argued that literacy brokering implicates emotional work, or what she calls "literacy as affinity—a discursive repertoire comprised of language of empathy, personal experiences, and even social relations embedded in the literate experience" (p. 58). CE not only mediated teaching and learning but also created affinity and empathy crucial for building a "dwelling place," felt among some professors for their students as evidenced by their understanding of and efforts to help students struggling with Standard English.

The professors' accommodative strategies bear implications for teaching English-medium content courses in translocal contexts. First, to assess learning, teachers may focus on short-answer questions in addition to essay questions to put less pressure on the students' essay-writing ability while allowing them to communicate subject knowledge adequately. Second, despite the professors' adaptions, writing still played an important role in facilitating learning. Teachers can design a variety of writing tasks, such as personal narratives, poetry, article summaries, and research reports to facilitate learning, as suggested by Young (2006) and as conscientiously practiced by Professor Walker. Third, teachers are familiar with the ways of reasoning and communicating in their disciplines, but they need to turn that familiarity into explicit, teachable awareness. Then they can effectively instruct students on disciplinary genres and conventions using workshops, worksheets, and feedback on their writing. Fourth, while requiring students to perform writing tasks in English, teachers should allow them to use other linguistic and nonlinguistic symbol systems to plan their writing and to organize their thoughts (Kibler, 2010;

Jäppinen, 2005; Johns, 1998). We should train our students to shuttle between their first- and second-language academic communities (Canagarajah, 2006; Casanave, 1998; Cho, 2010; Gentil, 2005; Jarratt, Losh, & Puente, 2006). Making connections between subject matter and students' home cultures will motivate them to learn and help them to develop translingual academic abilities such as cultural mediation skills (translation, interpretation, and explanation) and personal voice.

In addition to content teachers, academic institutions are also literacy sponsors and brokers critical to students' scale-jumping success. The professors' rescaling efforts raise questions for higher education in English-dominant nations, to which a majority of the summer school students were heading. First, with continuing influx of international students in these contexts, to what extent should universities and colleges adjust their assignments to meet the needs and skills of such students? Second, if they are going to adjust their assignments, how does that change curricular objectives, course expectations, and learning outcomes? Third, if we recognize that students, both international and domestic, are able to draw resources from multiple languages and cultures in facilitating subject learning, should learning and the assessment of learning be performed solely based on monolingual and monocultural norms? These questions beg in-depth research on how content teachers and academic programs in these institutions are adjusting or can adjust their curricular objectives, course expectations, and assignments to meet the needs of the increasing number of multilingual students from outside English-dominant nations. Content teachers and academic programs need to work together as part of the system project to help the unprivileged move between literacy regimes and ascend scale levels.

In this chapter I have demonstrated that the privileged can make space for CE and grassroots practices in academic literacy regimes, which in turn will help to retain local meanings and voices in translocal spaces. In view of her students' weak essay writing, for example, Professor Walker created opportunities for them to use oral English, visuals, and short written sentences and phrases to answer exam questions. Some professors allowed their students to speak either Chinese or a mix of Chinese and English in groups when brainstorming and scaffolding thoughts before writing. A psychology professor even allowed Chinese expressions on exams. Their openness to CE directly or indirectly encouraged the students to connect local issues with global or academic ones. Despite these strategies for accommodating CE, some monolingual assumptions continued to reign among the professors. While they typically didn't mind their students using other languages within groups, most of them upheld the idea that academic essays need to be composed in a single language and a single style, that is, Standard English. They, except for Professor Walker, didn't seem to recognize that their students could and probably should further develop their academic transliteracy and further develop their ability to function academically across languages and cultures. As literacy educators, as I will discuss in chapter 6, we can foster such ability in our students by helping them identify and marshal their literacy resources.

6

Academic Transliteracy

> I am now in the poor transition stage of Chinese and English dilemma: my Chinese is declining due to lack of practice, and my English is not improving very much. . . . For social networking generation, I use "Renren" instead, to update myself with the Chinese culture and keep in touch with my Chinese friends. As for English, hopefully by taking this class, I will improve in English writing skills and feel more comfortable with it. —Tacy, "Literacy Autobiography"

What is most striking about this confession probably comes from this writer's yearning for literacy in two languages. That yearning is expressed at the end of a literacy autobiography that a student, Tacy, wrote in the summer school that I described in the last chapter. She was in my English writing class. Having grown up in Shanghai, Tacy went to the United States for high school and then entered the University of California, Los Angeles (UCLA). After reflecting upon her transnational literacy experience, she concluded her narrative by expressing a strong desire for advanced bilingual literacy. Her desire indicates that after years of learning how to cross English-dominant literacy regimes (from grassroots social-networking to academic literacies), she viewed literacy across languages as equally indispensable. Transnational mobility spawned her desire to be a better linguistic and cultural juggler. She remained hopeful that she could improve her bilingual skills, and she literally paid a premium to enroll in my writing course.

The fields of writing studies and second-language writing are hardly ready to help multilingual students develop bilingual literacy, or what I would call *transliteracy*. While bilingual literacy, or biliteracy, tends to compartmentalize literacy development into separate languages, transliteracy emphasizes blurred boundaries between languages, between modalities, between cultures, and between identities. Much of the pedagogical practice in the two interrelated fields has rested on monolingual assumptions: English is a discrete linguistic system, developed by native speakers and formalized by the state-sponsored apparatus comprised of schools, standard exams, and publishing houses. For multilingual speakers writing in English, monolingual "native speakers" constitute their default audiences. Certainly, these assumptions have been challenged by scholars in applied linguistics, education, and writing studies. One theoretical challenge is the notion of biliteracy—the ability and practice of functioning literately in two (or more) separate languages and speech communities (Gentil, 2005; Hornberger, 1989; Hornberger & Skilton-Sylvester, 2003). Tacy's yearning for the ability to read and write in both Chinese and English evidentially supports the biliteracy challenge of traditional monolingual assumptions.

In this chapter, taking a cosmopolitan perspective, I will first review and critique the biliteracy-related research involving English literacy. Because of the symbiosis of English and other languages in many societies, a clear demarcation between languages is often hard to achieve. The ability to function literately in separate languages is an ideal supported by monolingual and nationalist assumptions. Instead, for multilingual/multidialectal writers, the symbiosis of languages and dialects makes writing hardly a job of a single language or dialect, hence a reason for translingual literacy, or transliteracy. English writing, though a local language practice, mediates multiple cultures and subjectivities, as Tacy reminds us with her simultaneous engagement with the popular social network Renren (人人, or everyone) in China while taking my English class. Transliteracy necessitates the ability to navigate between cultures and between identities, with the intent to foster cosmopolitan attitudes and practices. The English for academic purposes (EAP) class can be an important site for developing students' academic transliteracy, enabling them to perceive and practice linguistic and cultural crossings and to marshal resources for co-constructing meaning with academic and nonacademic audiences. Focusing on three Chinese students in an EAP class, I will analyze the language and cultural relations in some of their writing acts. As English teachers, even though we are supposed to teach Standard English, what is involved in student writing processes is far more complex than the simple reproduction and propagation of this particular Cosmopolitan English (CE) style and the single culture that assumably accompanies it. Understanding these dynamics will enable us to help students navigate and capitalize on language relations in their literacy development.

Moving from Biliteracy to Transliteracy

In view of the intimate relationships between English and other languages, literacy scholars have paid an increasing amount of attention to biliteracy. Biliteracy refers to multilingual speakers' ability to function literately in more than one language community. This concept draws attention to the fact that multilingual students and scholars typically need to read and write across two or more languages as they move between national contexts and between audiences of various linguistic backgrounds. Biliteracy effectively leads us away from treating the teaching of English literacy as solely within the realm of English, and it calls our attention to English's intimate connection with literacy in other languages.

Anglophone research on biliteracy thus far has focused on individuals who shuttle between academic contexts defined by nation or language (Casanave, 1998; Canagarajah, 2006; Cho, 2010; Shi, 2002; Shi, Wang, & Xu, 2005). For example, Casanave (1998) studied the writing activities and attitudes of four Japanese scholars who had received their graduate training in the United States and then returned to work at a Japanese university. While focusing on two of the four scholars who were starting their careers in Japan, Casanave found that they juggled "two sets of values and expectations" (p. 175). They faced difficult decisions regarding what scholarly activities to pursue, what values to place on those activities, and what shape their professional identities would take. All four scholars found writing in Japanese and English to be central to their professional lives, and all perceived differences in the "two writing worlds" despite many broad commonalities (p. 175). Canagarajah (2006) examined a Sri Lankan scholar's writing in three linguistic contexts: Tamil in a local publication, English in a local publication, and English in an international publication. When writing in Tamil and English for local publications, that scholar deviated in significant ways from the relatively standard introduction section of English research papers in the West (Swales, 1990). In contrast, he conformed to the Western standard introduction structure when writing for the international publication. These studies underscore the fact that different national and linguistic contexts entail different values, expectations, and challenges for scholarly writing.

Building on the existing work, we can consider another fact about biliteracy: that multilingual writers typically don't work within a single linguistic system, a single modality, a single national culture, or a single community. Although on many occasions these writers produce texts in a single linguistic symbol system, the process of generating texts goes beyond that system. In fact, Hornberger and Skilton-Sylvester (2003) define biliteracy essentially as "any and all instances in which communication occurs in two (or more) languages in and around writing," where "instances" can refer to "an individual actor, interaction, practice, program, situation, or society" (p. 35). When writing is viewed as a situated communication, the multilingual writer draws from sources of a multilinguistic and multicultural nature in the composing process (Chew, 2005; Engelson, 2011; Fraiberg, 2010; Jämtelid, 2002; Lee & Barton, 2011; Martin-Jones & Jones, 2000; Sebba, Mahootian, & Jonsson, 2012). Writing as a situated communication can be illustrated by the work of entry-level new hires in Hong Kong banks as observed by Chew (2005):

> Some amount of Chinese-to-English translation work goes on so that much of the gathering of information is carried out in Chinese whether it is talking to colleagues, clients, the media and other professionals in the industry. This information is then translated into English for the written product in the form of memos, minutes of meetings, reports, rules and regulations for bank customers, opinion and complaint letters from customers. . . . If the research content is international in nature or deals with international companies, the reading materials are in English. Technical and computer manuals are also read in English. (pp. 430–431)

While the new hires produce standard bank documents in English, the communications leading up to and following the production of those documents are rendered through the modes of speaking and writing in Standard Chinese, Cantonese, Standard English, regional Englishes, and necessarily nonlinguistic symbol systems. Behind these systems are overlapping professional cultures that cross national and regional boundaries and that the new hires must engage with. We certainly cannot view the "memos, minutes of meetings, reports, rules and regulations for bank customers, opinion and complaint letters" as the beginning or the end of a communication; instead, they are links in a complex, dynamic communication system, or in the "ecology of language practice" (Pennycook, 2010, p. 104). Therefore, instead of viewing biliteracy as the endgame when nurturing students' English for specific purposes, we should view both the writing process and product as integral to a local communication, to a practice in which writers engage multiple interlocutors and objects in order to collect, consolidate, synthesize, and organize information for better communicative effect. We need to go beyond texts and seek to understand the material and translingual processes involved in constructing these texts.

Biliteracy studies sometimes also overlook the fact that a multilingual writer's literacy practice can be complicated by audience. When writing in English, for example, a writer may need to communicate with an audience that cannot be easily pinned down to a single language or a single culture. It might be a cosmopolitan audience who, like the writer, has crossed the arbitrary lines demarcating languages and cultures. Constructing a text always entails negotiation between writer and reader, and alignment between the audience addressed and the audience invoked: "Rather than relying on incantations . . . writers conjure their vision—a vision which they hope readers will actively come to share as they read the text—by using all the resources of language available to them to establish a broad and ideally coherent range of cues for the reader" (Ede & Lunsford, 1984, p. 167). Dialoguing with interlocutors inhabiting multiple languages and cultures makes audience alignment especially challenging. The writer needs to provide sufficient details or cues for the reader to align with an invoked audience that is often multiple, mutable, and shifting. In addition, as each possesses a unique configuration of multilingual and multicultural experiences, the reader and the writer may not share the same rhetorical values, such as persuasion, efficiency, and clarity. The reader thus needs to work extra hard in constructing meaning, sometimes having to tolerate ambiguity, miscommunication, or incomprehension (Ede & Lunsford, 1996; Pratt, 1991).

Biliteracy studies have not paid sufficient attention to the shifting subjectivities and identities formed as multilingual writers negotiate multiple speech communities and discourses. Transliteracy underscores not only the multiplicity but also the fluid, shifting nature of subjectivities and identities generated by such writers' literacy practices (Li, 1994; Rampton, 1995). In probably the most influential literacy development model yet, Hornberger and Skilton-Sylvester (2003) described biliteracy in terms of four nested continua characterizing contexts, media, content, and development. These two scholars are primarily interested in how contexts, media, and discourses mediate one's development of a biliterate repertoire. Situated in the field of education, the two scholars defined development as the improvement of functional and cognitive skills. Transliteracy highlights the possibility and necessity of one developing appreciation for and new identification with a range of cultures and communities, or a cosmopolitan disposition, by reading and writing across languages and modalities.

Among studies of academic biliteracy, Gentil (2005) showcased the tensions between the biliteracy framework and students' transliterate practices. He studied three Francophone students in an English-medium university in Quebec for two and a half years. One of the issues he explored was how the students developed biliteracy as they negotiated academic discourses with professors, peers, and other mediating agents in and across English and French. Writing of one of his participants, Katia, a doctoral student, he characterizes biliterate development as the appropriation of "transliteracy," or "the ability and practice of writing and reading across languages, that is, of writing in one language while reading (and speaking) in another, back and forth" (p. 452). Katia had to constantly engage multiple disciplinary and vernacular discourses across languages. Some of these discourses were competing or mutually exclusive, making her feel as if she was shuttling between different worlds. On an academic level, she had to interconnect the Anglophone and Francophone discourses and literatures of her field of study, linking elements among webs of discourses that seemed to be only loosely interrelated. On a more personal level, she tried to bridge "two worlds" that are mutually incomprehensible and sometimes suspicious of one another by shuttling daily between her Francophone home context and her Anglophone institution of higher education. While Katia defines these "two worlds" using discrete languages, Gentil underscores her simultaneous engagement with different styles of these two languages and her efforts to cross multiple cultures.

Most Anglophone studies of academic biliteracy have focused on individuals' negotiations with disciplinary discourses and their interactions with academic and nonacademic contexts, giving one the impression that academic biliteracy arises out of disciplinary activities. Gentil (2005), for example, studied the three students' attitudes toward developing academic biliteracy and how they negotiated discourses in their disciplines (engineering, chemistry, and cultural studies) with various literacy brokers. Cho (2010) studied the challenges that four Korean scholars had encountered in their biliteracy development. These scholars fostered their academic literacy largely by using English in their disciplines while reserving Korean for nonacademic purposes. Cho identified three impediments to their development of academic biliteracy: the heavy use of Chinese characters in high school and university texts, the lack of academic books and journals written in Korean, and the lack of an established academic register in Korean. Overall, these studies underscore individuals' negotiations in developing academic biliteracy across disciplines.

While engaging disciplinary discourses is critical for academic transliteracy, the EAP class serves as another strategic site for transliterate development. This class has been traditionally used in the United States for developing students' academic literacy solely in English. Students engage cultural discourses by producing several papers ranging from personal experience essay to argumentation essay for an idealized English monolingual reader. Such a course typically focuses on writing as a process including drafting, revising, peer editing, and proofreading. The course teaches students to pay close attention to all parts of their essays, that is, introductions, thesis formulation, topic sentences, paragraph development, conclusions, as well as organization and research. Perceived as novices to the academy, students learn the conventions of research writing and the skills of audience engagement and critical thinking. Adopting a cosmopolitan perspective, an EAP teacher can tap into the multilingual and multicultural nature of a class, school, and society at large for transliterate development. Students can learn how to communicate with academic and nonacademic audiences of different languages and nations by marshaling their resources. Students like Tacy, quoted in the epigraph, yearn for biliteracy, and they seek EAP classes for improving their English reading and writing abilities. Like the subject teachers I described in the last chapter, EAP teachers can meet these students halfway in their efforts to cross literacy regimes. And we can do better in helping them develop literacy across languages, cultures, and identities.

Taking a transliteracy perspective, EAP teachers can do two key things in class. First, we can intervene in students' writing processes by directing their attention to resources, audiences, and consequences across languages. Speaking of a translingual approach to language studies, Pennycook (2010) emphasized paying attention to resources, audiences, and ideological consequences: "If we adopt a translingual model of language . . . to look at English use, the relationship to be understood is among interlingual resources (what language resources people draw on), colingual relations (who says what to whom where) and ideolingual implications (what gets taken from what language use with what investments, ideologies, discourses and beliefs)" (p. 86). In writing studies, seeing linguistic difference as a resource for making meaning, a translingual approach asks similar questions: "What might this difference do? How might it function expressively, rhetorically, communicatively? For whom, under what conditions, and how?" (Horner, Lu, Royster, & Trimbur, 2011, p. 303). In short, we can call students' attention to their resources and audiences, and also to the material and ideological ramifications of their writing. We can help students perceive what different styles of CE may achieve for audiences addressed and invoked. Second, we can encourage students to engage discourses across languages both in and outside their majors. Writing will enable them to identify and analyze connections among these discourses. In Gentil (2005), for example, his participant Katia had to connect the loosely interrelated Anglophone and Francophone academic discourses in her domain of study. A transliteracy pedagogy involving these two things may enable students to recognize intricate language and cultural relations and to develop new transcultural identities through their engagement with these relations.

To illustrate the viability of cultivating academic transliteracy in an EAP course, I will draw on a course that I taught in the summer school in Shanghai. The course was designed as an equivalent of first-year writing offered in American universities. The students, all Chinese, either had returned from their studies in North America, or they had just completed high school and were going to college in the fall. Therefore, they had had varying amounts of exposure to academic English. They were inspired to attend the summer program by the prospect of earning credits transferable to North American universities.

To introduce the students to academic inquiry and communication, I adopted a sequenced writing assignment approach. I developed this particular version of that approach based on Leki (1992) for teaching academic writing to English-as-a-second-language students. The approach consisted of four interconnected writing assignments: personal experience, interview with experts, literature review, and final report. In the personal experience assignment, students selected a topic, recounted a personal experience related to the topic, and raised questions or hypotheses for further inquiry. The interview assignment asked the students to use interviews to further explore the topic. In the literature review, students identified at least three scholarly articles on the topic and summarized them. Then, they reorganized the information they collected and delivered it as a coherent argument in the final report. The approach, according to Leki, has several benefits. First, students practice a variety of academic writing skills such as generating ideas, organizing, editing, and citing. Second, because the assignments are linked, they don't need to start anew for each one. In a sense, each assignment serves as a draft for a larger work in progress. Third, students become empowered, developing authorial expertise and confidence by researching, selecting, and molding information on specific subject matter. And, finally, they will not only better understand writing as a process wherein one makes choices concerning communication, but they will also develop a sense of discourse community. The sequenced assignment approach aligns well with the pedagogy of multiliteracies articulated by the New London Group (1996). The pedagogy of multiliteracies deals with designs of meaning for better social futures. Through sequenced assignments, students acquire concepts, ideas, and discourses related to their topic and academic writing conventions (available designs). Then they creatively apply and combine these available designs (designing) to create new meanings grounded in their sociohistorical context, personal interests, and life experiences (the redesigned).

To understand how my students develop academic transliteracy, I adopted teacher research: that is, I studied my class from a researcher's perspective. Teacher-researchers raise questions about what they think about and observe in their teaching and in their students' learning. They collect students' work in order to evaluate performance, but they also see students' work as data to examine the teaching and learning that produced it. Procedurally, teacher-researchers develop questions, investigate the questions with their students systematically, collect and analyze data from their classes, examine their assumptions and beliefs, articulate their theories, and share their research with a wide audience, including both teachers and students (Crookes, 1993; MacLean & Mohr, 1999; Nunan, 1989). Though similar in procedure to traditional education research, teacher research emphasizes a reflective process whereby teachers examine and change their own classroom practices. The advantages of teacher-researchers being able to explore questions with their students and improve their teaching at the same time make teacher research opportune for the present inquiry. However, the limitations of teacher research have to be acknowledged in this study. I came into the study with assumptions and even biases. I assumed that there aren't clear-cut boundaries between languages, between cultures, and between identities. I believed that the ultimate goal of literacy education is to cultivate students' ability to engage and identify with strangers, to become global citizens. I was concerned about how to cultivate transliteracy in my own students. I understood that given the specificity of the instructional context and design, the generalizability of the study would become an issue. Following Borg and Sanchez (2015) and Richards (2003), however, I hoped that providing a rich description and interpretation of my class would make my study interesting and relevant to those in other situations with similar educational goals.

I collected data consisting of my teaching journal, student writings (literacy autobiographies, major papers, and reflection papers), and recorded conversations from teacher-student conferences. Student consent was received at the beginning of the semester. In each step of their research, the students might communicate with or invoke various audiences, adopting myriad resources and strategies. Thus, I analyze each assignment as a link in the communication process. I identify the interlocutors addressed and invoked before moving on to linguistic and nonlinguistic resources mobilized by students in a particular assignment. Recorded conversations at teacher-student conferences offer a glimpse of how an EAP teacher, as a "literacy broker" (Lillis & Curry, 2006), enabled a multilingual student to identify appropriate resources to engage multiple cultural discourses. These conversations also showcase multilinguals' negotiation for meaning when engaging certain styles of CE. I listened to the recorded conversations right after a student-teacher conference and jotted down the various resources and cultural discourses that we discussed and the ways in which I called a student's attention to them. I also identified the negotiation strategies used by the interlocutors and noted the features of their English. Then I listened to these conversations again at the end of the semester to double-check my notes. Finally, I examined my notes to identify the most widely adopted types of resources and cultural discourses that emerged in our conversations. The student authors were later shown my analysis and given an opportunity to check the accuracy of my representations and interpretations of their data.

In my analysis I will focus on three students—Tacy, Wenyuan, and Shumin—who represent broad, mobile literacy experiences commonly found among the summer program students. Tacy went to the United States for high school and college and had just finished her first year as an accounting major. Wenyuan attended high school in China and went to Boston University, majoring in communication studies. Having just graduated from high school in China, Shumin planned to attend a Chinese university and to major in English. Among them, Tacy and Wenyuan had more exposure to academic English than Shumin, and Wenyuan and Shumin had more exposure to academic Chinese than Tacy.

Setting the Agenda for Transliterate Inquiry

In their personal experience essays, the students constructed multiple audiences and voices. Some of these audiences were outside the conventional boundaries of Chinese nationality. In her essay, for example, Tacy established the need to explore the usefulness of volunteering in modern societies by evoking transnational audiences:

> Some people want to add a line in the resume to show that they are well developed. High school seniors use volunteer experience to grab the attention of the college admission administrator; when looking for a job, college students put the volunteer line to leave a good impression on Human Resources staff. Some people want to earn reputation by showing their generosity in charity, especially for celebrities.

Having studied in the United States, Tacy clearly had American high school and university students in mind, and having served on the Volunteer China committee, she also had people inside and outside China in mind. She actively recruited participants for Volunteer China programs on the summer school campus and later interviewed some Chinese volunteers for her interview paper. She posed a question for her topic, querying about the meanings of volunteering: "As we can learn from life, more businessman, successful people, celebrities, and students are joining the volunteer team. The team grows bigger and stronger every year, yet the progress made in charity is not that obvious. Are 'volunteers' here for themselves (further development), or are they really here to make a change?" After this setup she goes on to relate two personal and drastically different volunteering experiences: one in Moldova and the other in the United States.

Conversations with transnational audiences necessitate the use of resources from more than a single culture. Tacy wants to engage those who are hesitant or doubtful about the usefulness of volunteering. Although she was physically in China when writing the essay, she addressed a mixed audience; there is not a one-to-one mapping between the context and the imagined audience. For example, she says, "People might disagree with me in saying that volunteer motivation does not matter, as long as people are working on the same thing and sharing the same goal. But I feel sad. I do hope, as president Obama hopes, that the world will be in peace." The most striking resources used in her rendition probably come from the references that index American education practices and values—volunteering, resumes, graduating seniors, human resources, and celebrities. Her mention of President Obama gestures at another alignment with American students. These cultural references, however, can potentially engage other audiences, as American education and business models have influenced most nations across the globe. In China, for example, requiring volunteer experience for college admissions has become common practice. In addition, President Obama's appeals for cosmopolitanism made in his memoirs and speeches alike have enchanted an international audience (Selzer, 2010), including Tacy.

A few essays invoked voices from local audiences, thus requiring a different set of resources: writers rendered individual local voices in English (regardless of the language originally spoken in) and necessarily used linguistic and cultural mediation skills, such as translation, interpretation, and contextualization. For example, Shumin invoked her father's and her roommates' voices. She chose to study friendship because she was "disturbed" by the issue of "how to make best friends and even keep the friendship forever." In her essay she recounted disagreeing with her father on the subject of friendship:

> My father thought that students studied art who academic records must be not so well so that they could not help me a lot whether in study or in life. He even thought that my classmates in high school were so excellent that the most friends I made, the more help I could get. Once he said: "You had better not keep in touch with your friends you made before." But I always recollect the beautiful days, happy smiles and the loud poems which are kept in my mind deeply.

Shumin worked on a topic that is deeply rooted in and inseparably connected to local culture: her father discouraged her from making friends with art students. And though he most likely spoke Standard Chinese or a local dialect, she represented her father's admonition in English and as a direct quotation. The quote, carefully chosen and rendered, evokes vividly a stern father who is biased against art students. His bias came from the prevailing belief in China that only students who don't have good grades choose to pursue the arts. Pressure from her father to pursue good grades led to Shumin's challenges in establishing and maintaining meaningful friendships. She felt that she was misunderstood by her boarding school roommates, so she tried to address them in her essay:

> I was not aware that until I was ignored by my roommates sometimes. It was difficult for me to change this situation because my roommates thought I was so absorbed in study that they were embarrassed to disturb me. How eager am I to tell them what is real inside me. What I communicated with them was something shallow like study problem, comments about our teachers, or difficulties in life. Obviously, the life was not what I looked forward to. Maybe it was easy to make friends but hard to be real friends. So what can I do next?

Obviously Shumin had her parents and her roommates in mind when she chose to write about friendship, a topic of great importance to her. Presenting their voices in English, she synthesized their comments originally made in Standard Chinese or a local dialect. Shumin used English in her personal endeavor to engage the friendship issue across multiple discourses—national, home, and school. Shumin's personal experience essay, inexplicitly embedded with Chinese linguistic and cultural elements, set the agenda for her transliterate inquiry for the rest of the semester.

Representing Local Informants

How to represent local cultural values and practices in a translocal space was the challenge of the interview assignment, which asks the students to communicate directly with experts on their topic. It is an opportunity for them to listen, to open themselves up to the views of both researchers and individuals who have personal experience with the topic. The central issue for the assignment is how to synthesize information and represent interviewees truthfully and fairly. The most compelling consequence of the assignment was the students' choice of diverse interviewees, representing different nations, genders, social classes, and linguistic backgrounds. Because the professors at the summer school represented multiple academic fields, they became popular interviewees. Interviews with them were typically conducted in styles of English. Through phone calls, e-mails, and face-to-face interactions, the students also interviewed their high school teachers and friends in styles of Chinese.

When it came to reporting these interviews, multilingual choices had to be made. Most of the time, the students paraphrased interviews solely in English. In contrast to this class norm, Shumin explicitly blended Chinese and English scripts in her writing, which opened up a student-teacher conversation on how to handle non-English symbols in academic writing. In the beginning of her essay, Shumin introduced her interview questions:

> First of all, I formulated various kinds of specific questions which I need to explore and some of which were: What is the definition of friends? Do you agree with Confucius's principle of making friends (子曰: 友直、友谅、有多闻, 益矣; 友便辟、友善柔、友便佞, 损矣。). And what about your principle? During these decades, what change most among your different kinds of friends? Does your friends' characters, hobbies and pursuits are similar to yours?

When articulating these questions, Shumin wanted to usher in Confucius as an interlocutor. However, she chose not to translate Confucius's words on making friends. At a student-teacher conference, we discussed how a textual choice might help break down cultural and linguistic barriers:

> Xiaoye (X): And here I thought it's cool that you have Chinese here.
>
> Shumin (S): I cannot translate into English.
>
> X: Can you translate this into English as well? You can keep this Chinese. But it would be better if you translate into English somewhere here, but you still provide Chinese.
>
> S: If I translate, I think its most origin[al meaning is lost], 就是感觉, 反正我觉得 (I feel, anyway I feel), which I think some reader does not, may not understand this sentence.
>
> X: I understand it. If you translate this into English, then more people can understand you. More people, more people. If you don't, that's fine. You do not need to change it.

Shumin had not originally translated the Confucian expression for fear that she would be unable to capture its original meaning. Her belief in an original meaning residing in Chinese and her distrust of English's ability to capture it made her choice to blend the two scripts inevitable. Ideas are indeed very much culturally situated, and one cannot easily extract them from their context. It is this very tension that I wanted students to experience. Recognizing Shumin's fear, I suggested that by providing the idea in both scripts, more readers could understand her. My multilingual identity and my understanding of Confucian teaching rendered some weight to my suggestion, and taking my suggestion, certainly a powerful one in the instructional context, Shumin reworked the paragraph as follows:

> I formulated various questions which I need to explore and some of which were: What is the definition of friends? Do you agree with Confucius's principle of making friends? For instance Confucius said: "Straightforward friends, generous friends and erudite friends are beneficial to you. Stubborn friends, changeable friends and flattering friends are harmful to you." (子曰: 友直、友谅、有多闻, 益矣; 友便辟、友善柔、友便佞, 损矣。). And what about your principle? During these decades, what change most among your different kinds of friends? Does your friends' characters, hobbies and pursuits are similar to yours?

In the revision she compromised with non-Chinese speakers in offering the translation. However, she didn't compromise entirely. Consciously or unconsciously she retained her accents by deviating from Standard English in multiple places, such as the inconsistent use of tense ("I formulated various questions which I need to explore") and nonstandard syntax ("Does your friends' characters, hobbies and pursuits are similar to yours?"). Yet, her provisional translation both conforms to the standard way scholars mingle other linguistic symbol systems with English and enables her to integrate local cultural meanings in a translocal space emphatically.

While most students chose narrative essays for recounting their interviews, one student mixed genres and adopted visuals as an additional resource. Wenyuan was deeply concerned about moral degradation in contemporary Chinese society. For the assignment she interviewed ordinary citizens in Shanghai about their attitudes toward life. In her essay she inserted pictures taken both with and of her interviewees. While interviewing people on the street, she ran into a homeless man begging in front of a Starbucks coffee shop, a popular stop for the rising middle class in Chinese metropolises. In describing her encounter with the man, she blended into her narrative Chinese song lyrics and a public service announcement (PSA) that she had originally designed for a subway advertisement competition:

> Near Raffles city there was a church. I heard someone singing 桃花盛开的地方. A few steps closer, I noticed he was a beggar. In front of him was a poor plastic bottle. I stayed there for a long time because all the songs he sang were my father's favorites and he was about my father's age. I gave him a coin and took some pictures of him. I did not interview him because I felt somehow inappropriate. However, I was sure something unexpected must have happened to him. It is ironic that just a few steps away, there was a Starbucks, a foreign coffee brand that comfortably fits the feeling of Shanghai which is what an urban and international city should carry; yet, the urbanization makes the city cannot accept a Chinese man singing beautiful songs.

The author didn't interview the man, but she constructed his voice using one of his songs and her own PSA, integrating two cultural discourses. 在那桃花盛开的地方 (In the place where the peach flowers are blossoming) was a song written in the early 1980s, which conjures peaceful images of a village and a peach orchard during a warm and blossoming spring. The lyrics expressed the upbeat sentiment of a China transitioning into the post–Cultural Revolution era. The man sung these songs of the past probably to express nostalgia or to express a longing for a peaceful life difficult to obtain in a Chinese metropolis. He might be a migrant worker who had lost his job or simply a beggar from outside Shanghai. For the author the Chinese lyrics captured the man's own sentiment.

The contrasting images and words of the PSA (figure 6.1) lent the homeless man additional voice. An image of the beggar is juxtaposed with an image of people leisurely sitting in front of a Starbucks. The PSA reads at the top, "Together in Shanghai." The author explained in an interview that the word "together" (同) was positioned at the intersection of the horizontal and the vertical lines, signifying the metaphorically shared space of both images. The ideogram, 同, depicting one mouth (口) within a compound (冂), means people come to gather in a household or a state, reinforcing sharedness in the Chinese cultural tradition. In the center the statement reads, "We should not only act like ocean which embraces hundreds of rivers but also pursue the virtue of tolerating difference." The last line argues visually by using larger and larger font sizes. The word 大 (virtue) sits diametrically opposite to the word 同 (together), making a cosmopolitan argument: only when we embrace difference will we be virtuous and strong. The caption at the bottom reads, "We have every reason to let foreign friends drink the original coffee; we have more reasons to let the non-locals find a home in Shanghai." Designed originally as a subway advertisement, the PSA spoke to the Shanghai residents on behalf of the homeless man, calling for openness and accommodation toward nonlocals. The advertisement unmistakably uses irony to convey the student's criticisms: the city embraced "foreign friends" from outside the nation but failed to do the same for nonlocals within the nation. In both the original advertisement and the interview essay, the PSA gave voice to the otherwise "voiceless," the marginalized, in the Chinese drive toward development and globalization.

While crossing the boundaries of genre and language, the author was suspicious of language and meaning's ability to travel across nations. As a communication studies major, Wenyuan had learned design programs, such as Photoshop and Illustrator, in a design and media class in the United States, where she designed PSAs, compact disc covers, and magazine covers. When she returned to Shanghai and saw a PSA competition notice, she decided to participate. Reflecting, in a student-teacher conference, on her choice to use the PSA genre, Wenyuan claimed that without the feelings and experiences concerning Shanghai that most Chinese people share, American audiences would not understand her:

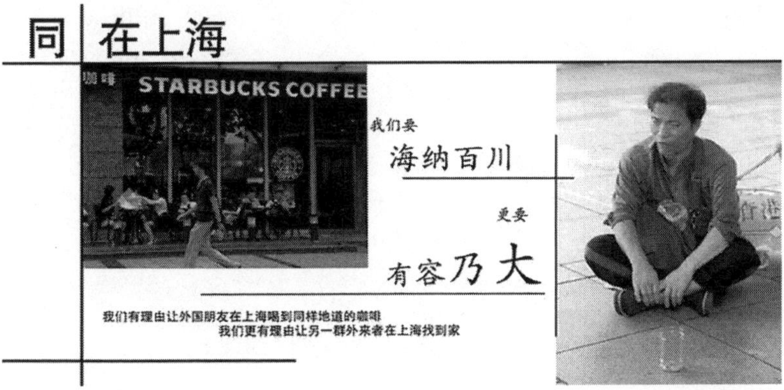

Figure 6.1. Wenyuan's public service announcement, portraying an ironic juxtaposition of a Starbucks coffee shop and a homeless man that is intended to give the "voiceless" a voice.

> I don't think people understand how I feel Shanghai or Chinese are struggling currently in the way of modernization. It's affecting people, and especially people of my age, or people has similar experience. I don't think people are really thinking about 以人为本, though it's advocated by the government. From this crash, high-speed train crash, I feel, this is, more and more people learned and know what the government tried to hide from.

Two high-speed trains collided and killed forty passengers near Shanghai that summer, which appalled Wenyuan. 以人为本 literally means "to take people as the foremost" in government service. A reformulation of the old slogan "To serve the people (为人民服务)," it was proposed by the Communist Party as a working principle in the twenty-first century. Wanting to participate in this political discourse, Wenyuan adopted the PSA genre and graphic design techniques learned in the United States to advocate the 以人为本 principle in Shanghai. Her decision to assert the PSA in the essay arose from her audience awareness: the instructor spoke Chinese and welcomed the skilled mixing of words and images. Though the PSA best captured her moral sentiment, Wenyuan believed that her American teachers would not understand it because they would be missing the cultural information necessary for extracting meaning beyond the words and images. Therefore she gave up explaining or translating the PSA in her essay, limiting her addressees to dual English- and Chinese-speaking readers like herself.

In conversation with interlocutors of diverse linguistic, cultural, and disciplinary backgrounds, the writers performed synthesis, summary, paraphrase, and direct quotation in translation. Often information was provided or exchanged in one language and then represented in multiple linguistic or nonlinguistic symbol systems. In her transcription and translation, Shumin showed a strong distrust of English's ability to fully capture the Confucian teaching and opted for Chinese script. Wenyuan spoke on behalf of the voiceless by integrating song lyrics and a PSA into her academic discourse. While she did translate her interviews, she doubted the translatability of the full meanings indexed in her heavily coded PSA. These two authors' beliefs about what a language could and could not achieve dictated the ways they marshaled resources in constructing the interviewees' voices. Retaining Chinese script in their texts created a "metonymic gap" (Ashcroft, 1999, p. 174), which reminded the audience of their style of English and their distinct linguistic and cultural identities.

Interacting with Scholarly Voices

As unprivileged novices in academia, students found handling scholarly voices challenging in the literature review. This assignment asked that they summarize three published articles related to their topic, identify connections among them, and create a reference list following American Psychological Association style. Like the interview essay this assignment urged the students to open themselves up to views on their topic. They were not expected to engage the scholars directly until the final report.

Among diverse and discordant scholarly voices, capturing those pertinent to one's research was the foremost and intended challenge. How to determine appropriate search terms when using search engines and databases is a fairly frequent undergraduate writer's trouble. It became a common topic of student-teacher communication. Nevertheless, in the end it was about how to identify appropriate scholars, or for some students it was about identifying an academic field to engage. Further, for multilingual writers it was also about how to express certain ideas in different linguistic contexts or cultural discourses. For example, when Wenyuan turned in her draft, she had summarized two articles on Chinese cultural values published in communication and media studies journals—key sources in her field. She couldn't find a third article. In a student-teacher conference, we discussed the importance of shuttling across languages and across academic and nonacademic cultures in identifying appropriate search terms:

Wenyuan (W): I tried "culture movement."
Xiaoye (X): How about "morality" and "modernization," or "morality and economic development," 道德和经济发展? Why don't you try it, "morality and economic development," or "moral and economic development"?
W: 有没有那种就是关注人性流失的那种文章? (Are there any articles dealing with the loss of humanity?)
X: "人性流失" 这是我们中文的说法, 在英文里的说法就是道德观念, 道德啊, 因为人性具体的在生活中的表现是人际道德、价值观, "人性流失" 很抽象耶。 (We say "the loss of humanity" in Chinese; the right term in academic English should be morality because humanity is discussed in everyday life in terms of morality or moral values. The term "the loss of humanity" is vague.)
W: 因为太抽象了, 所以我不知道怎么去 . . . (Because it's vague, I do know how to . . .)
X: 因为学者思考问题会思考得很仔细, 他/她不会使用那么抽象的词, (Wenyuan: 嗯) 对啊, 所以的话很多的时候不是因为没有, 缺乏这个词, 而是你自己找得不对。所以我说这个逻辑就有问题。 (Because a scholar tends to think carefully about an issue, he or she will not use such a vague term. Thus, often it's not that there isn't such a term but because you haven't found the right one. So I say the logic [of "cultural movement" as a search term] is problematic.)

人性流失 (the loss of humanity) might be a common expression in contemporary Chinese society, but it is vague and too broad for a scholar to conduct research on. The exchange reoriented Wenyuan to the ways and the language in which social scientists typically think, helping her move between grassroots and academic literacy. As this reorientation unfolded, Wenyuan soon discovered that she had engaged the scholars prematurely. She had more than summarized the articles; she had performed her research and writing with a strong bias. She felt deeply that Chinese society had morally degraded, and she only wanted to read articles that supported her assertion:

W: I feel the whole process is not right 'cause I myself have already the idea [the degradation of Chinese society] and I tried to find articles that can support my ideas; not I read the articles and learn from these articles.

X: So I think you have to give up, give up your original idea. Maybe . . . because your original idea is a little bit narrow and superficial. The purpose of this paper is to push you to be open-minded, to see what has been written by scholars. You know, they have been discussing this topic for a long time, and I want you to read the discussions.

In this further exchange, I reminded her of the purpose of the literature review and, by extension, that of academic research: she needed to set her moral judgments aside temporarily and listen to the scholarly discussions, including those she disagrees with. Respectful and deferent, Wenyuan acted on my suggestions. In the final draft she reviewed an additional article from outside her field on how the conflicts between identity and diversity in an increasingly global economy have given rise to cultural protection in trade. She summarized the article in a somber and objective tone. Our exchange enabled her to transcend her prior knowledge and assumptions and to tie in another text, another disciplinary discourse, and other voices.

Representing scholarly voices accurately and fairly often required a series of multilateral, translocal negotiations. With their multilingual and multicultural experiences, students might impose unique indexical orders, or interpretative frames, on the scholarly texts they encountered and arrive at meanings unintended by their authors. Often my students had to dialogue with the audience addressed (me) and the audience invoked (article authors) simultaneously. The students didn't just represent the article authors; they also negotiated new meanings during our conferences. For example, in a conference with Shumin about her literature review, I marked the phrase "an age of economics" in her first paragraph. As a reader I didn't understand what it meant; as an instructor I saw it as an opportunity to discuss audience awareness. Our conversation illustrates not only the multiple audiences that a writer has to engage but also the reader's responsibility in audience alignment and meaning making:

Xiaoye (X): "In an age of economics," what does it mean?
Shumin (S): 在经济的时代, right? (In an economic age, right?)
X: 在经济的时代, what does it mean? 在经济的时代是什么意思啊? 中文我都不懂。 (In an economic age, what does it mean? What does it mean to say "in an economic age"? I don't understand it even in Chinese.)

S: 是 . . . . 嗯, 应该是跟 ancient 相对, 就 opposite 的那种。(Perhaps it means . . . enh, it should be opposite to "ancient," should mean the opposite.)

X: 那 ancient 的话就是现代了, 古代, 那就是现代啊, 为什么是经济时代? 经济时代和古代就不相对称吧。(The opposite meaning of "ancient" should be something like "modern." Ancient times versus modern times, right? But why it means "an economic age"? "An economic age" should not be the opposite of "ancient times.")

S: 那个文章里面的标题就是这个。(The article title contains this expression)

X: 它的标题就是 age of economics 吗? 你敢肯定吗? (Does the title contain "age of economics"? Are you sure?)

S: 我敢肯定。(I am pretty sure.)

X: Economics 是经济学的意思。在一个经济学的时代, 当然它一定要这样讲, 也是可以的了, 就是一般, 我们平时不这样讲了。好吧, 你保留。(Economics means the study of economy. If "an age of economics" is used in the article, then so be it. Typically, we don't use this expression in our daily life. Alright, then you keep it.)

Shumin and I negotiated the meaning of "an age of economics" through a series of alignments. First, she offered a Chinese translation, meaning "an economic age." Her translation was tentative, marked by the ending of "right?" I questioned this first meaning by asking "what does it mean?" Next, Shumin furthered this interpretation by contrasting the expression with "ancient," a word she had used in the preceding sentence of the same paragraph. Our exchange led Shumin to posit a second meaning, or a time reference, which I challenged immediately. Finally, she ushered an additional interlocutor, the article author, into the dialogue to defend her use of the expression. Once the new voice, or a new indexical order in alignment with a higher, scholarly scale, was introduced, I had to alter my interpretative footing from the literature review to the cited article. Though I still wondered what the expression meant, there was no immediate need to challenge an expression cited directly from a source text. We temporarily settled on a third meaning that would allow our reading to proceed.

From our negotiations for meaning arose a distinct style of CE. The series of alignments can be broadly understood as "footing" (Goffman, 1981) or "recontextualization" (Canagarajah, 2013a). Goffman (1981) defined footing as "the alignment we take up to ourselves and the others present as expressed in the way we manage the production or reception of an utterance" (p. 128). A CE style emerged in the temporal-spatial dimension of our negotiations, based on reciprocity of language practice. I first asked Shumin what the expression "in an age of economics" meant. She responded to my question by mixing Chinese and English phrases: "在经济的时代, right?" I performed the first alignment by imitating her language style: "在经济的时代, what does it mean?" When Shumin contrasted the expression with "ancient," she blended the term into a Chinese-dominant sentence structure. I performed the second alignment by, again, imitating her language style. Mixing Chinese and English elements carried us through this brief exchange. Reciprocity in language practice can be seen in my conversation with Wenyuan as well. After I offered a Chinese translation for a search term "morality and economic development," she switched to Chinese, and I followed suit. When she admitted that she had engaged the scholars prematurely, she switched to English, and I followed suit again.

In this CE style it is worth noting that Chinese resources served to anchor meaning for all of us, three multilinguals. We used it to gauge the meanings at which we each arrived. When I first asked Shumin what the expression meant, she immediately offered a Chinese translation. When judging her interpretation, I responded, "I don't understand it even in Chinese." After Shumin introduced the article author in her defense, I translated "economics" into Chinese to arrive at another meaning ("an age of economics," or an age in which economics has deeply influenced human activity). With "economics" instead of "ancient" as our frame of reference, we reached a new meaning. I also translated a search term into Chinese for Wenyuan. For all of us, Chinese and English were intermingled in our linguistic repertoires, which allowed us to search for meaningful references quickly.

Committing Personal Voice to Form

Marshaling available resources to assert the voice of the unprivileged novice was the challenge of the final report. After interviewing experts and reviewing scholarly perspectives, students had gained expertise on their topics. In their final reports they were to argue for their positions by drawing on their personal experience, the interview data, and the scholarly perspectives. In class we discussed audience, the writer's credibility, tone, logical reasoning and fallacies, and counterargument, all of which are rhetorical issues typically covered in an English writing course. In addition we read three sample essays, two by professionals and one by a student, with an eye to how each author addressed the above-mentioned issues.

Out of their literacy resources, students needed to identify an appropriate argumentative frame. Having been exposed to diverse cultural discourses and ways of persuasion, multilingual writers might face the challenge of selecting argumentative strategies workable for an academic audience holding a specific set of rhetorical values. For example, in Shumin's final report, she intended to argue that "we should make friends widely." After introducing her stance, she wanted to refute a point made by her father. She stated the point as follows:

> As a proverb goes: "Good companions have good influence while bad ones have bad influence" (近朱者赤, 近墨者黑). As I claimed in my personal experience, my father thought that I should make friends with some excellent students who could have great impact on me and helped me in study rather than some people good at painting or singing. So my father did not allowed me to keep in touch with one of my best friends who majors art in the rest of her life because she did not have a good command of some subjects. But I did not care much about one's grades. As far as I am concerned, every person has different ways to become successful and an excellent personality is the key to making friends. Parents want their children to be successful and lead a happy life rather than struggle for a whole life. Parents also think that if their children make friends with good people, they will behave good like their friends.

Then in the same paragraph she goes on to challenge the idea of "good people," particularly the difficulty in defining good or bad people. Shumin's eighteen-line refutation of her father's central point struck me as laborious and confusing. In the student-teacher conference, we discussed her strategy for countering her father and how she could establish her own argument:

> Shumin (S): 但问题, 这段的话不是要推翻这个观点吗? 其实这个观点也没有错误啊。 (But the issue is, didn't I want to refute the point in this paragraph? Well, in fact this point is not wrong.)
>
> Xiaoye (X): 这个观点没有错误啊, 但这个观点给我们, 你看, 要么是红的, 要么是黑的, 对不对? 把这个世界一分为二。 (The point is not wrong in general. But you see, this point suggests either red or black, right? It splits the world into two.)

S: 噢. . . . . . . (Oh . . .)

X: 其实他的观点一方面是对的, 就是说, 他的观点你仔细看一下, 它有两个, 一个是赤和黑, 一个是动作, 是吧? 你和红的人在一起就变红, 和黑的人在一起就变黑, 它的变化这个东西是没有错的。 基本上是这样, 它的意思就是说受周围朋友的影响嘛, 对不对? 但是, 就是那点没有错, 但是另外一点, 把这个世界分成红的和黑的, 这个可能是有问题。 (On one hand, your father's point is correct. If you take a close look, the point involves two dimensions, one dealing with red and black and the other with actions, right? When mingling with people of red you will become red; when mingling with people of black you will become black. The aspect of change is correct. Basically it means that one is easily influenced by his or her friends, right? This aspect is not wrong. But the other aspect, splitting the world into red and black can be problematic.)

S: 噢 . . . . (Oh . . .)

X: 你可以攻击他的这一点。 (You can attack him in this aspect.)

S: 噢 . . . . (Oh . . .)

X: 对呀, 所以这就是我们所谓的逻辑分析。 作为读者的话, 你要说服他的话, 你要先提出一个问题, 提出一点, 然后再用一, 二, 三个小点来支持, 来论证它。 其实我们语文课里面也是讲这个东西呀。 高中语文课里面, 你们应该也讲过吧? (Yeah, this is what I meant by logical analysis. To persuade a reader, you can raise an issue, state a thesis, and then support and explain it with point one, two, and three. In fact, this strategy is introduced in our Chinese language class. You should have studied this strategy in the high school Chinese class, right?)

S: 讲过。 (We did.)

X: 其实英文和汉语没有什么区别。 (大声笑) 很多时候我们挣扎的话是语言的问题, 有的时候是一个点子你没有想到。 (In fact, there isn't much difference between English and Chinese. (laughing) We sometimes struggle with surface-level language issues; sometimes you simply haven't come up with a point yet.)

S: 嗯。 (Yeah.)

I stressed that the Chinese proverb used in her argument oversimplifies matters by dividing people into two kinds: good and bad. Our discussion provided Shumin a conceptual framework for refuting the proverb; in fact, she had already challenged the definition of good or bad people when she argued, in the same paragraph, that success means different things to different people. In the discussion I also elaborated on how, in addition to attacking her father's central point, she could establish her own argument. I suggested a deductive reasoning pattern since she had already staked out her claim in the first paragraph. My proposal served as a conceptual frame she could use to sort and select discursive materials for her essay.

Our discussion enabled Shumin to move from the local/personal scale evident in her early draft to a translocal/impersonal scale in her revisions. In the aforementioned paragraph she evoked her father in a narrative and cited the famous Chinese proverb used by him. In her new draft she removed her father's presence and adopted the logical framework I had suggested. By deleting the short narrative involving her father, she made the paragraph concise and more syllogistic:

> As a proverb goes: "Good companions have good influence while bad ones have bad influence" (近朱者赤, 近墨者黑). A saying also goes like this: "Every coin has two sides." So I suppose the former proverb is not totally right. First of all, I have to admit that if we get close to a person, he (she) will has a great impact on me. That is what I called good companions have good influence. Secondly, I have to explain that it is too simple to divide people into good or bad, because not all the people is perfect. Everyone has different specialties and are expert in certain areas. So we can not define people good or bad easily. All we need is a couple of eyes which is good at finding specialty on others.

Shumin pointed out that the position embodied in the first proverb was wrong, and then she used the second proverb to refute that position. It is hard to tell whether her father would find her revised argument more persuasive than her original one; nevertheless the revision clearly demonstrated a decontextualized, formal logic, elevating the text to a translocal/impersonal scale. In lifting her argument to a conceptual level hardly matched by her previous draft, Shumin shifted from addressing a father figure to engaging a general academic readership. The detachment from a particular, single audience was Shumin's foremost achievement in her revisions.

However, not every student favored deductive reasoning. Like Shumin, the class had been exposed to multiple argumentative schemes and strategies. They had studied argumentation in high school Chinese classes, reading classical and modern texts featuring argumentation, and practicing argumentative essays for college entrance exams. The Chinese education market was (and still is) flooded with exam-cracking reference books and classes. Some of the students had taken crash courses on writing for the Test of English as a Foreign Language (TOEFL) or for the SAT. Despite her familiarity with TOEFL and SAT writing styles, Wenyuan didn't find them helpful in staging her argument. In her final report she opted for a detoured argument to "give [the reader] my understanding about dreams, life, and culture." With twelve paragraphs this soul-searching essay covered the following ideas:

Para. 1: Dreams are defined as powers that both compel one to make life changes and that generate hope for the future.

Para. 2–3: The definition is illustrated by two Chinese students pursuing their dreams by making a documentary film and hiking across the United States.

Para. 4: To follow one's dreams requires great courage.

Para. 5: Many Chinese students' dreams are suppressed by various institutions, such as the college entrance exam system.

Para. 6: As a nation China faces conflicts between dreams and reality.

Para. 7–11: Modernization and globalization have robbed Chinese people of traditional values and contributed to many leading unhappy lives.

Para. 12: Young people should seek their own values.

In the essay Wenyuan integrated information gathered in her research. However, the reader doesn't come to her thesis until the last paragraph: "Globalization is certainly a global trend. No one can avoid it. But we young people in the nation have to be aware of the declining cultural China. When we have found ourselves' values, we can then get the inspirations to think about our dreams and really be comfortable of whom we are and be satisfied with our lives." The text falls loosely into an inductive pattern. Wenyuan first defines dreams using stories of peers fearlessly pursuing dreams in the United States. Then she shows that current Chinese institutions have suppressed young people's dreams, and she attributes the widening gap between Chinese people's dreams and their reality to modernization and globalization. She ends the essay with a call for young people to seek their own values. Among the twenty students in class, Wenyuan singularly chose an inductive pattern.

What prompted her to make this choice amidst heavy exposure to deductions exalted in high-stakes exams and celebrated in academic writing? In a student-teacher conference, she confided her motivation for defying the norm:

> Wenyuan (W): I know what TOEFL writing looks like.
> Xiaoye (X): I am not saying there is one way of writing argumentation. There are many ways, there are many ways. So I just want to find out why you are familiar with TOEFL writing or argumentation structure in the U.S. taught in other writing classes, but here you are using a structure that is very different.
> W: (smile) Sometimes different can be, (X: can be very good) can be very specialized. In my first writing class [in the United States], we have four or five essays. And for the last essay, like, this is pretty much the similar structure. At first, the professor said, so different and kind of not very familiar. But she said, it's good, and it's like I am doing a research paper, umm, it has a lot of layers, and like push you to see deeper, deeper, and deeper. The way I am organizing this is the way how I found the facts or the solution.
> X: Okay, okay, so here in this essay you want to show us the way you explored this issue.
> W: Yeah, cause I do not have that much confidence to really argue like those scholars said, like globalization or like the economic things. So I am trying to let the readers like, kind of, come into my mind and my way of thinking. So they can then, like empathy. Then they may understand why I am thinking this way.

This interchange reveals that Wenyuan had thoughtfully and strategically made her structural choice. Her success in negotiating with her American teacher about this structure gave her confidence to repeat it in a new context. Ultimately she wanted her argument to be both honest and unique. This "specialized" argument most truthfully captured her thoughts about dreams and about the future of Chinese society, enabling her to walk the reader through her research and thought processes. Opposite to what Shumin did, Wenyuan brought academic writing down a scale to accommodate locally situated, personal, and subjective meanings. And bringing her former English teacher, a member of the academic literacy regime, into dialogue with me lent credence to her textual choice.

My interchange with these two students highlights the connections between Chinese and English classes. Perpetuated by Anglo-American textbooks, inductive and deductive reasoning have been taught in English writing classrooms almost all over the world. The same notions were introduced into Chinese language classes a century ago (You, 2010). What I did in the student-teacher conferences was call the students' attention to the reasoning strategies they had previously acquired across linguistic and pedagogical cultures. The argumentative resources that they eventually used came from multiple sources—their prior Chinese and English language classes, their experience with standardized assessments, our class discussions, and our interchange at the conference. The revisions that they made resulted from their selective adoption of resources from these sources.

Academic Transliteracy with Consequences

In Anglophone scholarly discussions of academic biliteracy, there is a tendency to compartmentalize literacy resources, to divide them and ascribe them to specific languages and national cultures. When writing in Chinese, presumably one would employ idioms, metaphors, argumentative schemes, and genres from Chinese languages as well as adhere to the norms of academic institutions in China. And when writing in English, presumably one would employ idioms, metaphors, and genres familiar to Anglo-American speakers of English attempting to meet their cultural and rhetorical expectations. My analysis challenges the clear demarcation of resources according to language or national culture. In their essays and communications, the students constantly drew on what traditionally have been labeled Chinese or English. Whether they had studied overseas or not, the students used Chinese languages and dialects and resorted to their knowledge of local and translocal audiences, cultural practices, and institutions. The ability to search information, to engage an audience, and to select a textual scheme is required in all writing regardless of the representational system used. Communication technologies have promoted the global spread and relocation of certain literacy practices, such as searching information online, documenting sources, web authoring, and integrating multiple modes. My students adapted semiotic choices to audiences, both addressed and invoked, regardless of the language they used.

While blurring linguistic and cultural boundaries, my analysis shows the pervasiveness of a monolingual ideology. Repeatedly the recorded conversations exposed a nationalist and monolingual consciousness among the interlocutors. For example, when discussing the expression "loss of humanity" with Wenyuan, I stated, "'人性流失' 这是我们中文的说法," literarily meaning "'the loss of humanity' is an expression in *our* Chinese language." I suggested that Chinese is the national language that I shared with the student but English is not. While my statement can be viewed as a strategy for establishing rapport, in reflection it clearly shows my deeply seated nationalism. In another instance, when discussing the expression "an age of economics" with Shumin, I stated, "在经济的时代是什么意思啊? 中文我都不懂" (What does it mean to say "in an economic age"? I don't understand it even in Chinese). And later, after having come to a newfound meaning of that same expression, I remarked, "就是一般, 我们平时不这样讲了" (Typically, we don't use this expression in our everyday Chinese). In both comments I resorted to Chinese references to gauge the meanings we had arrived at. These comments, while showing my awareness of the students' expectations and perceptions, also reveal my unjustified confidence in native speaker intuition. Monolingual thinking is also observable in the students' comments. For example, Tacy declared in her literacy autobiography that she desired to improve her Chinese and English writing during the summer. She compartmentalized writing skills according to language and nation, wanting to improve her Chinese writing by engaging her Chinese friends on a social network based in China and to improve her English by writing in an English composition course.

The students and I did have moments when we consciously combated this imposing monolingualism. We challenged the notion that either Chinese or English constitutes a discrete system by mixing both languages in our conferences. Reciprocity in language practice gave rise to our CE styles. When discussing with Shumin how she might restructure her final report, I reminded her that the same deductive scheme I suggested was also taught in high school Chinese classes. Deductive reasoning transcends a particular language or a nation. Both Shumin and Wenyuan adopted Chinese as an additional representational resource in their writing; Wenyuan even inserted an untranslated PSA written in Chinese. They doubted whether English translations would be able to capture the full meanings of some Chinese expressions, not to mention their own feelings and sensibilities attached to these expressions. They not only subverted the conventional norms of English writing but also constructed alternatives.

By breaking away from monolingual and monocultural expectations, the students found opportunities to develop transliteracy, that is, writing for academic and nonacademic audiences by marshaling resources from different languages and cultures, and most importantly, cultivating empathy and respect for the Other. Writing in English, they invoked audiences in local and translocal contexts. Working on the sequenced writing assignments, they were able to connect discourses inside and outside their majors as well as discourses inside and outside their nations and cultures, across languages. For example, for their interview essay assignment, the students conversed with their American professors as well as their Chinese friends and high school teachers. In their literature review essay, they reviewed scholarly essays published in English as well as in Chinese. In their final report they wanted to persuade, again, local and translocal audiences by synthesizing and consolidating information collected in previous assignments. Ultimately the students were forced to step outside their national and cultural frames to engage unfamiliar audiences. For example, by narrating her volunteering experience in Moldova, Tacy wanted to arouse empathy in her transnational audiences, to argue for the importance of helping others. Given an opportunity to blend genres and blend modalities, Wenyuan made a visual argument for cosmopolitan practice in her interview essay. Shumin and Wenyuan were compelled to reevaluate both their decisions not to translate certain Chinese expressions in their interview essays and their choices concerning argumentation structure in their final reports.

Academic transliteracy thus has ideological and material consequences. A college writing class constitutes a translocal space where linguistic and cultural signs circulate and sometimes collide. Students come from different places with differing experiences, interests, concerns, and values. Undoubtedly such a class should teach students academic literacy skills so that they can succeed in college and in life. What is equally critical is that the course facilitate the students in addressing issues that matter to them, their communities, and beyond. The course can mediate in the process of students forging new cultural identities in their everyday lives. Tacy certainly experienced the power of CE in forging new political and cultural identities, a power that inspired her to become a skilled English user and to come to my academic writing class. In her literacy autobiography she related some of the civic realities on UCLA's multilingual campus:

> Over the year I learned about the immigration issue and unfair treatment, the existence of undocumented students, the education weakness, the withdrawing economy, and a whole public school system. Most of the students in USAC (undergraduate students association council) are politic science major, but certain amount of them are not native American, and they speak English with accents. However, they still won themselves respect and applaud. I see how my Filipino friends in USAC sent countless E-mails to student body, encouraging them to call the government and fighting against the $100 million cut to UCLA and $1.5 billion cut in California education, approved by California governor Brown; I see how my Korean and Indian friends in USAC gave tons of speech in the middle of Bruin Plaza, encouraging undocumented students to defend for themselves in AB 540 law. The fact that stating idea clearly was number one in communication appeared more and more frequently.

Tacy was inspired to enhance her communicative capacity so that she could participate and persuade in civic discussions at UCLA and in broader arenas. Crossing linguistic and national boundaries, she had come to identify with her new locale, a practice that was clearly cosmopolitan. Tacy chose to write about international volunteering, Shumin about friendship, and Wenyuan about Chinese youths' dreams because these issues mattered to them. English writing offered them an intellectual space for voicing concerns and dialoguing with their audiences. The class enabled the students to articulate their connections and identifications with local and translocal communities. Some of them, such as Tacy and Wenyuan, became involved members in their respective localities. Tacy actively recruited volunteers on the summer school campus, and Wenyuan participated in a subway advertisement competition. Transliterate inquiry matters, not only in improving the students' abilities to cross linguistic and cultural boundaries, but also in enabling them to cause positive material consequences in local or translocal contexts.

Although they may find transliteracy interesting, some EAP teachers may wonder how they can facilitate transliterate development if they don't share a similar linguistic and cultural background with their students. Admittedly, my sharing such a background with my students was an advantage, but EAP teachers without this benefit can still draw on their literacy experiences to guide their teaching. Such teachers are experienced in academic English literacy for sure, but they also have varying amounts of experience with literacy in and across other languages, modalities, and cultures. They can reflect on their experience and identify connections between literacy practices in English and those in other languages, modalities, and cultures. In class they can highlight these connections and ask their students to search for similar ones in their experiences. However, when facing teachers whose configurations of literacy experiences clearly differ from their own, students may distrust those teachers as readers of their texts, like Wenyuan did with her American writing teacher. When students read and write in languages and about cultures unknown to the teacher, their institutional roles can be reversed; teachers can learn from students by inviting them to translate or explain ideas in their texts. Both parties need to recognize the challenge of audience alignment in a multilingual text and work extra hard on it by attempting various coding and decoding strategies. In short, while drawing on their literacy experience, EAP teachers need to continue their own transliterate development.

In this chapter we have examined multilingual students' composing processes as locally and translocally situated practices, involving reading, writing, and talking across languages and cultures. A CE perspective emphasizes that English is always intertwined with other languages and dialects in these writers' rhetorical repertoires. Their literacy resources are not compartmentalized (easily attributable to discrete languages and cultures) but instead are the result of language and cultural boundary crossing. Up to this point in the book, I have focused on multilingual speakers outside Anglo-American nations, who are traditionally called "non-native speakers of English." In the next two chapters I will show that a cosmopolitan perspective is equally crucial for students and teachers who grew up speaking English. They have lived among speakers of other dialects and languages and, no doubt, have either learned some of the languages and dialects encountered in their communities and schools or have appropriated portions of them as part of their communicative repertoires. These students and teachers also need a transliteracy pedagogy that will enable them to recognize and marshal their resources for communicating at school, at work, and beyond.

7

Language Relations in English Studies

> 我非常喜欢你的动人的故事! 我的爸爸, 妈妈也离婚了。我小的时候, 没有爸爸让我伤心了, 但是, 我的妈妈跟你的妈妈一样, 她鼓励了很好的习惯。 OK, I have to use English now, because my Chinese isn't so good. This is an excellent essay—I really like the topic you picked. . . . I found myself wondering if you got to see your dad at all growing up, or was it just you and your mom? Maybe you could include a sentence or two explaining if your dad was a part of your life.
>
> —Ashley, an e-mail

I was pleasantly surprised to read Chinese in Ashley's e-mail. I taught an upper-level rhetoric course cross-listed under English and Asian studies at Penn State University in the spring of 2011. As part of the course, I connected my students with undergraduates at a Chinese university. Students on both sides shared and critiqued each other's essays. In her response to a Chinese student essay, Ashley began with a personal story in Chinese before delving into her critique: she shared with the Chinese peer her experience growing up with divorced parents.

It is apparent that Ashley used the narrative to establish a rapport with her Chinese collaborator. Her confessional tale was especially effective at bolstering ethos, as the essay she was critiquing was on parent-child relations. Growing up in a single-parent family was an element of life that both students shared even though they lived more than ten thousand kilometers apart. Narrating her story in her peer's home language further enhanced interpersonal identification. While we can ascribe a rhetorical function to this translingual practice, "foreign languages" actually served multiple functions in various contexts in this class. Some students used Chinese or Japanese in their notes and term papers to express sophisticated concepts; some talked to me using a mix of Chinese and English. I could discern in those moments my American students' enthusiasm for using "foreign tongues" to explore and establish connections across cultures, a passion that has been almost entirely ignored by the field of writing studies in the United States (except Marko, 2012; Marko et al., 2013; Marko, Osorio, Sepenoski, & Catalani, 2014; Merritt, 2011). College students are keen on implementing the tools and symbols that they have acquired or are acquiring, be they smart phones, software programs, or languages. By tapping into students' passion for these tools and symbols, we can not only improve their meaning-making competencies but also create a space for addressing local and translocal civic issues.

In this chapter I will first engage scholarship that addresses language diversity in the writing classroom. I want to suggest that the majority sentiment in U.S. writing studies has continued to hover around nationhood and disciplinarity. In our study and teaching of language issues, we continue to focus on English—its varieties, styles, and genres—and its imagined relations with other languages within the nation, that nation being, for this chapter, the United States. To attend to cross-language relations in academia and in our lives, we need to transcend our locality and engage our students in language relations across nations and disciplines. Toward that aim, I will introduce a transliteracy pedagogy that I adopted a few years ago for English majors and minors. By first introducing texts that feature code-switching, this pedagogy teaches American students language analysis and then engages them in studying and practicing transliteracy. Tracing two students' writing practices outside my class reveals that my pedagogy was actually part of an extensive transliteracy pedagogy already at work in English studies at my institution, a finding that challenges writing studies to adopt more cosmopolitan perspectives.

Language Relations in Writing Studies

Writing studies in the United States, a field born within English studies, has shown an indelible and solitary loyalty to the English language. English studies grew out of the nation-building project and has remained a field devoted to the study of English language and literature in service of the nation-state ever since (McComiskey, 2006). In the United States, the rise of writing studies had an intricate relationship with the first-year college writing course historically offered through English departments. This writing course has provided writing studies a set of long-lasting intellectual issues to address, and hence an institutional raison d'être. Although more and more autonomous departments of writing and/or rhetoric are arising, they and English departments continue to share a preoccupation with English, the default, though not official, national language of the United States. Up to this point an English-only ideology has long fixed writing studies within the broad field of English studies (Horner & Trimbur, 2002; Miller, 2010).

Over the last decade, though, writing studies scholars and academic organizations have launched a wave of criticisms against the monolingualist ideology perpetuated by the implicit English-only mandate. Notably among them are books, such as Canagarajah (2013a, 2013b); Horner, Lu, and Matsuda (2010); Horner and Kopelson (2014); Schroeder, Fox, and Bizzell (2002); Smitherman and Villanueva (2003); and Young and Martinez (2011). The National Council for Teachers of English (2011) announced its "Resolution on the Students' Right to Incorporate Heritage and Home Languages in Writing." The Conference on College Composition and Communication issued position statements such as "Students' Right to Their Own Language" (issued in 1974 and reaffirmed in 2003), "Multiple Uses of Writing" (2007), and "Teaching Second Language Writing and Writers" (issued in 1999 and revised in 2009). While these works of scholarship and position statements have collectively offered a powerful challenge to the English-only mandate, they continue to wrestle with issues surrounding the teaching of writing in English. The focus on English, because it both unites English studies and remains the dominant representational system in American universities, suggests the imposing power of the state and the monolingualist ideology in writing studies.

For more than a decade, scholars such as Bruce Horner, John Trimbur, and Min-Zhan Lu have repeatedly called for paying attention to cross-language relations. However, their calls have inspired nearly negligible cross-language practices in the study of writing (Horner, NeCamp, & Donahue, 2011), and even less in the teaching of it. Recently Trimbur (2010) called for the promotion of biliteracy and multilingualism in writing studies: "The question traditionally asked in writing studies is how cross-language relations inhibit or facilitate students' mastery of academic literacy in English. I think the questions needs to be reframed, to ask how the available linguistic resources can be tapped to promote biliteracy and multilingualism" (p. 38). Yet, most writing scholars and teachers continue to teach, speak, and write in English. While there are reported efforts to accommodate students' home dialects, with the exception of Artze-Vega, Doud, and Torres (2007); Fredericksen (2002); Hanson (2013); Marko (2012); Marko et al. (2013); Marko, Osorio, Sepenoski, and Catalani (2014); and Merritt (2011) I have come across little Anglophone scholarly work addressing how one teaches biliteracy in the English studies classroom. Most of us have remained armchair strategists, or as a Chinese idiom goes, we have been discussing war strategies on a piece of paper (纸上谈兵).

Teaching reading and writing across languages is not a stretch for writing studies. It is a turn that the field has to make in order to attend to the kinds of writing happening on the ground. As Trimbur (2010) reminds us, in addition to writing in English, college students also write in Spanish, French, German, Japanese, and Chinese in their foreign language classes. Even in their English writing, as the early chapters have revealed, they could employ other languages in school and out-of-school contexts. If we also take language to mean the discourse of a discipline, then students juggle disciplinary registers on a daily basis. To attend to translingualism in academia, writing studies can embrace these types of writing practices, already occurring, within its realm of study and teaching. Writing studies can transcend disciplinarity marked by its historical connections to English studies and branch out into other disciplines, for all disciplines employ written symbols. Indeed, I am advocating studying and teaching transliteracy within and across disciplines.

To the end of not being strategists on a piece of paper only, we can start from what we typically do well; we can start from the teaching of reading and writing of English. In our English classrooms we can take steps to engage our students in the types of transliterate practices possible within and cross disciplines. As Horner (2010) reminds us, depending on our institutional contexts, there isn't a single set of strategies or tactics for combating monolingualism. Similarly, writing teachers can find ways to teach transliteracy specific to their local situations. I would like to introduce a pedagogy that I used to engage American undergraduates in critically examining English monolingualism as well as in practicing transliteracy across disciplines, which then led me to discover an extensive transliteracy pedagogy already at work within English studies.

While sharing some strategies with Artze-Vega, Doud, and Torres (2007) and others, my pedagogy differs in significant ways. Teaching Latino/a students first-year writing in Miami, Florida, these teachers adopted a bilingual approach. In alignment with bilingual maintenance programs, they emphasized students' ability to access two distinct social, cultural, and literary worlds as resources for thinking and development. In the classroom they invited students to examine bilingual literary works by established Latino/a authors. The students analyzed the varied ways in which these authors blended Spanish and English as well as the rhetorical maneuvers they employed in doing so. Then the students used their home language, Spanish, for free writing and for translating Spanish texts into English. They were taught to imbed Spanish texts and voices in their English-dominant writings, either translating or not translating the Spanish texts. Fredericksen (2002) reported a Spanish-English professional writing program at the University of Texas, El Paso, which had adopted similar pedagogical strategies. While my pedagogy also includes multilingual reading and writing assignments, it departs from that of Artze-Vega, Doud, and Torres (2007) and Fredericksen (2002) in two important ways. First, they developed their approaches specifically for students from Mexico and Latino/a groups and promoted these approaches for these students only. My pedagogy was directed at American college students in general. Second, while they focused on college writing courses, my pedagogy encourages reading and writing across languages both inside and outside English studies.

Connecting literature, rhetoric, and education, I have taught an upper-level English class called World Englishes in Literature and Education multiple times since 2009. I used the term "World Englishes" because of its currency and not as an endorsement. Housed in the English department, this course was offered under various generic course titles, such as Issues in Rhetoric and Composition, Honors Seminar, and Senior Seminar. Typically students taking this course were majors in English or in secondary education with English as their minor. Some also double- or triple-majored in Arabic, Chinese, French, Asian studies, business, international studies, and psychology. Consisting of native-born American students, the class was predominantly white, occasionally having one or two ethnic minority students.

Different from other reports of teachers introducing World Englishes to American students, my teaching focused on critiquing the bounded perspective to nation, language, and culture inherent in World Englishes thinking. Teaching methods previously reported either introduced World Englishes to students in short-term experimental studies (Brown & Peterson, 1997; Kubota, 2001b; Wetzl, 2013), or the pedagogy was described sketchily (Lovejoy, 2003), or the method reported was a class activity that raised students' awareness of diverse English styles without resorting to the World Englishes construct (Lueck & Sharma, 2013). In contrast, I devoted an entire semester to exposing students to different styles of English and to scholarly debates on literacy education inside and outside the United States. When introducing the various English styles to students, I didn't dwell on linguistic terms but rather situated these styles in their historical and socioeconomic realities. Students were encouraged to be empathetic audiences, understanding that these styles resulted from speakers' and writers' struggles to create meaning in their contexts.

The class started with three novels by multilingual/multidialectal authors (such as Chinua Achebe's *Things Fall Apart*, Raja Rao's *Kanthapura*, Salman Rushdie's *Haroun and the Sea of Stories*, Ha Jin's *Waiting*, and Xiaolu Guo's *A Concise Chinese-English Dictionary for Lovers*) and a scholarly text on the transformation of English in postcolonial literature (Bill Ashcroft's *Caliban's Voice*). Next the class moved into the topic of English education. They first read a scholarly text on the teaching of English writing in China (my book *Writing in the Devil's Tongue*), followed by a book on the Ebonics debates and African American Vernacular English, or AAVE (John R. Rickford and Russell J. Rickford's *Spoken Soul*), and a book on the literacy education of African American children (Keith Gilyard's *Voices of the Self*).

Aligned with the pedagogy of multiliteracies (New London Group, 1996), my teaching also focused on the design of new meanings. In addition to completing the assigned readings, the students participated in a border-crossing activity with Chinese college students and completed a sequenced writing project. In the border-crossing activity—like the peer-review activities reported in Anderson, Bergman, Bradley, Gustafsson, and Matzke (2010) and Willard-Traub and Dressen-Hammouda (2014)—the students commented on each other's writings and developed friendships by communicating via e-mail and Skype. The significance of this activity in engaging American students in constructing meaning via Cosmopolitan English (CE), or diverse styles of English mingled with other linguistic and nonlinguistic symbol systems in translocal contexts, will be detailed in the next chapter. In the sequenced writing project, the students completed four interconnected assignments—research proposal, literature review, data analysis, and final paper. They were asked to study the use of English in any context and medium. As expected, some chose to study literary texts; others examined English in nonliterary contexts, such as music, movies, anime, high school classes, and dance studios. The students were encouraged to examine texts and contexts that interested them or mattered to their future careers. With concerted efforts to understand CE, the students' literacy activities helped to construct a "dwelling place," where they explored together language practice in context and sought an ethical use of language.

Starting from Code-Switching

To engage the students in exploring language relations, the first step is to call their attention to those relations. Scholars have proposed different pedagogical tactics for accomplishing this, most consisting of exploring the relations between various English styles and genres (Ball & Muhammad, 2003; Lovejoy, 2003; Lu, 2010). For example, Lu (2010) described a real-life scenario in which a Russian translator couldn't discern the meaning of "knowledge worker," used in a book by Bill Gates, and she posed a query online. Then Lu proposed an assignment in which her students would respond to the query by defining the term from multiple subject positions—an administrator at Microsoft headquarters, a student, and someone holding a perspective peripheral to that of the Microsoft administrators. One benefit of such an assignment, according to Lu, lies in the potential for the students to "initiate 'thick' descriptions of the peculiar circumstances and relations endorsed by the kind of vocabulary and lexicon standardized by U.S. corporations such as Microsoft and generate deliberations over the need and right of diverse users within and outside the United States to 'use' rather than 'imitate' such hegemonic usages" (p. 53). Such a pedagogical tactic, though, still hasn't transcended what has traditionally defined an English studies course, that is, the teaching, study, and practice of English reading and writing.

To call students' attention to language relations, we can take a more proactive step by discussing (from a bounded perspective to language) a translingual phenomenon such as code-switching. Thanks to the influences of monolingualism, our students are accustomed to the notion of language as a discrete system, particularly in writing. In my teaching I often start a class by exposing the students to code-switching in literature, one of the "available designs" in my class. We read an essay, "The Limitations of Code Switching in Chicano/a Literature" (Schmidt, 2011), written by one of my former undergraduate students and published in *Young Scholars in Writing*. Code-switching can be understood in various ways depending on how one defines a code. In literature, most scholars and teachers use the term to refer to the phenomenon of different dialects and languages appearing in the same text (Schmidt, 2011). Code-switching often indexes a speaker's social class, identity, and voice; the audience's assumptions and prejudices; and the specific literary effects the author intends to achieve. The topic of code-switching brings multifaceted sociopolitical issues into sharp relief and can potentially intrigue the students. Starting from literary code-switching and gradually moving toward the nature and functions of codes, the students will be introduced to the complex social relations and issues marked but often masked by this everyday practice. Ultimately, an exploration of code-switching raises students' awareness of the boundedness of codes versus the fluidity of language practice.

When my class read Chinua Achebe's (1994) *Things Fall Apart*, code-switching was an "open sesame" to critical language relations in writing practice. Throughout the text, there are several types of code-switching, between English and Ibo, between one Ibo dialect and another, and between narrative and song lyrics or fairy tales, each marking a particular power relation in context. In the story an instance of code-switching occurs when Ikemefuna, Okonkwo's adopted son, is walking in a forest with a group of men armed with sheathed machetes. He will soon be killed by Okonkwo, who is walking right behind him. The men are supposed to send Ikemefuna back to his home village, which he hasn't seen for three years. He wonders how his mother is doing and sings a childhood song in his mind as a way of figuring out whether she is still alive. While other song lyrics are rendered in English by Achebe, this is the singular place in the novel where they are not. In class we discussed this linguistic choice and its effects on the reader. The following is a segment from that discussion:

> Jarinil: Perhaps by leaving us in the dark, it gives us the feeling that he is having, ah, ah, his loss and in desperation. We also don't know what's being said here, and maybe this feeling is, emh, exclusive to him, and so he, like the boy, he knows what he's singing but he is not, emh, with everyone else in this. This is just his own battle.
>
> Xiaoye: Yeah. That makes sense. Think about the language. You know, although they don't live very far apart. His village, although, maybe is on the other side of a mountain, or two mountains, as far as that, but he is speaking his, they speak a different dialect. And this dialect is maybe just impenetrable for, for, for Okonkwo, and that's something he can hold on to himself. He can have a conversation with himself as a little boy.
>
> Meryn: I think it's also interesting that in the first song, it's something that's not so strange to a reader that's not Ibo. Because in scenes like wrestling match, in sports events, we sing songs and cheers and stuff like that. But then this instance is really strange to us, like the idea that somebody has a dream and the oracle says that this kid is dangerous and you have to kill him. And so like just walk and kill him. So I think that keeping it in reinforces how strange that seems to us, how far it's from our culture maybe. (August 30, 2011)

In this brief exchange the interlocutors offered three readings of Achebe's code-switching. Jarinil saw the impenetrable song lyrics as signaling a battle Ikemefuna was having with himself, feeling loss and desperation. Code-switching suggests the boy's personality and feelings. Taking a realistic linguistic approach, I suggested that the boy was simply having a conversation with himself in a dialect inaccessible to his companions. Code-switching underscores cultural differences and agency. Meryn viewed the untranslated lyrics as contributing to the construction of a mythic culture in the story. Code-switching suggests the intricate relationship between people, place, and language. It's important to note that although none of us understood the lyrics, we all attached an appreciative reading to this linguistic strategy. By choosing not to translate, Achebe achieves some dramatic effects crucial to the story. Additionally, a professor who was openly sympathetic to a translingual reading probably positively influenced the opinions voiced by the students who might otherwise have viewed this CE style negatively.

Writers of fiction have every right to, and often do, cross linguistic boundaries, so do scholars. As the class transitioned from fictional to scholarly worlds, our discussions on code-switching shifted gears, moving into a new realm. The two scholarly texts by African American authors provided ample translingual examples for discussions. In his award-winning literacy memoir *Voices of the Self*, Gilyard (1991) alternates his chapters using different styles/codes, a strategy that has always mesmerized my students. Speaking in a strong AAVE accent in the odd-numbered chapters, he narrates his childhood in New York City, where as a boy he shuttled between AAVE in his home community and Standard English in his school community. In the even-numbered chapters, using his life experience in the preceding chapter for illustration, he challenges some preconceived notions held concerning literacy education for ethnic minority students. In these chapters he adopts Standard English and a serious, formal tone. In Rickford and Rickford's (2000) award-winning work *Spoken Soul: The History of Black English*, the authors blend AAVE and Standard English seamlessly when discussing serious topics. For example, in the following passage that opens a chapter on the rhetoric of black preachers, sermons, and prayers, AAVE cadences are unmistakable:

> With their repertoire of styles and their passion for pageantry and dramatics, black preachers in the traditional black church don't merely deliver sermons. They hold court. When they testify for "King Jesus" in the tradition of the ancestors, the approach is eloquent, compelling, and certain to kick up dust. For the black

> church, which must reward the suffering of the stepped-upon and ward off despair in hard times, necessitates men and women who are on fire with the Lord, and who ain't too proud to perspire when delivering the Word. Ministers who can "take a text" from the Bible and "break it down" to the level of everyday people are adored. Intensity and fervor are almost always desired; "dead bones" preachers need not apply. In the many incarnations of the black church, the Living Word tends to be sung, shouted, clapped, hummed, stomped, and testified to in a majestic way that moves and moves and moves. (p. 39)

In the same chapter the authors point out the key features of the language used by black preachers. Some are certainly observable in the above passage: repetition (e.g., "in a majestic ways that moves and moves and moves") and manipulation of voice texture (e.g., "For the black church, which must reward the suffering of the stepped-upon and ward off despair in hard times, necessitates men and women who are on fire with the Lord, and who ain't too proud to perspire when delivering the Word"). On the book cover Geneva Smitherman describes their writing style as "rich and powerful . . . and funky and bold." Reading these books, my students experienced firsthand the multifaceted effects—be they of emotion, humor, or dignity—that the blending of AAVE and Standard English can achieve in scholarly writing.

In addition to cultivating students' appreciation for diverse CE styles, teaching them "design grammars" (Gee, 2007; New London Group, 1996) is also critical for preparing them for transliterate practice. As most of my students believed they had grown up speaking Standard English, they didn't feel competent enough with grammar to dissect their language and examine it under a magnifying glass. According to them, English grammar was minimally taught in secondary schools; they tended to develop grammatical knowledge in foreign language classes. They lacked the tools necessary for examining translingual practice. Only after they had become increasingly interested in the English symbol system did I introduce them to some basic linguistic concepts. I again used Rickford and Rickford (2010), who delineate the features of AAVE in one of their chapters. In one class meeting, after we had gone through every AAVE feature introduced by these two authors, I handed the students a short excerpt from Alice Walker's (1982) novel *The Color Purple* (pp. 4–5) and asked them to identify in the text as many AAVE features as possible. To help them develop their meta-language, I urged them to explain their identifications in front of the class. What my students achieved in solving this puzzle was enlightenment, not only enlightenment on a dialect that they had heard or heard about for years, but enlightenment on their own language. They gained some confidence and competence in analyzing English.

Transliteracy Possibilities in Student Writing

After the class had gained familiarity with language issues in literature and education, they plunged into their own inquiry on language practice, an opportunity to design new meanings grounded in their sociohistorical context, personal interests, and life experiences. For their term papers they were asked to study English in any text and context. I didn't prescribe a specific context for their text selection, but I did require an academic context for their inquiry and communication. They needed to complete three short papers—research proposal, literature review, and data analysis—before constructing their final paper. Although the final product was a traditional research paper, the inquiry process and the objects under scrutiny ended up being multilingual, multimodal, and multicultural, thus making the final paper a product of transliterate practice. The students not only became aware of the artificial boundaries between languages and between cultures but also crossed these boundaries and formed identification with the Other.

A close analysis of their inquiry process reveals four major areas in which the students demonstrated transliteracy possibilities. First, a few students branched into their other majors, making their inquiry cross-disciplinary and their papers transliterate. Take Meryn, who was majoring in English, French, and international studies as an example. Intrigued by our discussions about the works of multilingual writers, she wanted to "identify causes and effects of writing in a language that is not the author's own" (research proposal). Specifically, she wanted to examine *Things Fall Apart* by Chinua Achebe, *Lolita* by Vladimir Nabokov, and *Salomé* by Oscar Wilde. *Salomé* was a calculated choice. Meryn wanted to write her honors thesis on Wilde to fulfill one of her English major requirements. She was also a French major, and *Salomé* is a one-act play written in French.

In her analysis of *Salomé,* Meryn tried to determine the reasons for and the effects of Wilde's use of French. She first cites Wilde, who emphasized the aesthetic effects he hoped to achieve with this language choice, and then she cites his two French friends Philippe Julian and Adolphe Retté, who emphasized the importance of the Anglican accent in Wilde's French.

Next, in searching out her own answers, Meryn analyzed a dialogue from the play that takes place between Salomé and Iokanaan. After providing the dialogue in French, Meryn went on to offer a linguistic analysis, which I include below in full:

> This passage reveals several of Wilde's methods at work. As Salomé and Jokanaan (Iokanaan in French) converse, their discourse is rife with scriptural quotes and allusions that would have automatically justified the play's censoring according to British law. Verbally making love to Jokanaan's body, Salomé directly quotes the Biblical Song of Solomon (Song of Songs/*Cantique des Cantiques*). In fact, throughout the entirety of *Salomé*, Wilde references Song of Songs, almost as if he is re-writing the Bible. For instance, as the lovers in Song of Songs verbally adore each other, they use metaphors such as, "Tes yeux sont des colombes," (1:15), and "Comme un pommier au milieu des arbres de la forêt, tel est mon bien-aimé . . ." (2:3), the way that Salomé verbally deconstructs Jokanaan's body and adores him using metaphors. Additionally, the lovers urge each other saying, "Fais-moi voir ta figure, fais-moi entendre ta voix . . ." (2:14), just as Salomé begs Jokanaan to let her touch him. With such striking Biblical illusions, it is no wonder that Wilde used French as a tool to avoid the censor.
>
> Aside from the use of French itself, this passage also shows how Wilde manipulates the language. In this passage (and in Salome's other praises of Jokannan), Wilde deliberately uses feminine nouns. Describing Jokannan's body, Salomé uses the feminine nouns, "neiges, montagnes, vallées, roses, reine, aurore, feuilles, and mer," in comparison with the only masculine nouns, "corps, pieds, jardin and sein," which, meaning "body" "feet" "garden" and "breast" have feminine connotations throughout the text, despite their masculine gender in the French language. Herod, for instance, fixates on Salome's naked feet as she dances. When Jokannan rejects Salome, however, her language switches, using mostly masculine nouns. In this passage, the masculine nouns "corps lépreux, mur, plâtre, scorpions, nid, and sépulcre" contrast with the two feminine nouns "vipères, and choses." Salome's feminine language of love, and masculine language of rejection begin to create an image of Salome's peculiar sense of femininity.

> Finally in this passage, either out of ignorance or on purpose, Wilde seems to be playing with the formal/informal "you" in the French language. In the lines where Jokannan rejects Salomé, Wilde conjugates the verb "approcher" with the formal "vous" subject to refer to Salomé, but then immediately uses the informal "ta" possessive pronoun to refer to her. This mix-up on the part of Jokannan seems to reveal a mixed feeling about Salomé: on the one hand he sees her as an inferior, while on the other he respects and even fears her.
>
> Thus, the effects of Wilde's use of French are manifold. On one hand is a veiled (at least to the British readership) use of Biblical citation, and on the other is an interest and exploitation of aspects of the French language that English doesn't afford the writer (namely gendering and formal and informal pronouns). Throughout his play, these themes constantly reappear and generate an added level of meaning to the characters and their relationships with each other. Like Achebe, Wilde is asserting his freedom to use language in the face of criticism, while like Nabokov he is undoubtedly playing with language. (final paper)

Several observations can be made about the translingual choices that Meryn has made in her analysis. First, she has joined English with French studies. While Wilde is widely studied in English literature, his only French play, while important, seems to be a misfit in the English canon. Although he composed the play in French, his work overall has been marginal in French literary scholarship because he was not French nor was he considered significant among authors of French. What Meryn has achieved here is a text that illustrates the cosmopolitan dimension of French, or the intricate connections between these two national literatures and across disciplinary boundaries. Second, Meryn's linguistic analysis reveals what Wilde has achieved in breaking down linguistic and cultural boundaries. His use of biblical allusions in French freed him from British censorship; his playful and manipulative use of French helped construct the multiple faces of the central figures in *Salomé.* Third, while providing the examples from the French play, Meryn refrained from translations. During her research she discovered scholars of British literature often don't translate French passages in their writings, and she chose to emulate them. Her language choices evidence a conscious effort at communicating to multilingual readers.

Given the opportunity to study English as used in everyday life, some students examined genres other than literary and print ones, acts that constitute the second area of transliteracy possibilities. Some of their topics dealt with anime, American movies, and Western music. While the students set out with the idea of studying English use, they all ended up studying the relationship between English and other languages in these genres, as English is often used in combination with other symbol systems in film and music. These genres offered them not only opportunities to explore language relations in popular culture but also opportunities to connect the discourses of popular culture with those of the academy. For example, Josh loved alternative rock and stored several hundred songs on his iPod. For his research he set out to study the rhetorical strategies evident in the song lyrics of this favorite band, Dispatch. He first reviewed five scholarly articles and concluded that songwriting typically deals with topics such as place, identity, gender, memory, art, and poetry. In his own paper he wanted to examine how these topics had been addressed in Dispatch's songs. When analyzing the topic of place, he wrote,

> Lyrics in alternative rock music have a special quality in that, when paired with music, they can vividly portray a place in the listener's mind. Dispatch demonstrates this quality in their songs "Elias" and "Carry You." Typically, alternative rock groups are liberal in their political standing. Dispatch is a band with liberal political views, similar to other alternative rock groups like Pearl Jam, Guster, Red Hot Chili Peppers, OAR, and many others. One way they demonstrate this is visible in the way the band tries to use their music to effect positive change in places that could use the support of their listeners. Specifically, Dispatch advocates for people to help with the AIDS crisis in African countries like Zimbabwe. Their song "Elias" is about a man with HIV from Zimbabwe who the band members met when traveling in Africa, and the lyrics describe the feeling of Zimbabwe to those who listen closely. The biggest way "Elias" captures the spirit of Zimbabwe is that the band members use traditional African instruments in the introduction, and the opening lyrics are written in the language spoken in the country known as Shona. The words are, "Dai Jesu achoinekwa, ndaizofara naye (If I could meet my Jesus I would be very happy with him) Taizofara naye (We would be happy with him) Kwaziwai (How are you?) Makasimba, here? (How are you feeling?) Ndakasimba kana makiskimbawo (I am

> fine and I hope the same for you)" (Songfacts). The first part about meeting Jesus references the fact that many people in Zimbabwe are suffering so much from the AIDS epidemic that they would welcome death. In fact, the chorus of the song begins with the words, "If you die will I get word that you're gone?" The members of the band wonder if they will even know if Elias passes away from the disease. The inclusion of Shona and the sorrowful tone of the song give the listener a sense of how terrible the situation in Zimbabwe is. (final paper)

As the passage reveals, despite Dispatch being an American band, its songs were not written entirely in English. When the band members traveled in Zimbabwe, they ran into speakers of Shona. Shona joined English to become a key feature of their song "Elias." As Josh explains, the use of Shona and African musical instruments constructs a specific place in the imaginations of Dispatch fans. The song "Elias" eventually led to the establishment of the Elias Fund in 2005; its mission is to help spread hope and opportunities in Zimbabwe and to "[engage] the current youth culture of the United States by encouraging a positive identity centered on social justice" (Elias Fund, n.d.).

Uncovering the above information about Dispatch songs has meant crossing cultural and linguistic boundaries for Josh. Before taking my class, like other Dispatch fans, he loved the music style and lyrics of Dispatch songs. After we discussed multilingual issues, Josh started delving into instances where Dispatch invoked multiple linguistic symbol systems, and he explored the cultural meanings behind them with great interest. Unlike Meryn, though, Josh provided English translations for the Shona lyrics in the above passage. His language choice conformed to the typical practice in academic writing. Josh wasn't alone. Students who studied English use in conjunction with other languages in popular culture tended to provide translations for these additional languages. Josh explained that because he had not understood the Shona lyrics, he searched online for their translations. Other students also researched online to translate a language they didn't understand. As young scholars they took it as their responsibility to seek the meanings of such passages and to introduce them to the academic readership. Like students in Hanson (2013), they used the Internet as a critical resource for bridging the discourses of popular culture and the academy.

Though these aforementioned examples have replicated the typical academic styles and tones, one of the students, in his literature review, managed to address a rather serious topic using an overtly playful tone. This is the third type of transliteracy possibility, the ability to blend styles and tones in addition to blending languages and cultures. This style of writing requires more authorial attention and can sometimes be intensely difficult to construct. Joshua was a big fan of the American TV series *Star Trek*. He wanted to study the blending of English and Klingon, a fictional tongue in the show. After citing a few scholars to establish Klingon as a legitimate language, he concludes his literature review in the following fashion:

> This, as with my earlier attempts to establish the legitimacy of *Star Trek* (and now specifically Klingon) as an acceptable thoroughfare for academic interests, structurally bolsters the integrity of the primary goal of this paper; namely, to do a "close-reading" of an episode of *Star Trek* (which, in this context, is the text that will serve as my primary source). A close-reading wouldn't be possible, wouldn't be valid, and wouldn't really be necessary if Klingon (as a language) was employed only as a cheap acoustic embellishment. But this isn't the case; what I've proven (by way of asserting that Klingon is a functioning, complete language) is that any dialogical transitioning between English and Klingon is an example of code-switching. Just as with code-switching in *Chicano/a* literature, for example, there is a sub-textual reason for *why* it is being employed. This "why" is the question that loiters at the heart of my paper, impatient to be answered.
>
> The manner in which this question will be addressed still needs pinned down, though; it would be improper, or insufficient, to treat with it purely in terms of a televised, fictional phenomenon. As I've previously intimated, something else, something larger, is at work. This view is, incidentally, held by Stephen Burt, who in an article titled "Of Disembodied Mind Sparks and Speakers of Klingon: A New Model of Science Fiction," states that [. . . .] It is with this article in mind that I feel confident in both addressing and *stressing* the importance of the subject matter. The immediacy of the language, of the code-switching (in other words, that which will feature prominently in a selected primary source), can and should be "treated as important in its own right. . . ." *Star Trek* (as a cultural and political phenomenon) is palpably relevant, ripe for analysis, and, by extension, bolstered by the insights gained from the immediately preceding article, so is the employment of Klingon. With this information/supportive evidence in place, my

> aim, simply put, is to analyze a given sequence in which Klingon/English code-switching is employed, and to try and distill down exactly what it achieves.

Like Meryn and Josh, Joshua was interested in the "sub-textual reasons" behind individuals' shuttling between languages. In synthesizing scholarly views and proposing his research focus, Joshua constructed a distinct voice. This voice is achieved as he implements multiple strategies: the use of contractions to mark a colloquial tone ("But this isn't the case; what I've proven . . ."; "As I've previously intimated, something else, something larger, is at work."); the use of figures of speech such as alliteration ("it would be improper, or insufficient"), metaphor ("thoroughfare"), personification ("This 'why' is the question that loiters at the heart of my paper, impatient to be answered."), rhyming ("addressing and *stressing*"), and repetition and parallelism ("A close-reading wouldn't be possible, wouldn't be valid, and wouldn't really be necessary . . .") to enliven the otherwise serious tone. Joshua told me that some of his former English teachers had liked his style and some had not, indicating that his style wasn't entirely rejected by an academic readership. It has to be emphasized though that this artful style didn't come from Joshua naturally. Like other multilingual writers (Canagarajah 2006, 2013a), he took a substantial amount of time to craft it, consciously shifting between registers. When I expressed my appreciation for the style and encouraged him to develop it in his final paper, he politely declined, explaining that he didn't have enough time to do so. However, it cannot be emphasized enough that Joshua's efforts have illustrated the stylistic possibilities in academic writing, a genre often viewed by students as sounding monolithically formal, dry, and cold. Joshua's writing reminds us what an undergraduate can do in deconstructing this stereotype.

The ways in which the students crossed boundaries are certainly impressive, but what they often reaped in the end was enlightenment, which I consider the fourth transliteracy possibility. For every instance of translingual practice, there is always "a sub-textual reason," as Joshua has reminded us. Regardless of their topics, my students have invariably explored the subtext of and the reasons for crossing linguistic boundaries: that is, they grounded their analysis within specific historical, political, economic, or cultural ecologies. Eventually they gained the understanding that language as a local practice doesn't entirely conform to the standards set by any individual or institution. The deviations are culturally and sometimes politically meaningful; they aren't errors or markers of inferiority. Examining the transactions between English and other languages enabled the students to attend to the issues of the Other. In the process they had to wrestle with their own linguistic and cultural assumptions and arrive at new ones. They had to shuttle between a text and its subtext to arrive at such enlightenment.

In Joshua's final paper, for instance, he explored the use of English and other languages and in doing so arrived at enlightenment. In the passage quoted below, he offers his subtextual explanation for why Klingon was used alongside English, the default language of Hollywood and American society at large. Echoing other scholars of *Star Trek*, he suggests that the multilingual scenes are emblematic of the "ethnic-ness" of American society at the time of the show's production:

> It is here, too, that we see the first significant instance of code-switching employed. Kurn barks the phrase "Mev yap" (meaning "That is enough") in response to the outpouring of Klingon aggression from Worf. The import of this first implementation of Klingon as a spoken language is actually not so apparent—it serves to underscore the essential "ethnic-ness" of the plot (if you'll forgive my use of a rather sloppy phrase), and it mirrors the real-world tendency of bilingual speakers to slip into dialectical speech patterns when the situation demands. Furthermore, I would argue that the entire exchange would reek of inauthenticity if code-switching was *not* employed. As Jutta Weldes suggests, *Star Trek* in general is a highly reflective cultural text; by extension, the enhanced sense of *ethnicity*, of cultural disparity and uniqueness, which is only as strong as it is because code-switching *was* employed, beacons forth. From this vantage point it is relatively easy to connect the dots and assert that, in a general sense, society (specifically American society) at the time of this episode's construction was hyperaware of, or perhaps particularly interested in, the overarching idea of ethnic difference.
>
> However, as I've previously intimated, the main thrust of this episode is not a pluralistic celebration of all things ethnic; rather, in terms of pure narrative, it is a story of how disenfranchisement and dishonor can be dealt with. Here I must again telescope the plot, so as to effectively demonstrate those integral instances in which code-switching is employed to further this storytelling aim. The following sequence, just to flesh things out, is subsequent to a scene in which Kurn is severely injured by those malign governmental forces that want to keep his (and Worf's) family in

> a state of disrepute: [An interchange between Worf and Picard is quoted]. Here, Worf tremulously asks Captain Picard to assist him in expunging his family's name. Picard, to show his unequivocal respect and support, flawlessly delivers a line of formal Klingon, essentially accepting the request with absolutely no reservations. Again, the vitality, the vibrancy, of this moment would be lost had code-switching not been employed. If Picard had even responded in deliberately ceremonial, somber English, the gravity of the moment would have been substantially diminished.
>
> To gain an even deeper understanding of the importance of this sequence, one is obliged to look at what is immediately going on, both contextually and thematically. Though Picard may not be privy to all the nuances of ritualized Klingon honor exercises, he still respects the ethnically imperative urgency of Worf's request. Didactic (and slightly patronizing) as it may sound, it is not really a stretch to assert that *Star Trek: The Next Generation* is trying to inspire in viewers and fans a similar appreciation for the cultural needs of others—and just as an aside, this is actually a recurring trend in the *Star Trek* series; in a way not wholly dissimilar to parables or fables, they (generally) attempt to convey life lessons and display ethical behaviors.

Thus subtextual reasons for the use of Klingon are multifold: a reflection of ethnic and cultural disparities in American society, the need of the story to deal with disenfranchisement and dishonor, and a lesson for American viewers on how to handle cultural differences ethically. Collectively these reasons locate language representations in *Star Trek* squarely at the vertex of American cultural politics in the mid-1980s. The multilingual scenes were a media response to the cultural and political discourses surrounding ethnicity and multiculturalism. In presenting his somber analysis, Joshua has partially recoiled from the playful style used in his literature review, although traces are still visible (such as the use of "bark," "telescope," and "the vitality, the vibrancy").

What the students have achieved in my class is transliteracy, the ability and practice of making meaning across languages and cultures, resulting in appreciation for other peoples. They enhanced their awareness of the complex language relations implicated in English use. Taking this awareness into their own inquiry of language practices in various texts, media, and contexts, they read in and researched other languages. They enacted cross-language relations in their writing by citing texts in other languages (with or without a translation) or by blending styles. More importantly, some students arrived at new linguistic and cultural understandings of the Other and themselves. My follow-up study with some students indicates that their newfound skills and abilities spilled over into other English courses, where professors were equally supportive of their transliterate practices. My class turned out to be part of an extensive transliteracy pedagogy already at work in the English department. To understand this pedagogy and arrive at some implications for writing studies, I next turn to two students' writing practices after they left my class.

Transliteracy Pedagogy in Writing Studies

Two students continued to read and write across languages and cultures in other English classes. Meryn incorporated her analysis of Wilde's French into her honors thesis, and Joshua experimented with blending languages in poetry writing the following semester. After Meryn completed her thesis, I interviewed her and her thesis advisor, Professor Emily Harrington, about her writing process. I also collected drafts of her thesis and a second-reader report. Two of the drafts had embedded comments from her advisor. I interviewed Joshua and his teacher, poet and professor Robin Becker, about his poetry writing process and collected from him four multilingual poems written for Professor Becker's class. The fact that Meryn and Joshua employed transliterate practices across subject areas and only elicited positive responses suggests shared goals and efforts among their professors, who valued the multilingual relations in CE.

Meryn's initial inquiry into Wilde started in a British literature course. In an interview she revealed that her work in *Salomé* didn't start in my class but had germinated in a seminar on decadence, a literary movement in France and England of the late nineteenth century, taught by her thesis advisor the year before. The class read Lord Alfred Douglas's English translation of *Salomé*. Meryn "hated" it and thought the translation was "lousy," which inspired her inquiry into translation issues with the French original for her seminar paper. Professor Harrington, a specialist in nineteenth-century British literature, played a catalytic role in initiating this transliterate inquiry. She assigned a translation of *Salomé* as a class reading and pointed out some issues with the translation in class. While Meryn originally delved into the project by comparing the English translation with the French original in her seminar paper, the professor steered her in a more productive direction by insisting, for her honors thesis, that she study the two texts on their own merits. The professor's insistence arguably resulted from a perspective heavily influenced by her focus on and teaching of decadence. As Meryn later explained in her analysis of *Salomé*, Wilde's interest in form over content is clear, as he gives asymmetrical attention to the part over the whole, illustrating his broader connection to the decadence movement, a transition between romanticism and modernism in British literature. Havelock Ellis defines literary decadence as "an anarchistic style in which everything was sacrificed to the development of the individual parts" (cited in Gagnier, 2010, p. 2). Such an interest in the part over the whole is characteristic of many decadent texts, in which the import of the individual word supersedes that of the sentence. Leading Meryn away from textual comparison at a technical level, the professor in effect emphasized studying *Salomé* in the historical and cultural contexts of its production, particularly its significance in the decadence movement.

Meryn continued to converse with her advisor after my class. She first wrote a section called "Pourquoi en Français?" for her thesis on why Wilde chose to write in French. However, she didn't know where her thesis was going. Further conversations with her advisor helped her discover her thesis. She finally argued that Wilde's play is both an interpretation and a translation of a large body of source texts, including but not limited to the Bible, various poems and paintings, and cultural-historical interpretations of the Salomé figure. As a translation, Wilde's text focuses on language and medium to articulate the *way* in which his sources mean, rather than what they mean. Meryn titled her thesis "Salomé's Veils: Language, Interpretation and Translation." She explained the process of arriving at her argument in the interview:

> But after reading that first draft of the section that I wrote. . . . I used something like Oscar Wilde used language to veil his text and made connection that Salomé did use veils. Emily recommended reading Benjamin because he has an essay on Goethe's *Elective Affinities* . . . and when I was reading it, I just browsed through the table of contents and saw he also had an essay on translation. So I read that and thought it could really be applied to *Salomé*. And I read the part about beauty, semblance, and veils . . . And that's really when my argument kind of coalesced. (April 27, 2012)

As Meryn struggled to construct a thesis, her advisor recommended Walter Benjamin, who eventually provided a much-needed interpretative frame.

Among the ideas that Meryn cited from Benjamin, the following probably came to help her the most in pinning down her argument: "a translation, instead of imitating the sense of the original, must lovingly and in detail incorporate the original's way of meaning, thus making both the original and the translation recognizable as fragments of a greater language" (cited in Oswald, 2012, p. 15). This quote enabled Meryn to recognize that in a broad sense Wilde's text was a translation of multiple sources (including English and French versions of the Bible) and that Wilde translated by capturing the *ways* these source texts meant by focusing on forms (words) rather than simply on meanings. In the final version of her thesis, Meryn ended up citing twenty-nine scholarly sources, three of them in French.

A cohort of multilingual English faculty sponsored, to use Brandt's (2001) term, Meryn's study of Wilde. Meryn chose Professor Harrington as her advisor and Professor Janet Lyon as her second reader because they spoke French. When she asked me whether she needed to translate the French quotes in her term paper for my class, I told her not to because I could read French. When Meryn wanted to show Wilde's use of language against other sources from which he drew, she would leave his text untranslated. She translated only when she was dissatisfied with an author's translation, as she was with Douglas's. In our interview, she explained how the faculty supported her study of translingual practice in British literature:

> She [Professor Harrington] said not to [translate] because it kind of complicates things, because then I add my translation in there, and she speaks French, so, and both my two readers are able to read French, so we just kept it. . . . And I think Lisa Sternlieb [English honors advisor] is also able to read French. . . . I think a lot of British literature specialists also have a proficiency in French because of the influence, the French language influence on British literature, and British literature on French literature too. The two are really connected, so, and it is even hard to read something like Charlotte Brontë without speaking French. (April 27, 2012)

In addition to the French-knowing readers, Meryn's knowledge of the translingual nature of British literature also gave her confidence to leave the French text untranslated. In their comments on Meryn's drafts, her two readers praised her linguistic and rhetorical analysis of the French text. Professor Harrington made a few comments on her linguistic analysis in the margins of two drafts, which corroborated Meryn's account that both readers spoke French. In fact, in the second-reader's report, Professor Lyon offered a multilingual response, indicating the profusion of transliterate practice in literary scholarship:

> On [Meryn] Oswald's reading, Wilde's strange French—literal, non-idiomatic, naïve, grammatically unstable—creates a deliberate incommensurability between the story (one might say the *fabula*) of Salomé on the one hand, and its ethereal transmission as a kind of symbolist *Gesamtkunstwerk*, a synthesis of affect, dramatic movement, repetition, and visual spectacle, on the other. As Oswald says repeatedly, *Salomé* illustrates Wilde's concern with the way that art means, rather than with meaning itself; for Wilde, in her words, "*Salomé* is an expression of art brought to life."

A specialist in modernism, Professor Lyon italicized two terms signifying their "foreignness" although both had entered English language. Originating from Russian formalism and used to describe a narrative construction, *fabula* refers to the chronological order of retold events while *syuzhet* refers to the telling of events in narrative form. *Gesamtkunstwerk*, German in origin and used in aesthetics and architecture, refers to a work of art that makes use of many art forms or that, at least, strives to do so. In using terms that originated from other languages, the professor added new theoretical perspectives to Meryn's reading of *Salomé*. Unwittingly they also served a pedagogical function as Meryn admitted that she had not known what *Gesamtkunstwerk* meant prior to receiving the report from Professor Lyon.

While my class turned out to be a stepping-stone in Meryn's inquiry, it was a launching pad for Joshua's multilingual experimentation in poetry. Growing up in rural Pennsylvania, Joshua didn't find relevance in learning Spanish in his all-white high school. In college, influenced by the cosmopolitan atmosphere on campus, he took two semesters of French. When studying, in my class, the interplay between Klingon and English in *Star Trek*, he was intrigued by multilingual practice. The following semester, when taking a poetry writing course with Professor Becker, he was intrigued again when the professor mixed Yiddish into one of her poems, "The Sounds of Yiddish" (Becker, 2013). The class dealt with the technical aspects of poetry writing, including rhythm, rhyme, and meter. The general focus of the class was on how to be creative, on how to understand the form first and then deviate from it. Joshua saw the class climate as conducive to his language experimentation. He noted that while the class read translated poems, only his professor's poem involved explicit switching between languages. He described the professor's attitude toward his multilingual experimentations as "appreciative," though she "did not applaud them yet" (July 10, 2012).

Joshua sought authenticity through blending languages. In one of the four poems, he inserted a Latin expression, "Deus Vult," in writing about a leper in Jerusalem during the crusades. The leper dreamed that God would spare him the indignities of sickness. Mixing Latin into a Standard English–dominant poem, Joshua hoped to bring some historical and cultural weight to the story. Among the rest, which portrayed lives in French-speaking Louisiana, he inserted French expressions. The following is one of them, and it depicts scenes of an approaching hurricane:

> Thunderheads roll like death
> Over the sugarcane, and servants race
> to board up shutters. Spanish moss
> flutters and falls in clumps, and the trees
> bend with the wind. The bayou roils,
> black made silver by motion and lightning
> coming closer. Grandmother, the creole,
> waits on the porch for the hurricane,
> watching. All know fear, the people,
> the wild eyed horses being drug
> screaming from the stable,
> but not her—*Dieu peut nous noyer*
> *ce soir.* The storm has yet to come
> great enough to drown her; she
> weathers them all, the unmoving eye
> of the hurricane, ancient face flickered white
> by the awesome blaze of thunderbolts.
>
> (emphasis in original)

Joshua had to reconcile authorial intention with the linguistic resources available to him. Originally, he wanted to capture a southern accent. He could hear it because he had a childhood neighbor from Louisiana, but he wasn't sure how to represent it in writing. In addition, he felt that he lacked credibility because he didn't speak it himself. Therefore, he chose to compose the poem predominantly in Standard English and to add authenticity to his work by incorporating the French expression. His translingual choice compensated for the cross-modal challenges of moving from sound to script and for his perceived lack of authenticity in using Standard English instead of a southern dialect.

The two students' reading and writing beyond my class evidences a transliteracy pedagogy at work. In Professor Harrington's literature class, students read texts in translation or in languages other than English. They wrote papers analyzing these or similar texts. The professor also directed the students to read critical works on these texts or on translation theories (cf. Venuti [1996] and Wittman & Windon [2010] on teaching literary translation in English studies courses; Alemán [2008] and Schwartzward [2008] on a multilingual and interdisciplinary approach to study literatures of the Americas in North American English studies). After engaging these literacy exercises, Meryn gained a deep appreciation for translingualism in British literature and enhanced her skills in using academic English and French. In the creative writing class, Professor Becker used translated poems and her own multilingual poem as class readings, and she appreciated students' efforts to construct the voices of the Other (cf. Unger [2008] on the MFA program at the University of Nevada, Las Vegas, for its emphasis on cultivating cosmopolitan writers through international experience and literary translation). Joshua used his knowledge of French to authenticate his representations of the life experiences of French-speaking Louisianans. As Anglo-American literary canons continue to expand, an increasing number of multilingual texts involving languages other than the traditional ones of European origins, such as French, Latin, German, Greek, and Italian, will enter literature and language arts classrooms, giving students opportunities to apply their knowledge of different languages in reading and writing.

In view of the transliterate practices in these areas of English studies, a question concerning writing studies naturally arises: if these areas have been engaging their students in reading and writing across dialects and languages, why should we continue to emphasize a single dialect (Standard English) and a single style (formal or academic style) in the writing classroom? A similar question was raised by Lu (1994) in the context of addressing multiculturalism in writing studies and was reiterated by Horner, Lu, Royster, and Trimbur (2011) and Horner, NeCamp, and Donahue (2011). One response is that with limited resources, writing teachers need to focus on Standard English for academic or formal purposes. However, this and the last two chapters have shown that academic settings don't exclude, but instead often require, the use of multiple languages, genres, and styles. Another response might be that some writing teachers have not received subject and foreign language training that these area teachers have. They lack the ethos and skills necessary for engaging students in writing across languages, not to mention for assessing their multilingual writings. The way that I taught World Englishes in Literature and Education can offer one answer to this challenge.

My class was institutionally labeled as upper level and writing intensive. In addition to required readings, the class was involved in an extensive writing project: centering on a chosen topic, the students completed four interconnected papers. They were given the opportunity to explore English use in any text and context. They typically chose texts, genres, media, and contexts that they were already interested in, which motivated them to spend time reading secondary sources and analyzing language relations in the primary texts. They mobilized their knowledge of English and other languages; when they lacked such knowledge, they resorted to online and offline resources. Most of the topics that my American students chose and the language relations that they studied were unfamiliar to me. Their research proposals, literature reviews, and data analyses educated me along the way, preparing me for their final research papers. Although they produced texts predominantly in English, their composing processes involved reading and writing across dialects and languages.

Transliteracy can be promoted in the first-year composition course (a staple of writing studies in the United States), which, at different institutions, has been taught for various purposes and using a variety of approaches. Nevertheless, across the board it places an emphasis on raising students' awareness of the rhetorical situations and composing processes they will encounter or use when addressing academic and general audiences. In this course we can engage students in analyzing texts written in CE, texts that have clearly crossed linguistic and cultural boundaries. For example, they can read sections of the texts used in my World Englishes class. Or they can read from multilingual/multidialectal literary anthologies (Ahmad, 2007; Shell & Sollors, 2000). For example, *Rotten English: A Literary Anthology* edited by Dohra Ahmad (2007) is an anthology of CE, with poetry, short stories, novels, and critical literary essays drawn from different parts of the world. Many American universities require their undergraduates to take foreign language courses and/or general education courses related to international culture. In first-year composition we can encourage students to examine the accented texts they inevitably encounter in their everyday lives by drawing on the knowledge they gain in these other courses. They can study texts and artifacts from social media sites, bulletin boards, churches, or local ethnic restaurants. The class can discuss the translingual choices made when producing these objects and explore together the sociocultural subtexts behind these choices. Students can be directed to studies on youths' attempts to blend languages and styles in nonschool contexts (e.g., Lam, 2009; Lee, 2002, 2007a, 2007b; Lee & Barton, 2011; Jacquemet, 2005; McGinnis, Goodstein-Stolzenberg, & Costa Saliani, 2007) and be invited to examine their own or peers' language practice in similar contexts. For the writing assignment, students should be given liberty to select texts or artifacts for examination with the aim of unveiling the multifaceted ways in which English is used in context. Like my students described in this and the previous chapter, they can create multilingual texts by capitalizing on their diverse linguistic and cultural resources.

To promote transliterate practices, English studies and writing studies need to strengthen their ties despite their disciplinary divides. They need to recognize that literary scholars, writing researchers, and creative writers typically read and write across languages and cultures. In the college classroom, their students are doing the same but with much less interest in defining or defending disciplinarity. In my class, for example, my students were intrigued by translingualism represented in literature, academic texts, and popular culture. They explored the sociopolitical reasons speakers move between languages and writers construct multilingual protagonists. Further, the students attempted blending languages and styles in their own papers, adding new rhetorical strategies to their literacy repertoires. The students' transliterate practices have unequivocally supported calls for building closer ties between English studies' subfields. For example, Hesse (2010) justifies such a move between writing studies and creative writing by highlighting the rhetorical power of the aesthetic: "The aesthetic has a rhetorical force even as the belletristic can carry information and idea. It is the rhetorical force of image and identification, metaphor and symbol, of narrative arc and character as actor and acted upon, of Burkean ratios enacted in possibility rather than constrained by given formation" (p. 48). Writing studies will find allies in transliterate practice if, taking a CE perspective, it reassesses its relationship with English studies.

In addition to English studies, we can promote transliteracy across disciplines. At the graduate level, the fact that many departments have a foreign language requirement, instituted to allow students to read articles in languages relevant to their field, suggests that transliterate practices are already part of the process of text development. Like graduate studies in rhetoric and composition, as Horner, Lu, Royster, and Trimbur (2011) suggested, "the challenge is to incorporate more multi- and cross-language work into graduate curricula" (p. 309). Some of us often get the chance to teach or co-teach undergraduate courses in other humanities, social sciences, business, and law departments. We can study how scholars read and write across dialects and languages in these fields and then design assignments that allow students in these fields to perform similar and relevant activities. For example, Dr. Walker, professor of sociology introduced in chapter 5, asked her students to write about two lectures given on education issues, one of which was delivered in Chinese. In my own class described in this chapter, the students studied language relations in Harry Potter movies, Japanese anime, and French music bands, topics also examined in media and performance studies. Students should be given the liberty to choose their own material, material that interests them. The assignments should encourage students to make full and creative use of their linguistic and nonlinguistic resources. Similar to those of the English studies courses, the purposes of such activities include encouraging a cosmopolitan language perspective in students and allowing them to discover that human activities are connected and mediated, not by a single dialect, but instead by multiple dialects, languages, and nonlinguistic representation systems. Analyzing and enacting the interplay of language and social activities in their fields of study requires the ability to read and write across languages. As students' literacy resources are continually enlisted across disciplines, they gain a better understanding of the cosmopolitan language perspective, benefiting them and their field of study.

While students' transliterate practices described in this and the previous two chapters are impressive, we need to note that these students are humanities majors and have proficiencies with multiple languages and dialects. In contrast, science and engineering students might insist that they are die-hard monolingual English speakers. They could further claim that they grew up only speaking Standard English. Approaches to transliterate development for these students therefore have to be modified. These students may indeed not have to interact with natural languages other than English in their schoolwork. This fact alone doesn't mean they aren't multilingual. First, science and engineering majors typically work with multiple symbol systems, English being one of them. Recognizing and crossing these systems constitutes an essential part of their communicative repertoires (Fountain, 2014; Poe, Lerner, & Craig, 2010). Second, even for those who insist that they only communicate in Standard English, their English is always sedimented, involving the work of recontextualizing language, ideas, conventions, and interlocutors in each context. Their English shows remarkable variations when examined in a temporal-spatial frame (Lu & Horner, 2013). Therefore, a transliteracy pedagogy for these students can first call their attention to the types of boundary crossing that they need to perform daily. Then literacy brokers, be they language teachers and/or professors in their majors, can design activities where students study masterful ways of crossing in their fields and practice these ways in their oral presentations, lab reports, and research papers. The ultimate goal is to cultivate both empathy and appreciation for the ways that linguistic and cultural crossings take place within and outside their fields.

In this chapter I have shown that a transliteracy pedagogy is currently practiced across some English studies areas in my university. Professors in these areas require their students to read and write across languages, often resulting in the latter's new identification with the Other. Taking a cosmopolitan perspective, I also managed to raise my students' awareness of the language relations imbedded in English. They completed a sequenced writing project exploring such relations in various texts and contexts. The classes I described in this chapter can serve as examples and offer possible strategies for teaching transliteracy in English studies. However, we must keep in mind that multilingual students come from both within and outside the nation. What we often have in place in English or writing studies departments are teacher development programs designed for teaching students from within the nation. Such programs hardly accommodate students from outside the nation, called "international students" or "second-language writers," who are often placed in a separate program or department but now increasingly show up in our writing classrooms. A CE perspective collapses this nation-based division, forcing us to recognize that students from inside and outside the nation all use both English and other linguistic and nonlinguistic representation systems. This realization compels us to revise and retool our teacher development programs, and to this aim I turn in chapter 8.

8

Crossing Borders in Teacher Development

The field of writing studies has united in recognizing the crucial part that language differences play in the teaching of writing. In 1974 the Conference on College Composition and Communication (CCCC) in the United States declared that students had the right to use their home dialects in acquiring standard written English (Committee on CCCC Language Statement, 1974). After a national firestorm ignited by the Oakland Unified School District's resolution in the 1990s, the CCCC called for more research on how educators could best build on existing knowledge about Ebonics to help African American students expand their command of Standard English (CCCC, 1998). In the new millennium, the CCCC exhorted us to address the needs and challenges of second-language writers, including international-visa students, refugees, permanent residents, as well as naturalized and native-born citizens (CCCC Committee, 2009). The past four decades witnessed the field strengthening its effort to address issues arising from language differences, to help a wide range of writers, from dialectal to multilingual.

These policies, as well as much of the pedagogical practice on the ground, while trying to be inclusive, have unwittingly reified and reinforced national, disciplinary, and institutional boundaries. With pressures from outside the classroom, these U.S.-based policies place Standard English, the idealized national code, at the center of teaching writing. They intend to contain or eliminate language differences rather than to value them as resources in student writing. They divide students into camps, from dialectal and Standard English groups to first- and second-language groups, primarily based on their relationships with the default national code. These students are then placed in separate programs to be taught by specialists of different disciplinary training (Atkinson & Ramanathan, 1995; Matsuda, 1999, 2006). Only in recent years have writing scholars recognized the need to bridge these nation- and discipline-anchored divisions. They recognized that writing always involves drawing resources from multiple languages and dialects across genres, styles, and contexts, defying clear national and ethnic lines (Canagarajah, 2006, 2011, 2013a; Horner, Lu, Royster, & Trimbur, 2011; V. A. Young, 2004). Taking a Cosmopolitan English (CE) perspective, this book has also emphasized that dialectal, first-language, and second-language writers can be multilingual/multidialectal, performing transliteracy inside and outside classrooms.

Even within national and disciplinary frames, Anglophone research on how we can prepare writing teachers to work with multilingual writers has been, at most, limited (Hirvela, & Belcher, 2007; Matsuda, Saenkhum, & Accardi, 2013). Among the published studies, Coxhead and Byrd (2007), Ferris (2007), Hyland (2007), and Weigle (2007) discussed strategies they used in preparing second-language writing teachers to handle issues of vocabulary and grammar, genre, response to student essays, and assessment in academic writing. Focusing on preservice or in-service teachers, Lee (2010, 2011, 2013) and Seloni (2013) examined how a teacher development course broadened their perspectives on teaching writing and how it helped them construct new identities as writing teachers. Taking a sociocultural perspective, Villamil and de Guerrero (2005) examined how metaphors could help Puerto Rican teachers enrolled in an MA program in TESOL (Teaching English to Speakers of Others Languages) to construct theoretical notions of second-language writing. Taking a similar perspective, Worden (2015a, 2015b) studied the development of writing teachers' pedagogical content knowledge in teaching activities. Canagarajah (2016) introduced the principles (practice-based, dialogical, and ecological) and the classroom resources that he adopted when training novice teachers for teaching translingual writing. These scholarly discussions focus on teacher education programs in applied linguistics, TESOL, or secondary education, not in rhetoric and composition. Further, except for Canagarajah (2016), most of them have not taken a cosmopolitan perspective on English and the teaching of writing.

To dislodge our national framework, we need to educate writing teachers and program administrators about a cosmopolitan one. First, in the age of globalization and new media, writers outside the academy don't compose within rigid programmatic, institutional, or national boundaries. They engage multiple discourses and communicate with diverse audiences, from academic to nonacademic, from domestic to international, by drawing resources from multiple languages and cultures. Second, with the rise of digital technologies, students no longer compose using one single language but design their work using multiple representational systems including words, images, sounds, and performances. From a cosmopolitan perspective, native dialectal students don't seem so different from so-called second-language students, or from mainstream native students. Being educated about CE and transliteracy will allow most American teachers to become conscious of their monolingual assumptions and to become better situated to teach multilingual students from inside and outside the nation.

In college writing courses in the United States, student writers from within the nation are rarely conceptualized as multilingual; hence virtually no teacher training instructs from this perspective. Teachers commonly deal with anywhere from just a few to a sizable number of writers from outside the nation. For this group of writers, teachers learn about second-language writing through practicum meetings, guest lectures, graduate seminars, or published sources. What they gain from these venues and sources tends to be conceptual rather than experiential knowledge. Instead, following a Vygotskyan perspective on concept development, both conceptual (scientific) and experiential (everyday) knowledge need to be united into a "true concept" (Vygotsky, 1986). Four decades ago, to respond to students' dialectal differences in the United States, the Committee on CCCC Language Statement (1974) asserted the value of experiential knowledge: "Empathy with the difficulties often faced by such speakers can be appreciated in indirect analogies with other situations which make one an outsider. But the most vivid sense of the students' problem is likely to come from direct experience" (p. 19). Thus, the committee recommended that teachers ratify their theoretical knowledge of language by living as minority speakers. The committee's suggestion aligns with the Vygotskyan perspective; however, though well intended, the suggestion is not without problems. First, it emphasizes the difficulties and ignores the benefits that multilingual speakers/writers experience. Second, the suggestion in reality can end up looking a lot like "slumming" or cultural tourism rather than really experiencing what it is like to use another dialect or language. Even with its merits, pedagogical or research efforts to immerse pre- and in-service writing teachers among dialectal students and multilingual students are rare.

To sensitize American teachers to the literacy practices of multilingual writers, we can bring them into direct contact with those from outside the nation. Working with such writers may enrich these teachers' understanding of multilingual writing, enabling them to perceive ways in which national and linguistic boundaries can be crossed, which will help them teach multilingual writers in general. Research shows that teachers tend to demonstrate more confidence working with language learners when provided opportunities to link conceptual tools with practical tools in their training experience (McDonald, 2005). After reviewing the current practices in writing teacher development, I will propose a border-crossing model for writing programs. In the model, communication technologies are used to introduce teachers to writers from outside the nation. When mediated by experienced teachers, class readings/discussions, and egalitarian interactions with multilingual writers, such training can help teachers connect conceptual and practical knowledge about the needs, challenges, and strengths of multilingual writers with the translingual and transcultural characteristics of their writing. Using a global partnership program that I developed with colleagues in China for illustration, this chapter explains how an infrastructure can be established in local programs and how this model may help teachers develop expertise in teaching transliteracy.

Developing Teachers of Multilingual Writers

Arguments for the need to develop teachers of multilingual writers have been made by scholars and professional organizations. For example, the CCCC Committee on Second Language Writing (2009) argued that college writing teachers, researchers, and administrators are to be held responsible for addressing second-language issues because the acquisition of a second language and second-language literacy would continue throughout students' academic careers and beyond. As for teacher preparation, the committee urged that "any writing course, including basic writing, first-year composition, advanced writing, and professional writing, as well as any writing-intensive course that enrolls any second language writers should be taught by an instructor who is able to identify and is prepared to address the linguistic and cultural needs of second language writers" ("Part Two" section). The committee's contention is that because second-language writers show up in all types of writing courses, virtually any writing teacher will have to be a second-language writing teacher.

While the committee's argument is sound, it was framed within a national and bilingual perspective, subjugating all multilingual writers to the English-only mandate in the United States. From a cosmopolitan perspective, the term *second-language writers* is problematic. It reinforces the ideas of nativity and linguistic boundaries. Students referred to by that term are often using English as their "third, fourth, or fifth language" (CCCC Committee, 2009, "Part one" section). But ordering languages based on an acquisition sequence isn't always useful. In reality, English is simply one of the representational systems in these writers' linguistic repertoires. In order of prominence and frequency of use, English may be their first language. The concept of second-language writing has long implied the adoption of native speaker standards and norms as the target of second-language learning and teaching. Anglo-American writing conventions and rhetorical preferences are established as the standards, thus casting the work of English users from other traditions as different, undesirable, or erroneous (Connor, 1996; Kaplan, 1966; Kubota, 1999, 2001a). Pedagogically, the label *second-language writer* tends to evoke the image of a deficient learner, failing to represent the rhetorical complexity and dexterity of the writer (Jordan, 2009, 2012; Ortmeier-Hooper, 2008, 2013). Hence, a decade ago Canagarajah (2004) advocated replacing "second-language writers" with "multilingual writers" to draw our attention to these writers' rich linguistic and cultural resources.

There are multiple ways in which American college teachers have been trained to teach multilingual writers. Of course, we have to remember that until now multilingual writers have been conceptualized in the field largely as those who didn't grow up speaking English, while those who did have been viewed as monolingual. First, in practicum meetings, new teachers, including graduate instructors and adjunct faculty, may receive an introduction to the identification of multilingual writers and the characteristics of their composing processes and written products. And throughout the year, guest lectures may be arranged, devoted to issues such as teaching grammar, responding to student writing, and assessing writing. Second, teachers are also educated using professional support materials and in academic conferences, such CCCC, the TESOL Convention, and the Symposium on Second Language Writing. In addition to the extensive treatises on teaching second-language writing (such as Bruce & Rafoth, 2004; Canagarajah, 2004; Ferris & Hedgcock, 2005; Leki, 1998; Matsuda, Cox, Jordan, & Ortmeier-Hooper, 2006), teachers learn about issues that multilingual students often face in a section devoted to English as a second language, or ESL, found in most writing handbooks. While sometimes useful, because most handbooks focus on grammar issues in this section, they give novice teachers an incomplete, static, and often false picture of multilingual writers. Third, teachers can also learn about teaching these writers by interacting with them in classrooms and writing centers, and by learning from other teachers and mentors in their teaching programs. Fourth, they can take a course devoted to second-language writing or multilingual writing at some universities. However, such courses are rarely required in graduate programs in writing studies (Matusda, 2006). Last but not least, these teachers can also work or study abroad (many already have), where they would interact with multilingual speakers and writers directly.

Given current institutional arrangements, new teachers usually lack opportunities for interacting with diverse multilingual writers in their respective writing programs.[1] New teachers have not yet taught these students, and veteran teachers have encountered, almost exclusively, multilingual students that grew up in the United States. What these teachers have learned about writers from outside the nation is conceptual knowledge derived from practicum meetings, academic conferences, workshops, and professional support materials. Even teachers who have taken a course in second-language writing will, many times, not have gained extensive experience with these writers. The benefits of interacting with diverse multilingual writers are apparent: teachers gain experiential knowledge of these writers and their writing, experiencing firsthand the ways in which writers and readers negotiate national, racial, ethnic, sexual, and linguistic boundaries; issues of multilingual writing discussed in professional sources come alive to them; and teachers develop skills in dealing with these issues in real contexts. We need to find ways to allow teachers to interact with diverse multilingual writers.

A Model of Border Crossing

The "direct experience" that the Committee on CCCC Language Statement (1974) called for suggests a crossing, migration, or assimilation into the dialectal and multilingual Other's cultures and contexts. An early champion of the "direct experience" call was the Language Curriculum Research Group of the City University of New York in the late 1960s and the 1970s. Inspired by the discourse of CCCC's "Students' Right to Their Own Language," the group arranged collaborative learning sessions that paired upper-division education majors with African American Vernacular English–speaking students enrolled in composition courses of the Language Curriculum Research Group. The preservice teachers helped the students revise and edit their essays using grammatical concepts they had learned in their coursework. The tutorials and discussions held with the students "deepened the preservice teachers' understanding of African American linguistic traditions and heightened their sensitivity to their students' rhetorical sophistication and critical sensibilities" (Wible, 2006, p. 457).

However, the "direct experience" called for suggests that writing teachers in American universities are solely monolingual speakers of Standard English, who need direct exposure to dialectal speakers, including both their language and culture. In reality, a large number of these teachers are multilingual, as the last three chapters have shown and as this chapter will show. So in addition to gaining continuous direct exposure to multilingual students from outside the United States, they need to recognize that they share some of the same experiences. They need to foster empathy (rather than sympathy) and to recognize similarity with their multilingual students. However, "direct experience," consisting of contact, conflict, struggle, ambivalence, and reconciliation, remains a powerful concept in teacher development, providing teachers with necessary skills for working with multilingual students.

Recognizing the need for direct engagement, particularly with writers from outside the nation, I propose a model of border crossing. My model is useful both as an institutional program and as a pedagogical strategy in teacher development. In this model, teachers and multilingual writers are connected through communication technologies, including electronic bulletin boards, blogs, e-mails, instant messaging, teleconferencing, and phones. Student writers share their work and their composing processes with the teachers. Through a dialogical process whereby students and teachers discuss student writings and reflect on their interactions, teachers gain firsthand knowledge of the writers' needs and resources and the features of their writing. In return, writers receive feedback from the teachers. In the interactions the teachers are led to recognize and enlist their own language and cultural experiences to reconceptualize issues of multilingual writing. In this model the teachers cross and re-cross artificial borders: the border between teaching "native" and "non-native" multilingual writers, the border between the teachers' language learning and teaching experiences, and the borders between writing programs, between universities, and even between nations.

The border-crossing model embraces decades of thinking on teacher development. Teachers should no longer be viewed as conduits, as knowledge sources channeling wisdom to their students. Instead, they are decision makers, and they would benefit from making their tacit knowledge and decisions explicit. From the perspective of sociocultural theory, teachers achieve expertise not only by obtaining content knowledge from expert teachers but more importantly through goal-directed interactions with their peers and their students during which they engage conceptual tools and artifacts in various contexts (Johnson, 2006, 2009; Lantolf, 2000; McDonald, 2005). The border-crossing model has the potential to generate numerous contexts where teachers can link their conceptual (scientific) knowledge and their experiential (everyday) knowledge as they reframe the way they describe and interpret their experiences with multilingual writers. Indeed, these new understandings enable teachers to reorganize and reframe their experiential knowledge, providing them a new and more productive lens through which to view and interpret their own teaching practices.

To understand how the model might actually work, in recent years I developed global partnerships. Global partnership programs are widely used in the teaching of business and technical writing (Anderson, Bergman, Bradley, Gustafsson, & Matzke, 2010; Connor, Davis, Rycker, Phillips, & Verckens, 1997; Herrington, 2008, 2010; Maylath, Vandepitte, & Mousten, 2008; Maylath, Vandepitte, Minacori, Isohella, Mousten, & Humbley, 2013; Sapp, 2004; Starke-Meyerring, 2005, 2006; Tesdell, 2013) but much less in other domains of writing studies (see Verzellaa & Tommasob, 2014, for first-year composition and Craig, 2014, for writing across the curriculum). Professor Zheng Chao, a writing program director in China, and I, as a professor in the United States, designed and implemented parallel semester-long activities each year since 2009 (Zheng, Du, & Wu, 2013). We connected faculty, graduate, and undergraduate students at Penn State University with undergraduate writers at Guangdong University of Foreign Studies in China. When undergraduates at Penn State were involved, parties at both institutions exchanged and critiqued one another's work. When faculty and graduate students at Penn State were involved, they critiqued the Chinese students' writings. By the end of 2015, we had conducted eighteen exchange activities. In fall 2009, ten American graduate instructors taking a graduate seminar were connected with twenty-five Chinese undergraduate writers. In this particular partnership program, we wanted to find out first, in light of the model, how we could develop an infrastructure for teacher development within our institutions and, second, how using such a model would help the graduate instructors gain expertise in the teaching of multilingual writers.

The instructors were taking a rhetoric seminar with me in the English department. Six of them were MA students and four were PhD students. All of them were multilingual: one grew up speaking Chinese and one speaking Spanish; the rest grew up speaking English with proficiencies in either French or Spanish. They gained proficiencies in these two "foreign" languages predominantly through classroom learning and study-abroad experiences. The instructors' experience with teaching writing ranged from one semester to three years. Four of them had prior experience in both classroom instruction and writing-center tutoring. The rhetoric seminar was intended to acquaint them with rhetorical theories and practices developed in different cultures and ethnic groups. The class studied texts from ancient Greece and ancient China and read about rhetorical practices in African American, Asian

American, and Chicano communities. For ethnic rhetorics, the class read Cintron's (1997) *Angels' Town: Chero Ways, Gang Life, and Rhetorics of the Everyday*, Howard-Pitney's (2005) *The African American Jeremiad: Appeals for Justice in America*, and a collection of essays edited by Mao and Young (2009), *Representations: Doing Asian American Rhetoric*. These texts amply show how, in various sociohistorical contexts, individuals negotiated multiple discourses by crossing national, ethnic, or linguistic lines. The instructors enrolled in the seminar were typical of new teachers in the English departments of American research universities: as graduate students, they had the opportunity to take courses in rhetoric and composition. However, none of them had previously taken a course on multilingual or second-language writing.

The Chinese students were English majors in their junior year, taking an English writing course. The course was taught according to an approach homegrown in their university called the length approach (Wang, Niu, & Zheng, 1999; You, 2010; Zheng, 2004). Instead of placing equal emphasis on the modes of narration, description, exposition, and argumentation, the course focuses on narratives and opinion papers. The students were encouraged to write as much as they could. When their essays were evaluated, in addition to conventional criteria such as content, organization, style, and mechanics, their length was also factored in, hence the length approach. In a social context where English was used little by the majority of students for daily communication, the Chinese teachers believed that meaningful output such as writing would enhance students' expressive competencies in English. In the writing course the students started with generic narrative writing and gradually moved on to professional genres, such as magazine feature stories.

Establishing an Infrastructure for Exchange

We implemented the exchange within our respective institutional structures. On the American side, I presented "direct experience" as an assignment in the graduate seminar. In the beginning of the semester, the graduate instructors were introduced to the Chinese students and were invited to evaluate their magazine feature stories. They were encouraged to comment on every article critically and independently. On the Chinese side, Professor Zheng also introduced the exchange as a class assignment. Some students who had taken a writing course in the spring semester were assigned to conduct field research and to write magazine features in groups or individually over the summer. After the fall semester began, with the help of their teachers, the students worked on their feature stories, creating several drafts. They then shared their work along with reports of their composing processes with the graduate instructors. Their work and reports offered the instructors an insider perspective on the students' literacy practices. The two parties corresponded by e-mail or on Skype. The students revised their articles after receiving feedback.

To facilitate the "direct experience," we built a multilingual online platform at the outset of the project. On the Chinese side of the writing program's website, we created a space to host the exchange. Filled with both alphabetic and ideographic symbols, the website provided the instructors an example of CE at work. We composed a brief English introduction to the activity and made the feature articles available online (figure 8.1). Held in an open-access space, these articles could be read by anyone. Under each article we installed a function to allow both parties to trade comments. This function was password protected; only the participants could post messages. We didn't require synchronized communication because there was a thirteen-hour difference between the two locations. However, some participants used Skype's voice-chat function during the exchange.

I facilitated the actual exchange in a number of ways. First, I handed out a printout of figure 8.1 to the instructors with every Chinese expression translated. I also furnished them with the universal log-in name and password. The instructors provided their actual names and contact information (such as

Figure 8.1. Border-crossing online platform, providing users with a "direct experience" of using Cosmopolitan English through activities and articles.

e-mail address, phone number, or Skype account) in their initial posts. Second, I divided the instructors into five groups, with each group having particular articles assigned and each member in a group responding to those articles independently. I asked them to respond to the articles as if they had been written by their own students. Third, over the course of the semester, the instructors were given three opportunities to discuss the exchanges in class. In these discussions they shared their observations and comments on the student articles, allowing for their conceptual and experiential knowledge to coalesce into "true concepts." I chimed in periodically to provide background information on English teaching in China or to point the discussion in a certain direction.

The student essays and the ensuing exchange gave the instructors firsthand experience with the students' transliterate practices. The students explored a variety of local and translocal cultural phenomena, ranging from business start-ups to cross-dressing to the impact of media on youths' lifestyles. They incorporated Chinese expressions and images into most of their essays, showcasing various styles of CE. In reports they produced on their composing processes, they explained their translingual and transmodal efforts. For example, a student reported on the lives of Chinese online store owners. She described her writing process as being mediated by both Chinese and communication technologies:

> We designed a questionnaire [in Chinese] and asked five online shop owners relevant questions through QQ or telephone [in Chinese]. Most of the interviewees were our friends or schoolmates. . . . Then we searched the Internet for more data, especially some statistics and typical examples, which were not easy to get from our interview but could be very persuasive argument in the article. (Liao Lulu)

QQ is a social media site popular in China, which provides an instant-messaging service. Self-reports like this one reminded the instructors that English writing often involves complex relations not only between languages but also between the modes of talking, reading, and writing. In some reports the students even included the transcripts of their interviews in Chinese, evidencing their translingual processes. The exchanges were also marked by the use of multimodalities: imbedded in the online postings and student e-mails were images, hyperlinks, and emoticons. The students offered the instructors insights into the multilingual and multimodal activities that Fraiberg (2010) has urged writing teachers to examine in their teaching.

The Zone of Proximal Development

The instructors cultivated their expertise for teaching multilingual students in a zone of proximal development (ZPD). According to sociocultural theory, a site of potential learning called ZPD arises or is created when participants collaborate to understand a concept or to solve a problem. ZPD marks the difference between what one can achieve independently and what he or she can achieve working in collaboration with others or with someone more expert (Lantolf, 2000; Vygotsky, 1978; Wells, 1999). Teachers, whether in practice or in training, can develop a greater understanding of teaching through reflective practice and goal-directed collaboration with other teachers. They internalize theoretical concepts as they appropriate what others say, in the process transforming themselves and their teaching. In the higher mental process of internalization, different psychological tools are formed and used to mediate the process, including concepts and metaphors (Villamil & de Guerrero, 2005; Wertsch, 1991).

To understand how the instructors developed expertise, I examined the discourses generated in the exchange. Specifically, the data consisted of the Chinese student essays, their reports on their composing processes, their public and private correspondence with the American instructors, the instructors' communications with the two coordinators, and discussions in the graduate seminar. Consent for using the data was received from both the instructors and the students at the beginning of the semester. I performed data analysis by first searching for moments in which the instructors' conceptual knowledge and their experiential knowledge were explicitly brought up and either agreed or disagreed with each other. Disagreements arose when their assumptions and values about writing came into conflict with the direct experiences they were having with multilingual writers. Reconciliation of the conflicts was critical to their internalizing key concepts in teaching writing. Once these moments were identified, I searched for themes, concepts, and metaphors that arose in these moments and assigned them different codes. Comparing the codes across different moments/scenes allowed me to identify the frequently occurring themes, concepts, and metaphors that mediated discourse in this transnational interactive space, which became a "dwelling place" for all participants. Focusing on a few frequently used concepts in the instructors' discourses, I went back to those moments to trace the instructors' evolving understanding of these concepts.

An examination of these discourses reveals that some concepts were catalytic in the instructors' development; in the process of the exchange they reformulated their understandings of these concepts. As suggested by sociocultural theory, the instructors would have to mobilize both theoretical constructs and experience in formulating and reformulating their notions of writing and writers. In class discussions and in their reflections, the instructors consciously brought to bear their experiences interacting with the Chinese students and their writing as they reconceptualized writing. They built on what they had already learned from previous experiences with teaching, tutoring, and reading about multilingual writers. In the next sections I will show how some concepts aided the instructors' reconfigurations of their conceptual and experiential knowledge about multilingual writing and writers. Further, I will explain how, under these broad concepts, they negotiated and crossed various boundaries. The concepts critical to the instructors' formulation and reformulation processes include, among others, audience, coherence, genre, and language.

Audience

When teaching first-year university writing in the United States, teachers generally assume that they share the same national culture with their students, with occasional exceptions. Most students in their classes grew up in the United States; in class the students write for American audiences, either addressed or invoked. However, when reading the Chinese student essays, the American instructors were forced to abandon these assumptions. Their expertise on responding to multilingual writing grew along with their coming to terms with the unstable, fluid, unfamiliar audiences constructed by the Chinese students. For example, in her comments on the student essays and e-mail correspondence, Heather repeatedly queried the students about their intended audiences. She also e-mailed me asking about it: "Is the writing meant for a Western audience? Or English speakers in China? Or both? One of the students used a word—'pagan'—in her piece. She said that the meaning of the word would be familiar to a Chinese audience, even if not to a non-Chinese audience." I told her the students wrote these articles as a course assignment (intended for their teachers) but that they were aware their articles would be read by the American instructors too. My answer certainly didn't eliminate the uncertainty surrounding the intended audience. At the end of the semester, Heather reflected on the challenges this issue had posed in her reading of the student essays:

> Specifically, I didn't know if the students were writing for a particular audience (American? Chinese English speakers?). More generally, I was unsure of whether or not my comments would meet the needs of the students. Were students looking for concrete advice from me (e.g. editing), or were they open to reading more rhetorically based comments that encouraged them to think about the effectiveness of the argument in relation to a particular audience and purpose?

The uncertainty of audience perplexed Heather, complicating her decisions in responding to the essays. The complication came from at least two entangled issues concerning the reader-writer relationship in multilingual writing: First, who did the Chinese students intend to address, an American audience or a Chinese English speaker? Second, what would the Chinese writer like to hear from the reader, editing advice or how to increase the rhetorical effectiveness of his or her argument? Articulating the conundrum indicates that Heather experienced, and also was reflective about, the double consciousness inherent in writing in English as an additional language. Multilingual writers of English often find themselves mired in ambivalence, trying to address both local audiences and the larger English-speaking world (Ashcroft, 2009). Certainly, even the so-called monolingual writer from within the nation can be indecisive in deciding whom to address in his or her papers—the teacher or other audiences. However, Heather's questions suggest that her prior assumptions about audience, as situated in a particular national culture, were challenged.

The instructors found the students' sometimes unsuccessful attempts at addressing American audiences confusing and at times even abrasive. The resultant misalignment of discourses and cultural and cognitive dissonance forced the instructors to confront their prior assumptions about audience and authority. As such an instructor, sensitive to gender and sexuality issues, Elaine, an African American, was troubled by the cultural incongruences revealed in some student essays. She commented on one such perplexing encounter in her reflection:

> I reviewed the essay of a student who wrote about homosexuality as a problem among Chinese teenagers. I asked this student, "How do you know that promiscuity is only common among homosexual college students? What about heterosexual college students—aren't some of them sexually active also?" His reply to my comments revealed a rather disturbing position that I didn't

> know how to respond to. He states, "I think the differences between our understanding is about the openness towards sex in your country and mine. I think generally, promiscuity is rather rare among the heterosexuals in my country. It's even somewhat a taboo. However, this is rather common among the homosexuals and all the statistic do point out that they're closer to sexually transmitted infections."

The student seemed to have an American audience in mind. However, the dialogue reveals that he held fast to some erroneous assumptions about sexuality in the United States. He was unaware that there are large segments of the U.S. population, Christian and otherwise, that strongly promote abstinence before marriage and monogamy afterward, and promiscuous girls are many times devalued or shamed in the media and in American society at large. When Elaine brought up her perplexity in the graduate seminar, I weighed in and offered a possible explanation for why the student considered homosexuality a problem. Chinese society had remained conservative relative to gender roles and sexuality but has in recent years started to open itself up to discussions and practices of alternative forms of sexuality. Although misinformed about American gender culture, the student participated in the burgeoning discourse on alternative forms of sexuality in Chinese society. While attempting to cross national and cultural boundaries to reach American audiences, the student revealed clearly that American audiences lack authority in some cultural discourses that these students were engaged in. Without being fully cognizant of the Chinese context, Elaine felt incapable of responding to the student other than in feeling "somewhat baffled and frustrated." Further, she wondered to what extent she could "be a cultural relativist and respect their opinions"—a profound cosmopolitan question. Refraining from taking either an assimilationist or an accommodationist stance toward language and cultural differences (Matsuda & Cox, 2004; Severino, 1993), Elaine keenly perceived the challenges in responding to writers mired in cultural misunderstanding or engulfed and engaged in their own cultural discourse.

Coherence

In the instructors' evaluations of the student texts, the most charged issue was coherence. Coherence is commonly understood as a text's unity, stemming from that text's connectivity of underlying ideas as well as its overall logical organization and development of thematic content (Halliday & Hasan, 1976). Coherence is not a property or a state inherent to a text; it is instead a process by which writer and reader, or speaker and listener, negotiate with textual and contextual factors to arrive at a unified sense of the text. Their sense of coherence will never match exactly but will always partially align (Bublitz, Lenk, & Ventola, 1999; Carrell, 1982). However, as pointed out by postmodern critics, rhetorical values such as clarity, consistence, and coherence reflect a Western ontology, a belief in language's power to capture a single-ordered world out there. Further, Hall and Ames (1995) suggest that these values are more "a consequence of the desire for ego-stability and self-identity than of getting at any truth of the matter" (p. 169). Insistence on logical coherence thus can exclude alternative narratives and meanings critical in intercultural communication.

In their written comments as well as in class discussions, the instructors noted internal contradictions in a few student essays. For example, in an essay on cross-dressing among Chinese youths, the author concludes, "But if it's only an action out of curiosity or imitation, it could be solved at the early stage, which is at home." Elaine wrote in her comments, "Why is this an issue that you feel needs to be 'fixed'? The juxtaposition of Sid's testimony, the background information you provide, and a great description of how dress affects behavior directly conflicts with your arguments about the negative effects of cross-dressing. It may help your argument if you acknowledge that cross-dressing could have both positive and negative consequences." Elaine expected the author to strike a balance in her conclusion. Similarly, another student wrote about Chinese youths, who, attracted to online video games and pressured by high-stakes exams, spend long hours indoors. The way the author concluded the essay irritated a few instructors. After presenting the opinions of those who both approve and disapprove of this indoor lifestyle, the author concludes, "A balance, however, is needed to be struck. And it mainly relies on the awareness and the attitude of the youth. 'My life is anything but boring. We just stay indoors a little bit longer than the others.' Yang Ming is quite proud of being of the 'Zhai'" (Meng Anni). Instructor Michael commented on this conclusion: "You suggest a balance is needed, but then the essay just sort of ends. As a reader, I'd like a bit more about this balance: what would it look like? How can it be struck? Has anyone proposed such a balance? You provide both sides throughout the essay—how can you put them together in this paragraph?" Michael expected the author to elaborate on how she negotiated the two sides of the cultural phenomenon—"zhai" (staying indoors for long hours or even days). These two instructors raised questions because their expectations were left unmet. Both suggested ways to improve these essays' arguments by addressing unity and coherence, constructs that writing teachers are familiar with.

In a class discussion, more instructors joined the critique, labeling these essays as lacking internal consistency. They exchanged evaluations and reached a collective verdict on the coherence issue. I then raised a series of questions to extend the discussion: "Do we see our students as coherent thinkers all the time? Should we expect our students to always think coherently? Do we think coherently all the time although we try to portray that in our writing?" These questions, centering on the key word *coherence*, spurred a train of responses from the instructors. Elaine immediately defended her aforementioned evaluation by emphasizing the ethical responsibility of a writer to strive for both internal and external consistency. She spoke passionately, using hand gestures for emphasis:

> But I do think it's important to call them on it and say if you are going to make a claim, do defend yourself. And make sure your life is consistent with what you are saying. Because I do think that we live in a culture where there is a cleavage between what people say and what people do. That creates anxiety, shame, embarrassment, and all kinds of crazy issues in people. People are not held accountable for, standing for their beliefs because of their desire to fit into groups.

Elaine's defense suggests that coherence doesn't solely deal with formal logic. It is also a cultural issue for her. On one hand, she believed that a writer must defend his or her claim at all costs; in later discussions, she called the failure to do so "a weakness." The writer needs to create a unified ethos inside the text. On the other hand, Elaine also argued for an external consistency in communication because, according to her, there was a lack of such consistency in American culture. Many individuals don't live according to the values they purport to embrace. Apparently Elaine was deeply troubled by such hypocrisy. Grounded in her experiences and values, she assessed coherence by searching for both an internally unified ethos as well as for alignment between this persona and the writer's actual lifestyle. She advocated bringing a culturally charged standard to bear in evaluating the Chinese student essays.

Elaine's notion of coherence was not accepted by everyone in class; a few instructors put pressure on it. For example, Sarah pointed out that one can explore many aspects of a controversy and still end up not deciding on an absolute position. And she thought that could still be a productive argumentative strategy to use. Then, another instructor, Kris, argued adamantly for internal consistency in student writing:

> Coherent to me is more about holding together. Does everything move towards the same direction? And so you can write a totally decisive paper about being indecisive. My stand on abortion is like it's complicated and I don't know. And I can write a very coherent paper saying that. But I feel coherence is more like do you undermine yourself or not.

Kris drew the class back to the conventional notion of coherence as logical unity. The class agreed that within American society the reader expects the writer to explain and defend his or her statements. Because the class understood coherence as a construct valued in American society, they seemed unable to answer the question of how to deal with coherence in a multilingual and translocal context. The uneasiness they felt about evaluating coherence again suggests that they were unwilling to take an assimilationist stance in dealing with language and cultural differences.

Discussion of the coherence issue in multilingual writing didn't end in class. A few instructors continued to wrestle with the issue outside the classroom. For example, Sarah consulted the student author on what she meant by the statement "a balance, however, is needed to be struck." The student responded in an e-mail:

> I think the internet is more likely to become a kind of force keeping the youth indoors rather than going out, which to some extent, prevents the youth from communicating with others in real life. And spending too much time indoors may not be good for our health. Therefore, we'd better keep a balance between the indoor activities and outdoor activities, at least on the time arrangement. (Meng Anni, November 3, 2009)

After being given an explanation grounded in the student's cultural milieu, Sarah, again and finally, reflected upon the coherence issue: "One of the problems students did seem to have in common was analyzing their evidence in a way that pointed toward a single argument; however, as we talked about in class, I think this was as much a product of writing to better understand a cultural phenomenon as it was of writing in a second language." Sarah saw "incoherent" writing as constituting and mediating the Chinese students' exploration of a cultural phenomenon, though they may not necessarily reach any conclusive argument. She also recognized that lacking a "coherent" argument could be identified by readers taking a particular cultural stance as a feature of multilingual writing. Taking the coherence issue a step further, Michael adopted a poststructuralist perspective on the relationship between author and text in his reflection: "I'd add that we shouldn't expect coherence between the essay and student either. I heard expectations that students might believe what they were writing. We can't know what a writer believes, only what the essay purports the writer to believe." By emphasizing that there is no inherent, fixed relationship between text and author, Michael highlighted the fluidity of the existing relationship. Both Sarah and Michael demonstrated willingness to explore other ways of organizing thoughts in a text. Although the instructors didn't solve the issue of evaluating coherence, which necessitates engagement with the complex and delicate relationships between language, culture, and self, they did arrive at some nuanced understandings.

Genre

Genre was another concept important to writing teacher development. Genres are "typified rhetorical actions based on recurrent situations" (Miller, 1984). Specifically, as Berkenkotter and Huckin (1993) explain, genres are dynamic rhetorical forms, developed in response to recurring situations, that evolve over time in response to genre users' needs. One's knowledge of genre comes from participating in communicative activities in daily and professional life. This knowledge involves both form and content, including a sense of rhetorical appropriateness. Through the use of institutional and disciplinary genres, humans constitute social structures and reproduce them when they draw on genre rules. Genre conventions reflect a community's norms, epistemology, ideology, and social ontology.

Genre emerged as a key term for discussion once the instructors learned they would read and evaluate some magazine feature stories, a genre they seldom taught. Along with these stories, the Chinese students also sent reports of their composing processes, where they explained how they had interpreted and constructed this genre in their social contexts. For example, a student stated,

> After reading the model essays on our textbook, I found the structure of feature writing were quite set: firstly, describe the subject with vivid language; do some analysis and reveal something within the surface; then use about three concrete examples to illustrate features of the subject; show the dilemma or raise a question; vaguely show your stance or indirectly answer the questions. (Liao Lulu)

The student derived her genre knowledge from a pool of samples written by both American and Chinese authors. In the textbook the students used, there were two feature stories adapted from American magazines and five written by Chinese students (Zheng, 2008). Reports like this one showed the instructors the process of students acquiring genre knowledge: they analyzed the characteristics of feature stories and appropriated them in their own writing.

As cultural artifacts, the feature stories allowed the instructors to perform genre critique by examining social values imbedded in genre activities. Bawarshi and Reif (2010) suggested that analyzing genres and their cultures critically can teach students "purposeful rhetorical uptakes for social action and can enable [them] to engage more critically in situated actions" (p. 202). For the instructors, genre critique opened a window to the worldviews and life experiences of the Other, which in turn led the instructors to critically engage their own teaching situations. For example, in class discussions and reflections, Bill tried to extrapolate from the feature assignment cultural implications about the Chinese students and Chinese society at large. He stated in his reflection,

> Something I found quite refreshing is that not only did the Chinese students have different genre expectations for their writing . . . but the political orientation is totally different. I attribute this to an historical hopefulness about markets, capitalism, and entrepreneurship that I do not fully share. I think this is because our capitalist system has become rigidified to a certain extent that work, even for the optimistic and ambitious, is often associated with necessity or drudgery, and not with the unqualified eagerness that I sense from the Chinese students.

Bill connected the students' genre performance, or their interpretations, expectations, and implementations of a genre, to a distinctly Chinese political orientation. While one may question Bill for having gone too far in his interpretation, when he explained it in class, everybody seemed to agree with him. Among the student essays that Bill used to make his point, one dealing with supermodels delved into the hardships common in the modeling business. The writer concluded her essay by suggesting that, despite these hardships, modeling remained an ideal career for her: "Though being a supermodel is a glorious job for a while, a difficult profession for a minute. It is still worthwhile" (Zhang Xiulan). The class's concurrence with Bill's extrapolation suggests that genre performance can tell the reader something about the writer, about both her attitudes and aspirations, and more broadly about the norms, ideology, and social ontology of the community to which she belongs. The student's confessional tale of her writing process confirms Bill's extrapolation:

> When I first came across this kind of writing, I was stunned because I knew nothing about feature writing. But as soon as the teacher said that we could investigate the job we were interested in, the first idea that struck me was model, which I have longed to be since I was in primary school, because they can always were beautiful clothes. . . . At last, I state my own opinion towards model because it is still an ideal profession for me no matter how harsh and short its life is. (Zhang Xiulan)

The student's sense of what feature stories could do was deeply grounded in her desires and sensibilities, mediated and shaped by her social context. Interpreting genre performance actively, Bill didn't view the feature stories as stand-alone written products but instead as artifacts mediating the matrix of and shaping the students' lives. At the same time, the "them-us" comparison (China versus the United States) made Bill and other instructors increasingly aware of the connections, or disconnections, between politico-economic relations and student writing in the United States.

Not only did the feature genre allow the instructors a glimpse of the Chinese writers' worldviews; it also encouraged them to reflect upon the norms and ideologies of their own community, a reflection that challenged them to reassess and revise their pedagogical assumptions. Feature stories are not commonly taught in college writing courses in the United States. The possibilities of the genre suddenly made, among the instructors, some long-held pedagogical assumptions seem odd. For example, Nadia was compelled to revise her assumptions about academic writing in her reflection:

> What really constitutes academic writing? Beyond this point, what are the objectives of English 15 or one like it? . . . If critical thinking is what we emphasize I feel that it is necessary to expand on the genres that are used generally. Ultimately I've found that the Chinese student's take on the genre taught me something about the beloved thesis statement. It doesn't need to be in the first paragraph or even on the first page.

For Nadia, genres uncommonly taught in American schools could also be used to encourage critical thinking. The students' enthusiasm for and successful writing of feature stories inspired her to assess the core values of the first-year writing enterprise that she was part of. As a result of her experience with this genre, some conventional wisdom about academic writing, such as that concerning thesis statements, started to crumble. The feature stories pushed Nadia to reimagine academic writing as necessarily subverting conventions (e.g., thesis statement) and crossing boundaries (e.g., genre), a form of translingualism. Similarly, this experience with feature writing inspired Sarah to teach multilingual and multimodal writing. She explained in her reflections, "Often, it is easy to focus on low-level issues in second-language writing, but the genre and topics of these essays made the content the focal point. I think this focus on the expression of creative, compelling ideas is essential, especially when we want our students to experiment with new languages or multimodalities." Sarah perceived an array of benefits that a new genre could yield, including encouraging student writers to use creative expressions, to relate compelling ideas, and to experiment with languages and multimodalities. Reflecting on the world of possibilities that feature stories might open up for them, the instructors clearly saw their teaching as a local-global practice, a practice within their institution and nation but also closely connected to the teaching of English and writing in other parts of the world.

Language

Only occasionally did the instructors bring up sentence-level issues in class discussions, paying it proportionately less attention than other issues. In their marginal comments on the student essays, they made grammatical corrections like most teachers would have done, in areas such as tense, word choice, sentence structure, and collocation. In their reflections a few of them praised the students for making no more errors than American undergraduates. Such an imbalanced attention to language issues may be accounted for in two ways. First, trained in literary and rhetorical studies, like the undergraduate English majors that I described in the last chapter, the instructors might not have yet fully developed terminological repertoires for addressing surface-level language issues. Second, in taking a seminar on ethnic rhetorics, they might have developed an appreciation for the Chinese students' linguistic choices. Thus they refrained from extensive discussion of grammar and mechanics in class.

In their correspondence with the students, however, the instructors addressed language issues more extensively and reflexively. They pointed out recurring issues, such as word choice and article use. It is worth noting that often the instructors didn't judge these issues against any absolute native speaker or grammarian standard. Without taking either an assimilationist or an accommodationist stance toward language differences, they contextualized their comments within American culture or emphasized their personal interpretations. For example, when asked by a student which pronoun should follow the noun "person," Heather offered her answer emphasizing the U.S. context: "In American writing it has become accepted to not indicate the sex of the subject if that information is not necessary to what you are writing." Similarly, Bill commented on a student's use of the term "white-collar" with an acute translocal sensitivity: "the term . . . in the U.S. is a slang term for which different people have widely different understandings. You seem to use it as if it had a more precise meaning for readers, different from simultaneous interpreters. This usage may be appropriate for your audience." While Bill viewed the term as imprecise or inappropriate for an American audience, he saw the possibility that it might be acceptable for the intended audience. The student wrote back to confirm her own take on the term: "I did not realize this as I took for granted that the word 'white-collar' means people who work in offices, like the employees in P&G I mentioned in the following paragraphs in my essay." While the student welcomed Bill's interpretation of the term, her response suggests that the term did mean something more narrow, specific, and positive in her cultural context. In contextualizing their comments, the instructors reinforced in both parties the idea that whether a writer is aware of it or not, linguistic choices are deeply grounded in a cultural context.

Recognizing the cultural specificity of linguistic choices can lead to successful translocal communication. In a few instances, the instructors appreciated the students' use of Chinese expressions. For example, commenting on the piece "Have You Been 'Zhai' Today?," Sarah praised the author for her skilled translingual strategy: "I think one of the things that you did very well was to define your topic. In fact, I liked that you retained the word 'zhai' and then defined it specifically for your audience in the second paragraph, as opposed to using an English synonym. I think it helps keep this idea culturally contextualized in your piece." The student explained what "zhai" meant and demonstrated its prevalence in China using interview and survey data. Sarah valued the rich cultural indexicality of such local terms. Indeed, zhai indexes a new lifestyle popular among Chinese youths affected by a pervasive online gaming culture and susceptible to the mounting pressures of high-stakes exams. In successfully employing strategies such as definition, translation, explanation, and recontextualization, the student writer was able to negotiate and to cross linguistic and cultural boundaries to reach her multiple audiences.

Language issues sometimes awoke the instructors to their own multilingual experiences, resulting in their own pedagogical treasure troves. In these moments of enlightenment, of self-realization, they felt connected to the Chinese students. For example, when a student revealed via e-mail that she did more translation than writing when composing her feature story, Nadia, one of the instructors, shared her experience of acquiring written Spanish: "I grew up in a Spanish speaking household so I was able to absorb a spoken Spanish which made writing clear grammatical Spanish more difficult for me. I heard a dialect and not that 'proper' grammatical way. I still find that I tend to translate my thoughts from English to Spanish." In referencing her own experience, Nadia confirmed to the student that people naturally draw on their diverse language resources when composing. When a student declared that "the use of articles is my killer," Nadia again empathized by drawing on her own experiences learning Spanish and working in the writing center. She wanted to assure these students of the universality of challenges associated with acquiring an additional language. What is most significant here, from the perspective of teacher development, is that Nadia actively probed her own multilingual experiences and used them as tools for interpreting and tackling the challenges of writing in English as an additional language. Nadia's example should encourage and inspire teachers of multilingual students to recognize the usefulness of their own past experiences in creating teachable moments.

Mediations along the Borders

The border-crossing model enabled us to find a strategic location to educate teachers about multilingual writers. Until recently most English departments or writing programs in American universities have been unable or unwilling to offer courses on second-language or multilingual writing. When these courses are offered, they tend to focus on scholarly readings rather than on "direct experience." Working within the constraints of such an institutional context, I opted to make cultural exchange part of a graduate seminar on rhetoric. In the seminar the instructors studied ways that individuals in various cultural contexts crossed national, ethnic, and linguistic lines in their rhetorical practices. They then linked their conceptual knowledge acquired through readings and class discussions to their work with the Chinese students. They developed richer perspectives on the teaching of multilingual writers by engaging their own linguistic and cultural experiences, other seminar participants, the Chinese students, conceptual tools, and various artifacts, including e-mails, Skype, and the course website. On the Chinese side, the exchange complemented well the writing curriculum of the university, helping the students enhance their knowledge of audience, coherence, and the genre of feature stories.

CE probably served as the most useful and widely used tool of the exchange. All parties mixed linguistic and nonlinguistic symbols as they moved between styles and between genres. The online platform was constructed using Standard Chinese and English. To maintain authority, the instructors adopted Standard English in their correspondence. In their feature stories the students also attempted to use this standard code, while also mixing it with images and translated Chinese expressions. In the students' online posts and e-mail correspondence, their English was blended with smileys and URLs, and included grammatical and orthographic deviations. In addition, student essays, reports of their composing processes, and instructor-student correspondence offered the instructors a precious glimpse into the situatedness of the students' language use, allowing them an understanding, though an incomplete one, of the histories, cultural contexts, and personal stories creating English in China.

Several key concepts mediated prominently the instructors' development of expertise. These concepts framed their evaluations of the feature essays, their border-crossing correspondence, class discussions, and end-of-semester reflections. Because these concepts constitute the primary domains of writing assessment, the instructors, understandably, used them heavily in their "mental lives" (Johnson, 2006, p. 236). While using these concepts to organize and make sense of their experiences working with the Chinese students, they were led to reformulate their understandings of audience, coherence, genre, and language, arriving at the "true concepts" in the Vygotskyan sense. The evaluation task that was built into the exchange propelled the instructors to expand their expertise in teaching multilingual writers even further.

Tracing the key concepts in the instructors' mental lives reveals that they came to understand many of the cultural and rhetorical complexities associated with multilingual writing. Like travelers arriving in a foreign land, they encountered situations that challenged, confused, and even shocked them. For example, they were perplexed by the ambiguity of audiences evoked and positions held in the student essays. Although the Chinese students kept the American instructors in mind, they didn't seem altogether successful in addressing them, as the latter raised a series of questions about audience. The students' "failure" revealed to the instructors the challenges of negotiating the double consciousness inherent in multilingual writing. In exploring the pedagogical motivations and sociocultural implications of assigning feature stories in college writing courses, the instructors marveled at the deep cultural meanings associated with teaching English writing in China. Through dialogical engagement with the Chinese students, they experienced firsthand the complex interplay between translocal values and writing in English as an additional language.

The challenging, confusing, and sometimes shocking experiences of the interchange inspired the instructors to confront and to reformulate their assumptions. In reading the student reports, they learned that these writers juggled several languages and modalities when constructing their feature stories. A single linguistic symbol system was simply inadequate for the communicative purposes of these writers. When teacher-student power relations were equalized to some extent in the online space (cf. Liu, 2011, for online communication among Taiwanese and American undergraduates), some Chinese students held fast to their biases about Chinese and American societies, unwavering when confronted with Elaine's suggestions for revision. Assessing writing in a translocal context proved a significant challenge for Heather and Elaine, as it forced them to reevaluate their assumptions about audience. Class discussions on coherence also revealed the opposing values held and contested among the instructors: Elaine connected coherence to the integrity of the writer while a few other instructors preferred to limit the term to the internal consistency of a text. The instructors came to realize that the coherence issue they attributed at first to the Chinese student writers turned out not to be an exclusively multilingual issue. Similarly, some of them didn't find surface-level language challenges a uniquely multilingual issue either.

The exchange awakened the instructors to their values and assumptions and challenged them to modify them.

As faculty, we intervened strategically when the instructors were struggling or having a difficult time finding their own answers during the interchange. Insiders to both Chinese and American cultures, we sometimes were able to redirect the instructor discourses and to offer critical lenses. For example, when Heather was perplexed by the audience issue, she sent one of us an e-mail requesting assistance. I advised that instead of hastily disparaging the writer for lacking audience awareness she might consider the possibility that the writer was struggling with a double consciousness. My comment on Chinese attitudes toward gender roles also redirected the instructors' conversation on the coherence issue. In border crossing, someone needs to provide insights about the multilingual writers and their cultures. That role was filled by coordinators of the exchange, the students, and the instructors who are multilingual themselves. All parties involved in the crossing were assets with insights valuable to the exchange.

The success of our border-crossing activity does not guarantee the model's success in other institutions or in the development of adjunct or tenure-line faculty. To implement this model, a writing program needs to embrace transliteracy as its pedagogical goal and to possess the right resources, such as trained or at least interested multilingual faculty, technological support, and already well-established connections across borders. The success of our teacher development practices had much to do with the instructors being students at the same time, a group that we could teach and shape. They had the opportunity to take a graduate seminar on cultural rhetorics and to participate in the exchange. In contrast, adjunct faculty may not have such opportunities for development. For the fortunate few who are retrained once every few years, a border-crossing activity can be implemented in their training courses. Tenure-line faculty may never receive formal pedagogical retraining. Fortunately, they have easy access to scholarship in multilingual writing and its teaching. Despite the challenges, I hope writing program administrators and literacy and writing scholars will be inspired by our border-crossing practices and adapt this model in their contexts.

While the global partnership program has allowed us to educate teachers about teaching writing across national and institutional borders, crossing can also take place along disciplinary, racial, and class borders that have divided and marginalized some multilingual/multidialectal writers. The model I propose here comes close to the style of teacher training practiced by the Language Curriculum Research Group of the City University of New York introduced in the beginning of this chapter. That program was able to cross racial and class lines in educating preservice teachers. Brodkey (1989) adopted a similar teacher development model that effectuated the crossing of class and gender lines. When she taught a graduate course on teaching basic writing, her white middle-class teachers corresponded with six white working-class women in an adult basic education class. They exchanged "literacy letters" on various topics, which allowed the teachers to learn about the reading and writing concerns of these adult students. Brodkey's analysis of their communications revealed both the affordances of and challenges in such a pedagogical endeavor. The border-crossing model joins these historical efforts to prepare teachers to deal with language and cultural differences.

Over the last four decades, writing studies has made great strides in terms of helping students with language differences. It moved from focusing on dialectal writers to embracing multilingual writers ranging from international-visa students and refugee students to permanent residents and native-born citizens. It is encouraging that some part of writing studies has abandoned the national framework and started treating American students as multilingual/multidialectal, recognizing their vast communicative repertoires. While the field has produced a critical mass of scholarship on the needs of multilingual writers from outside the nation and the characteristics of their writing, relatively little research has been conducted on how we may develop the large cohort of writing teachers to teach writing from a cosmopolitan perspective. At my institution the border-crossing model proved strategic in sensitizing teachers to issues of multilingual writing. The model, inspired by the "direct experience" mandate of the students' rights era, has transcended some of that mandate's problematic assumptions while addressing the fluid linguistic and cultural realities of globalization.

Conclusion: Transliteracy as a Dialogical Imagination

> It is sobering to say, but in certain ways I feel that the Chinese students actually outpace and eclipse my own—"mastery" (I feel *decidedly* preening and self-aggrandizing writing that) of English. Whether it stems from their culture, their work ethic, or simply their innate determination to produce quality material, I was at nearly every turn struck by their flair for, and skill with, writing. It is, as I've said, a sobering moment when a native speaker reads a piece written by a non-native speaker, and realizes that it would be beyond his or her own capabilities to craft a comparable piece. This is certainly true when it comes to description; almost invariably, I found that my correspondents had a way of beautifully and simply capturing the essence, or pith, of a moment. This is, in my opinion, one of Ha Jin's great strengths as a writer, and it was a pleasure to see that (in admittedly smaller doses) mirrored in the essays I read and critiqued. —Joshua, "Reflections"

I end the book with a reflection by Joshua, whom we met in chapter 7. He studied the English-Klingon mixings in *Star Trek* and employed transliterate strategies in his research papers and poems. His class border-crossed with a group of Chinese undergraduates by sharing and critiquing each other's essays. While equally subjective, his reflection contrasts sharply with the remarks made by the disgruntled first-year student that I introduced in the opening of the book. The striking difference lies in their attitudes toward other styles of English and, by extension, toward other cultures and other peoples—one disparaging and the other appreciative.

Joshua's reflection showcases just one route by which one may move from local to global in meaning making and in the end enlarge one's "geographic imaginations" (Reynolds, 2004, p. 6). He analyzed *Star Trek* and wrote poems in conversation with academic and ethnic audiences within the nation. In class we read Ha Jin's (1999) novel, *Waiting*, which won the U.S. National Book Award, and Joshua's expressions of appreciation for that work evidence his positive attitude toward ethnic writing. As an immigrant writer, Jin adopted English along with a style that is both linguistically transparent and realistic to depict Chinese individuals struggling within and against the restrictions of a communist state apparatus. Though sacrificing his Chinese, he borrowed "its strength and resources, in order to accomplish a style in his adopted tongue" (Jin, 2008, p. 60). Like Raja Rao, Xiaolu Guo, and Sapphire, Jin used transliterate strategies to fashion his English; preeminently he drew from American, Chinese, and Russian literary traditions for creative inspiration (Geyh, 2001; Zhang, 2002). One can observe in Jin's fictional and poetic depictions of Chinese humanity his "thoroughgoing assimilation to dominant American values through validating the cornerstone notions of 'freedom' and 'opportunity' that uphold the rhetorical infrastructure of U.S. cultural and political ideology" (Yao, 2010, p. 115). Jin appealed to American audiences, including Joshua, likely because he had embraced dominant American values in his works. He served as a linguistic and cultural mediator for Joshua, who came to appreciate the Chinese students' writing styles. Joshua's mind was opened and his communicative repertoire expanded as he progressed from analyzing and performing multilingual writing to appreciating the styles of an immigrant writer and to appreciating the styles of a group of total strangers.

The attitude of Joshua's reflection may be termed cosmopolitan as far as it exhibits critical empathy toward the Other. When reading multicultural texts or interacting with narratives of the Other, students are in danger of fostering a too-facile empathy. They may feel comfortable, happy, assured, and satisfied as some experiences of the Other resonate with theirs. For developing a truly cosmopolitan attitude, however, such narcissistic reading is limiting because it erases rather than appreciates differences. Instead, students need to cultivate critical empathy; that is, they need to contextualize the narratives in their historical materiality and allow for discomfort (DeGenaro, 2014). Seeking ways to fight racism in multicultural reading practices, Schneider (2005) proposed historical materialism as the foundation: "students become able and then perhaps willing to read history, its material effects, and present cultural forms in ways that at least create the possibility for intervening in the practices of everyday life that perpetuate inequalities" (p. 208). Similarly, a cosmopolitan attitude has to be cultivated through transliterate practices that are grounded in historical materiality.

The transformative experiences of Joshua and his classmates demonstrate that transliteracy has the potential to engender “a dialogical imagination.” Mendieta (2009) emphasized that cosmopolitanism necessarily presupposes “a form of suspended, delayed, on the way, universalism” (p. 254). It is the universalism of the Other, an “other” that is always historical and concrete. The Other needs to be included in a dialogical imagination, which “internalizes the other, alterity, in a non-imperial and non-obliterating way, in order to reconstitute itself” (p. 254). Engagement with a dialogical imagination can potentially give rise to a cosmopolitan vision and open up the spaces of mutual transformation. Indeed, appreciation for linguistic and cultural differences wasn’t innate for Joshua or his fellow classmates. They confessed in their reflections that they had held biases similar to those of the disgruntled first-year student. They arrived at their new attitudes by reading, researching, and writing in and about diverse styles of English, focusing on the multilingual and multicultural relations entangled in literature, popular culture, and everyday life. Some of them openly enacted these relations in their scholarship, creative writing, and interpersonal communications. Collectively, they constructed a “dwelling place” where they pondered how they could use language ethically across local-global contexts. They came to understand that one may use Cosmopolitan English (CE) to construct identities and voices along national, racial, ethnic, gender, and class lines, but CE itself always defies being pigeonholed along those lines. They came to view CE as consisting of linguistic choices that are deeply rooted in language users’ sociopolitical and economic realities. Certainly, their individual experiences with the linguistic and cultural Other in other courses and off-campus settings might have also affected their transformations (see Staples, Kang, & Wittnerb, 2013).

In contrast, the first-year student, refusing to accept unfamiliar styles of CE and the stories behind them, missed opportunities to sample other English styles, other languages, and other cultural meanings, and in the long run he or she probably missed valuable opportunities for transliteracy and self-transformation. Certainly, the student’s negativity towards my multiculturalist pedagogy has a positive side: it forced me to examine my teaching and to move away from a bounded notion of nation, culture, and language.

Studying literacy practices in schools and beyond can contribute to our understanding of cosmopolitanism. First, literacy activities in higher education depicted in this book can be viewed as a form of “banal cosmopolitanism”

(Beck, 2006), deeply grounded in individuals' everyday lives. However, this banal form has been almost neglected in studies of cosmopolitanism (Holton, 2009). As international students increasingly alter traditional higher education scenes in many nations, students' border-crossing activities warrant more attention in studies of cosmopolitanism. Second, as this book has illustrated, school literacy can provide an important site for examining dialogical imagination, which has the potential to give rise to a cosmopolitan vision and spaces of mutual transformation. Third, a neoliberal perspective may view literacy skills, including fluency with Standard English, as cultural capital of high market value, as universal, as potentially globalizing, but, following the tradition of New Literacy studies (Street, 2003), this book has viewed literacy practices as always taking place in sociopolitical contexts, thus begging for a materialistic and postcolonial angle to understand literacy skills as universal.

Joshua's experience, as was the case with the other students depicted in the book, admittedly was situated in specific locales and had its own sociocultural and economic characteristics. The students all had backgrounds in the humanities and had proficiencies in multiple languages. Most of them came from middle-class families and could afford a notoriously expensive American higher education. And some pedagogical scenarios were intensely mediated by a teacher who navigated among languages and among cultures and who shared with the students a similar socioeconomic status. The Japanese and Chinese online participants as well as the three creative writers examined in this book also developed their CE styles in certain national locations with certain cultural and economic capital. How far can transliteracy go in transforming individuals with different sets of sociocultural and economic characteristics? This is a question yet to be answered. Nevertheless, while acknowledging these ever-present contextual realities, we can still arrive at an expansive understanding of English and literacy education in the United States and beyond.

To be sure, CE has fundamentally challenged the conventional wisdom about English. Instead of a discrete symbol system anchored in nation or ethnicity, CE refers to English in situated practice, often with notable linguistic differences among interlocutors. These differences only become noticeable when one crosses boundaries of nation, region, class, ethnicity, or gender. Differences can be observed in both speech and writing, as reflected in one's pronunciation, vocabulary, syntax, and/or discourse structures. By emphasizing the fact that everyone speaks and writes with a difference, the notion of CE sets English in motion instead of treating it as an abstract, static system. More importantly, the notion draws our attention to the preexisting sociocultural relations and language ideologies that speakers and writers bring to bear in their meaning making. As their communication unfolds, these relations will evolve, expand, entangle, and mutate, giving rise to new relations, identities, voices, and ultimately a new culture. At the same time, the speakers' and writers' language ideologies may change as well. It is for their boundary-crossing potential that accented styles of English become cosmopolitan.

A situated practice perspective opens up an array of issues in the study of English-mediated meaning making in this globalized world. When we study English use in specific communities, it may be politically advantageous to identify and associate discrete symbol systems with those communities; however, it is idealistic, reductive, and simplistic when attempting a holistic understanding of language use. Such an attempt may miss the diverse linguistic differences within a community because they are often viewed as negligible deviants of the system. Differences are central to understanding English in situated practice because they index the speakers' linguistic and sociocultural relations. How do linguistic and sociocultural rules operate in a speaker's repertoire? How do users of English construct flexible identities by configuring and reconfiguring existing linguistic and sociocultural relations? How do users of English construct ethos using accent as a resource? How do students use accented styles of English to scaffold their learning? How will accents bring people together or drive them apart? These are critical questions of lasting significance for writing studies.

As CE is already the norm, English-medium higher education would be better off acknowledging CE and then availing itself of it. As students and teachers come from both within and outside the nation, CE is used in all aspects of schooling. While schools typically champion a different norm, that is, Standard English, learning takes place via the broader styles of CE. Therefore, schools should train students to develop skills in negotiating meanings across language differences, skills that are critical for collaborative learning. Both subject and language teachers can publicly recognize the positive roles of CE in the learning process, especially its ability to ease the anxiety of students who view their English styles and their cultures with self-doubt. Further, these teachers can exploit the multilingual and multicultural resources that invariably accompany students' English styles. These resources can be mobilized in the design of reading and writing tasks and group activities. Based on local educational traditions and resources, teachers must develop strategies to facilitate the movement of local meanings and values across literacy regimes so that students' literacy practices can effectively lead to subject learning and strong self-esteem. Accordingly, academic programs may need to adjust their curricular objectives, course expectations, and learning outcomes to accommodate students' diverse styles of English.

In literacy education, linguistic difference points to new responsibilities for language teachers. Conventionally, English teachers are supposed to help students, regardless of linguistic and cultural backgrounds, acquire reading and writing abilities in the idealized, mystified, and equally accented Standard English. With its accumulated cultural capital, this CE style certainly needs to be valued and taught in the curriculum. But we also need to be careful lest the linguistic and cultural relations accompanying students' CE styles be shut out of their school literacy practice and subject learning. Teachers can draw students' attention to their CE styles, not only to identify them but also to turn the students into adept listeners and readers of a broad spectrum of CE styles. Ultimately, students need to develop sensitivity to, appreciation of, and skills to negotiate with linguistic differences. In addition, teachers can design reading and writing activities to capitalize on students' available linguistic resources. In the writing classroom, for example, students should get the chance to hear, speak, read, and write in English and other languages. By marginalizing certain styles of English and other languages, a teacher runs the risk of occluding other ways of knowing and meaning making, ending up crippling their students' education.

Championing CE in schools will naturally lead to conflicts with existing assessment standards. As part of the state apparatus, schools are guards of national languages, holding as their responsibility the dissemination and maintenance of certain language rules. In English-dominant nations, such as the United States, language assessment rubrics tend to embody the rules of Standard English (Balester, 2012). In nations where languages other than English dominate, English is being taught just like a national language with rigid rules adopted from Anglophone nations. CE intends to challenge such nation-anchored language standards. While still valuing the cultural capital of Standard English, we need to recognize other populations' cultural and personal investments in other CE styles. We can reform the assessment standards by including diverse styles of CE on tests and focusing on students' ability to negotiate with these styles across contexts in constructing meanings (Flores & Schissel, 2014). To support this radical change, we can diversify the discourses and the genres that students interact with in the classroom, providing them exposure to CE and its ten thousand faces (Ryan & Barton, 2014).

The ultimate promise of CE is to correct the injustice incurred through conventional social classifications perpetuated by bigotry, regionalism, slavery, colonialism, nationalism, and now fast capitalism. For instance, the artificial, loose division between "native" and "non-native speakers" was historically established for various purposes, creating indelible psychological and social consequences for all. Using CE as a heuristic, we can educate our students about linguistic difference being the universal norm. CE does not promote relativism or ignore existing power relations and socioeconomic inequality. Instead, it calls our attention to local histories and cultural practices that give rise to linguistic and socioeconomic differences. Together with students, we can further explore the rich histories, experiences, and narratives behind these differences. Engaging students in such explorations through research, discussion, writing, and reflection, we can *hope* to foster in them a better appreciation for and understanding of the Other, who speaks with an accent. Joshua's reflection testifies to the possibility of such transformations in our students.

Joshua's reflection also engages a useful dialectics of CE. In previous chapters I have demonstrated the vitality of CE in various contexts in an attempt to collapse artificial but rigid boundaries between nations and between communities. Joshua drew on these boundaries to offer his nuanced reading of certain CE styles. He evokes communities ("their culture"), nations ("the Chinese students"), and nativity ("native speaker" and "non-native speaker") as anchors for his literate practice, and so did I in many places of the book. In doing so, he reminded me that these artificial boundaries are realities that we have to work with, for, and sometimes against. I believe this is the true meaning of CE. In the book, the Japanese, Chinese, Indian, and American writers of English constantly struggled with these boundaries. It is this constant struggle, this push and pull, and the tensions therein generated that have afforded meanings to CE. It is to search for these meanings in and beyond pedagogical contexts that we in writing studies have to take the cosmopolitan turn.

Notes

References

Index

Notes

1. Cosmopolitanism and the Future of Writing Studies

1. American undergraduates' negative responses to international instructors are often reported in local and national media; thus, my experience is not unique here. However, studies have revealed that students' negative responses are derived from more than just foreign accents (Hill, 1999; Rubin & Smith, 1990; Rubin, 1992; Samuel & Wane, 2005). For example, after studying American undergraduates' attitudes toward international teaching assistants, Rubin and Smith (1990) found that factors like instructor ethnicity and lecture topic, extraneous to the teaching assistants' speaking proficiency, tended to be more potent determinants of undergraduate attitudes and comprehension. Further, when students perceive high levels of a foreign accent, they tend to judge speakers to be poor teachers. Therefore, while the student in my class expressly complained about foreignness, his or her discontent could also be caused by other factors, such as the requirements of the first-year writing course.
2. Some may wonder what the rest of the class thought of my teaching. On a 1 to 7 scale, the class of eighteen students rated the overall quality of the course as 5.56 and that of the instructor as 5.50, suggesting an above-average teaching performance.
3. For example, Held (2010) summarized a set of cosmopolitan principles based on values articulated by previous scholars. According to Held, these principles can be universally shared, and they form the basis for the protection and nurturing of each individual's equal significance in the realm of human morality. These are the principles of "(i) equal worth and dignity; (ii) active agency; (iii) personal responsibility and accountability; (iv) consent; (v) collective decision-making about public matters through voting procedures; (vi) inclusiveness and subsidiarity; (vii) avoidance of serious harm; and (viii) sustainability" (p. 69).
4. Jenkins' (2011) definition is arguably the most influential one in ELF studies. ELF scholars defined ELF in markedly different ways over the last three

decades. They moved from seeing it as a linguistic system arising from interactions between non-native speakers (Firth, 1996; House, 1999) to seeing it as situated language practice among speakers with different first languages (Jenkins, 2006; Seidlhofer, 2011). They moved from seeing it as language practice (Pennycook, 2007) to seeing it as multimodal communication (Matsumoto, 2015). They also moved from excluding (Mauranen, 2012) to including English learners' use of English (Matsumoto, 2015) in studies of ELF.

5. Instead of viewing code as a discrete symbol system or a style of language use, Gilyard (1997, 2011) emphasized that it is a language user's ability to decide which dialect or style to adopt in a particular situation. To provide this understanding of code, he cited a definition originally from Michael Gregory and Susanne Carroll (1978): "Code controls the verbal repertoire of the individual, his capacity to encode meaning lexically and grammatically. Code therefore determines which options will be selected as appropriate to the given situation" (cited in Gilyard, p. 116). As the majority of scholars discussing code-switching in writing studies have viewed code as a discrete system or a style of language use, I go along with Gilyard in critiquing this discrete and static view of language.

2. Arts of the Dwelling Place

1. Also compare with Code's (1995) notion of "rhetorical spaces," which she defines as "fictive but not fanciful or fixed locations, whose (tacit, rarely spoken) territorial imperatives structure and limit the kinds of utterances that can be voiced within them within a reasonable expectation of [. . .] being heard, understood, taken seriously" (pp. ix–x). While both contact zone and rhetorical spaces seem to emphasize spaces and locations with relatively fixed power structures, dwelling places highlight individuals negotiating with power structures using a broad range of resources for forging new and often contingent values for co-presence.

3. Linguistic Creativity in the Diaspora

1. I tallied the numbers of Chinese college graduates from 1980 to 2008 using information provided by both the Department of Comprehensive Statistics of the National Statistics Bureau and the Department of Education of the People's Republic of China. During the twenty-nine years, China produced 30.4295 million college graduates.
2. In some instances, when a Chinese person calls out for "God," he or she simply may have translated it from the Chinese expression *tian na* 天哪

or *laotianye a* 老天爷啊, literally meaning "Good Heavens!" and "Good Lord!" In traditional Han thinking, heaven is perceived, on the one hand, as the supreme force that rules the universe and, on the other, as the spiritual entity to whom people bring their cares and worries. Therefore, whether "God" means the Christian deity or "heaven" in traditional Han thinking needs to be determined from the communicative context. With the confluences of Christianity and traditional Han thinking over the last several centuries, to separate these different meanings of "God" in discourses of contemporary China can be difficult.

3. When studying a variety of English, scholars typically seek out the unique sounds, expressions, and grammatical structures that define the variety as a linguistic system. Nevertheless, some of these scholars have often found statistically low and varied frequencies of these features in a variety. For example, when studying English spoken by undergraduate and graduate students in China, Xu (2010) identified the following syntactic and grammatical features of Chinese English, although their frequency of occurrence across the two groups was statistically low: adjacent default tense (1.6 percent, 1.7 percent), null-subject/object utterance (1.4 percent, 0.8 percent), co-occurrence of connective pairs (0.8 percent, 1.0 percent), subject pronoun copying (0.2 percent, 1.1 percent), yes-no response (0.5 percent, 0.7 percent), topic-comment (0.2 percent, 0.6 percent), unmarked object-subject-verb (0.3 percent, 0.2 percent), and inversion in subordinate finite *wh*-clauses (0.2 percent, 0.2 percent) (p. 69). Similarly, a statistically low frequency of occurrence for most of the linguistic features that define Philippine English was also found by Bautista (2008). Even in certain varieties where a higher frequency of occurrence for some linguistic features has been found, such as with AAVE, the frequency of a particular feature can vary across time, regions, and social classes (Rickford & Rickford, 2000). With the findings of these studies in consideration, it is questionable to view China English as a system with stable lexical, syntactic, and pragmatic features.

4. Transliterate Creativity in the Literature of Globalization

1. In discussing Kachru's theory of bilingual creativity, I have chosen to focus on the chapter "The Bilingual's Creativity and Contact Literatures" in Kachru (1990), where he has offered the fullest rendering on this topic.
2. In an interview with BBC China, Guo discussed her techniques for crafting "broken English" (Escolme, 2008). She says, "It's a very natural thing for me to do because I don't even need to use techniques, because I arrived in

this country from China only four years ago. . . . It's a very natural method. Consciously and unconsciously I use my own broken English to write."

3. On the back cover of the novel, a *Philadelphia Inquirer* review states, "A fascinating novel that may well find a place in the African American literary canon." In an interview Sapphire explained why in earlier years she was reluctant to adapt her novel into a motion picture. She worried that, instead of representing African American women respectfully, a movie would continue to perpetuate stereotypes of her people (Couric, 2009).
4. The literacy narrative approach described in the novel has also been inspiring in various teacher education and literacy programs in the United States (Alexander, 2006; Clark & Medina, 2000; Dill & Stafford, 1997; Polleck, 2011; Trier, 2007). For example, at Ohio State University, Clark and Medina (2000) designed literacy narrative reading and writing activities to shape preservice teachers' understanding of literacy pedagogy and multiculturalism. Polleck (2011) detailed how, in a book club, twelve urban Latina and African American females used adolescent literature, including literacy narratives, to understand their lives, communities, and families.

5. Crossing Literacy Regimes

1. Marston, Jones, and Woodward (2005) have offered the most systematic critique of scale as semiotized space-time. First, they argue that there tends to be conflation and confusion between scale as extensiveness on the horizontal plane and scale as a vertically imagined hierarchical ordering of space. Second, they see scale as deeply entangled with the micro-macro distinction in social analysis and its related binaries, such as local/global, agency/structure, static/dynamic, and concrete/abstract. Third, once scaled levels are taken as a given, they suggest that researchers often assume the hierarchy in advance or obey conventions of scale as a priori. Finally, they also view hierarchical scale as implying a transcendent position for the researcher. To offset these potentially problematic uses of the concept, Moore (2008) proposes that research projects focus on the scalar dimensions of practices rather than practices occurring at different scales. Further, Kell (2013) suggests that "claims related to verticality and power in relation to scale should come from the analysis of empirical data" rather than be presupposed (p. 9). Responding to these and other critiques of scale, Blommaert, Westinen, and Leppänen (2015) decided to take the notion of sociolinguistic scales out of "the rather unproductive complex of

spatial metaphorization" (p. 126) and to understand it as "spatiotemporal scope of understandability" for different signs in communication (p. 123).

2. The names of the professors in this chapter are aliases.
3. Over the last decade, numerous initiatives have been implemented in Asian, European, and North American (Mexican) universities to help content teachers transition from local languages to English in their instruction (Craig, Poe, & Rojas, 2010; Fortanet-Gómez, 2011; Harbord, 2010; Harder, 2009; Kam & Meinema, 2005; Poe & Craig, 2011; Wilkinson, 2004). In initiatives that focused on writing across the curriculum, subject-area faculty and language faculty typically worked together to identify and deal with issues in English-medium instruction. For example, before implementing the Bologna Process (a set of reforms intended to harmonize higher education in Europe), a team consisting of content and language teachers at Universitat Jaume I of Spain discussed the results of university-wide surveys on students' needs for courses delivered in English and on disciplinary differences in modes of teaching and pedagogical strategies (Fortanet-Gómez, 2011). At the University of Groningen, the Netherlands, the Expert Centre on Language, Communication and Education designed workshops in close cooperation with faculty members. In these workshops a course schedule was proposed in which several elements of teaching writing were integrated: choosing a specific disciplinary genre as the writing task, planning the writing process within a disciplinary module, selecting which elements of the writing process to support explicitly, and supporting writing in groups (Kam & Meinema, 2005).
4. In a corpus of IELTS essay tasks that they examined, Coffin and Hewings (2004) found that test takers from China and Greece extensively used pronouns (e.g., "I," "my") in a sentence initial position, and they showed a propensity for extrapositional overstatement (e.g., "It must be emphasized . . . ," "It is a fact that . . . ," "It is pointless . . ."). They also used hearsay rather than expert voices through direct or indirect quotations (e.g., "everyone claims," "some people think").

8. Crossing Borders in Teacher Development

1. Teachers trained in applied linguistics and TESOL programs are an exception. In general, these teachers have rich experiences interacting with diverse multilingual students but very little knowledge of writing. It is writing issues, not multilingual issues, that they must learn about through orientations, guest speakers, and textbooks.

References

Aaltonen, S. (2006). Exploring corporate websites as a setting for ELF research: The case of Ostrobothnian export companies. *Nordic Journal of English Studies, 5*(2), 189–220.

Achebe, C. (1994). *Things fall apart.* New York: Anchor Books.

Agutter, P. S. (1979). Precision testing: A method for improving students' written work in biochemistry. *Journal of Biological Education, 13*(1), 25–31.

Ahmad, D. (2007). *Rotten English: A literary anthology.* New York: W. W. Norton.

Albakry, M., & Hancock, P. H. (2008). Code switching in Ahdaf Soueif's *The Map of Love. Language and Literature, 17*(3), 221–234.

Alemán, J. (2008). Redefining national literatures in the Americas. *ADE Bulletin, 126,* 38–42.

Alexander, J. (2008). *Literacy, sexuality, pedagogy: Theory and practice for composition studies.* Logan: Utah State University.

Alexander, K. (2006). *Implicit response: Instructor values and social class in the literacy narrative assignment.* Unpublished doctoral dissertation, University of Louisville, Louisville.

Anderson, P., Bergman, B., Bradley, L., Gustafsson, M., & Matzke, A. (2010). Peer reviewing across the Atlantic: Patterns and trends in L1 and L2 comments made in an asynchronous online collaborative learning exchange between technical communication students in Sweden and in the United States. *Journal of Business and Technical Communication, 24*(3), 296–322.

Annbaby (1999). 上海冬天 [Winter of Shanghai]. Retrieved September 1, 2009, from http://www.moon-soft.com/art/annbaby/winter.htm.

Anzaldúa, G. (1987). *Borderlands/La frontera: The new mestiza.* San Francisco: Aunt Lute Books.

——. (2007). *Borderlands/La frontera: The new mestiza* (3rd ed.). San Francisco: Aunt Lute Books.

Anzaldúa, G., & Keating, A. (2000). *Interviews/Entrevistas.* New York: Routledge.

——. (Eds.). (2002). *This bridge we call home: Radical visions for transformation.* New York: Routledge.

Anzaldúa, G., & Moraga, C. (Eds.). (1984). *This bridge called my back: Writings by radical women of color.* New York: Kitchen Table/Women of Color Press.

Appadurai, A. (1996). *Modernity at large.* Minneapolis: University of Minnesota Press.

Appiah, K. (2007). *Cosmopolitanism: Ethics in a world of strangers.* New York: W. W. Norton.

Aristotle. (2007). *On rhetoric: A theory of civic discourse* (2nd ed.). New York: Oxford University Press.

Artiano, E. (2015). *Vexed tongues: A translingual approach to eighteenth and nineteenth century Atlantic literature.* Unpublished doctoral dissertation, Northeastern University, Boston.

Artze-Vega, I., Doud, E. I., & Torres, B. (2007). Más allá del inglés: A bilingual approach to college composition. In C. Kirklighter, D. Cárdenas, & S. W. Murphy (Eds.), *Teaching writing with Latino/a students* (pp. 99–117). Albany, NY: SUNY Press.

Ashcroft, B. (2009). *Caliban's voice: The transformation of English in post-colonial literatures.* New York: Routledge.

Atkinson, D. (2004). Contrasting rhetorics/contrasting cultures: Why contrastive rhetoric needs a better conceptualization of culture. *Journal of English for Academic Purposes,* 3(4), 277–289.

Atkinson, D., & Ramanathan, V. (1995). Cultures of writing: An ethnographic comparison of L1 and L2 university writing/language programs. *TESOL Quarterly,* 29(3), 539–568.

Atkinson, Y. (2000). Language that bears witness: The black English oral tradition in the works of Toni Morrison. In M. C. Conner (Ed.), *The aesthetics of Toni Morrison: Speaking the unspeakable* (pp. 12–29). Jackson: University Press of Mississippi.

Bailey, K. M. (1984). The "foreign TA problem." In K. M. Bailey, F. Pialorsi, & J. Zukowski-Faust (Eds.), *Foreign teaching assistants in U.S. universities* (pp. 3–15). Washington, DC: National Association for Foreign Student Affairs.

Balester, V. (2012). How writing rubrics fail: Towards a multicultural model. In A. B. Inoue & M. Poe (Eds.), *Race and writing assessment* (pp. 63–77). New York: Peter Lang.

Ball, A., & Lardner, T. (1998). Dispositions toward language: Teacher constructs of knowledge and the Ann Arbor Black English case. *College Composition and Communication,* 48(4), 469–485.

———. (2005). *African American literacies unleashed: Vernacular English and the composition classroom.* Carbondale: Southern Illinois University Press.

Ball, A. F., & Muhammad, R. J. (2003). Language diversity in teacher education and in the classroom. In G. Smitherman & V. Villanueva (Eds.), *Language diversity in the classroom: From intention to practice* (pp. 76–88). Carbondale: Southern Illinois University Press.

Bardovi-Harlig, K. (2006). Interlanguage development: Main routes and individual paths. *AILA Review, 19*(1), 69–82.

Baron, N. S. (2008). *Always on: Language in an online and mobile world.* Oxford, England: Oxford University Press.

Barron, A. (2012). Interlanguage pragmatics: From use to acquisition to second language pedagogy. *Language Teaching, 45*(1), 44–63.

Bauer, D. M. (1990). The other "F" word: The feminist in the classroom. *College English, 52*(4), 385–396.

Bautista, M. L. (2008). Investigating the grammatical features of Philippine English. In M. L. Bautista & K. Bolton (Eds.), *Philippine English: Linguistic and literary perspectives* (pp. 201–218). Hong Kong: Hong Kong University Press.

Bautista, M. L., & Bolton, K. (Eds.). (2008). *Philippine English: Linguistic and literary perspectives.* Hong Kong: Hong Kong University Press.

Bawarshi, A. S., & Reiff, M. J. (2010). *Genre: An introduction to history, theory, research, and pedagogy.* West Lafayette, IN: Parlor Press.

Beard, G., & Hutchins, H. (2002). *The adventures of super diaper baby.* New York: Blue Sky Press.

Beaujour, E. (1989). *Alien tongues: Bilingual Russian writers of the "first" emigration.* Ithaca, NY: Cornell University Press.

Beck, U. (2006). *Cosmopolitan vision.* Cambridge, England: Polity Press.

Becker, R. (2013). The sounds of Yiddish. *American Poetry Review, 42*(5), 15.

Belcher, D., & Braine, G. (Eds.). (1995). *Academic writing in a second language: Essays on research and pedagogy.* Norwood, NJ: Ablex.

Berkenkotter, C., & Huckin, T. N. (1993). Rethinking genre from a sociocognitive perspective. *Written Communication, 10*(4), 475–509.

Berns, M. (1988). The cultural and linguistic context of English in West Germany. *World Englishes,* 7(1), 37–49.

——. (1995). English in the European Union. *English Today, 11,* 3–11.

Besemeres, M. (2002). *Translating one's self.* Oxford, England: Peter Lang.

Bhabha, H. (2004). *The location of culture.* New York: Routledge.

Bhatia, V. K. (1993). *Analysing genre: Language use in professional settings.* New York: Pearson.

Bizzell, P. (1994). "Contact zone" and English studies. *College English,* 65(2), 63–69.

Blackledge, A., & Creese, A. (2010). *Multilingualism: A critical perspective.* New York: Continuum.

Blommaert, J. (2007). Sociolinguistic scales. *Intercultural Pragmatics*, *4*(1), 1–19.

———. (2008). *Grassroots literacy: Writing, identity and voice in Central Africa.* New York: Routledge.

———. (2010). *The sociolinguistics of globalization.* Cambridge, England: Cambridge University Press.

Blommaert, J., Collins, J., & Slembrouck, S. (2005). Spaces of multilingualism. *Language & Communication, 25*, 197–216.

Blommaert, J., Westinen, E., & Leppänen, S. (2015). Further notes on sociolinguistic scales. *Intercultural Pragmatics, 12*(1), 119–127.

Bolton, K. (Ed.). (2002). *Hong Kong English: Autonomy and creativity.* Hong Kong: Hong Kong University Press.

———. (2006). *Chinese Englishes: A sociolinguistic history.* Cambridge, England: Cambridge University Press.

Borg, S., & Sanchez, H. S. (2015). Key issues in doing and supporting language teacher research. In S. Borg & H. S. Sanchez (Eds.), *International perspectives on teacher research* (pp. 1–13). New York: Palgrave Macmillan.

Brandt, D. (2001). *Literacy in American lives.* New York: Cambridge University Press.

Brandt, D., & Clinton, K. (2002). Limits of the local: Expanding perspectives on literacy as a social practice. *Journal of Literacy Research, 34*(3), 337–356.

Brodkey, L. (1989). On the subjects of class and gender in "the literacy letters." *College English, 51*(2), 125–141.

Brown, G. W., & Held, D. (2010). *The cosmopolitanism reader.* Cambridge, England: Polity Press.

Brown, K., & Peterson, J. (1997). Exploring conceptual frameworks: Framing a World Englishes paradigm. In L. E. Smith & M. L. Forman (Eds.), *World Englishes 2000* (pp. 32–47). Honolulu: University of Hawaii Press.

Bruce, S., & Rafoth, B. (Eds.). (2004). *ESL writers: A guide for writing center tutors.* Portsmouth, NH: Boynton/Cook.

Bruna, D. (1984). *Miffy's dreams.* New York: Price Stern Sloan.

Bublitz, W., Lenk, U., & Ventola, E. (1999). *Coherence in spoken and written discourse: How to create it and how to describe it.* Philadelphia: John Benjamins.

Cabrera, N. L. (2009). *Invisible racism: Male, hegemonic whiteness in higher education.* Unpublished doctoral dissertation, University of California, Los Angeles.

———. (2014). Exposing whiteness in higher education: White male college students minimizing racism, claiming victimization, and recreating white supremacy. *Race, Ethnicity and Education, 17*(1), 30–55.

Callahan, L. (2003). The role of register in Spanish-English codeswitching in prose. *The Bilingual Review, 27*(1), 12–25.

Campbell, K. E. (2005). *"Getting our groove on": Rhetoric, language, and literacy for the hip hop generation.* Detroit, MI: Wayne State University.

Canagarajah, S. (1997). Safe houses in the contact zone: Coping strategies of African-American students in the academy. *College Composition and Communication, 48*(2), 173–196.

———. (2004). *Critical academic writing and multilingual students.* Ann Arbor: University of Michigan Press.

———. (2006). The place of world Englishes in composition: Pluralization continued. *College Composition and Communication, 57*(4), 586–619.

———. (2007). The ecology of global English. *International Multilingual Research Journal, 1*(2), 89–100.

———. (2009a). The plurilingual tradition and the English language in South Asia. *AILA Review, 22*(1), 5–22.

———. (2009b). Multilingual strategies of negotiating English: From conversation to writing. *JAC, 29,* 17–48.

———. (2011). Codemeshing in academic writing: Identifying teachable strategies of translanguaging. *Modern Language Journal, 95*(3), 401–417.

———. (2013a). *Translingual practices: Global Englishes and cosmopolitan relations.* New York: Routledge.

———. (Ed.). (2013b). *Literacy as translingual practice: Between communities and classrooms.* New York: Routledge.

———. (2015). Suresh Canagarajah on translingualism: A four part interview, part 1. Transnational Writing, a blog. Retrieved from https://transnationalwriting.wordpress.com/2015/08/04/suresh-canagarajah-on-translingualism-a-four-part-interview-part-i/.

———. (2016). Translingual writing and teacher development in composition. *College English, 78*(3), 265–273.

Carrell, P. L. (1982). Cohesion is not coherence. *TESOL Quarterly, 16*(4), 479–488.

Casanave, C. P. (1998). Transitions: The balancing act of bilingual academics. *Journal of Second Language Writing, 7*(2), 175–203.

———. (2002). *Writing games: Multicultural case studies of academic literacy practices in higher education.* Mahwah, NJ: Lawrence Erlbaum.

CCCC (Conference on College Composition and Communication). (1998). CCCC statement on Ebonics. Retrieved from http://www.ncte.org/cccc/resources/positions/ebonics.

———. (n.d.). Position statements. Retrieved from http://www.ncte.org/cccc/resources/positions.

CCCC Committee on Second Language Writing (2009). CCCC statement on second language writing and writers. Retrieved from http://www.ncte.org/cccc/resources/positions/secondlangwriting.

Chew, K.-S. (2005). An investigation of the English language skills used by new entrants in banks in Hong Kong. *English for Specific Purposes, 24,* 423–435.

Ch'ien, E. N.-M. (2004). *Weird English.* Cambridge, MA: Harvard University Press.

Cho, S. (2010). Academic biliteracy challenges: Korean scholars in the United States. *Journal of Second Language Writing, 19*(2), 82–94.

Chval, K. B., & Khisty, L. L. (2009). Bilingual Latino students, writing, and mathematics: A case study of successful teaching and learning. In R. Barwell (Ed.), *Multilingualism in mathematics classrooms: Global perspectives* (pp. 128–144). Bristol, England: Multilingual Matters.

Cintron, R. (1997). *Angels' town: Chero ways, gang life, and rhetorics of the everyday.* Boston: Beacon Press.

Cisneros, J. D., & Nakayama, T. K. (2015). New media, old racisms: Twitter, Miss America, and cultural logics of race. *Journal of International and Intercultural Communication, 8*(2), 108–127.

Clark, C., & Medina, C. (2000). How reading and writing literacy narratives affect preservice teachers' understandings of literacy, pedagogy, and multiculturalism. *Journal of Teacher Education, 51*(1), 63–76.

Clifford, J. (1992). Traveling cultures. In L. Grossberg, C. Nelson, & P. Treichler (Eds.), *Cultural studies* (pp. 96–116). London: Routledge.

———. (1994). Diasporas. *Cultural Anthropology, 9,* 302–338.

Code, L. (1995). *Rhetorical spaces: Essays on gendered locations.* New York: Modern Language Association.

Coffin, C., & Hewings, A. (2004). IELTS as preparation for tertiary writing: Distinctive interpersonal and textual strategies. In L. J. Ravelli & R. A. Ellis (Eds.), *Analysing academic writing: Contextualized frameworks* (pp. 153–171). London: Continuum.

Coleman, J. A. (2006). English-medium teaching in European higher education. *Language Teaching, 39,* 1–14.

Committee on CCCC Language Statement. (1974). Students' right to their own language. *College Composition and Communication*, *25*(3), 1–18.

Confucius. (1989). *The analects of Confucius*. New York: Vintage.

Connal, L. R. (2004). Hybridity: A lens for understanding Mestizo/a writers. In A. Lunsford & L. Ouzgane (Eds.), *Crossing borderlands: Composition and postcolonial studies* (pp. 199–217). Pittsburgh, PA: University of Pittsburgh Press.

Connor, U. (1996). *Contrastive rhetoric: Cross-cultural aspects of second-language writing*. New York: Cambridge University Press.

——. (2008). Mapping multidimensional aspects of research: Reaching to intercultural rhetoric. In U. Connor, E. Nagelhout, & W. V. Rozycki (Eds.), *Contrastive rhetoric: Reaching to intercultural rhetoric* (pp. 299–315). Amsterdam: John Benjamins.

Connor, U., Davis, K., Rycker, T., Phillips, E., & Verckens, J. (1997). An international course in international business writing: Belgium, Finland, and the United States. *Business Communication Quarterly*, *60*(4), 63–74.

Connors, R. (1981). The rise and fall of the modes of discourse. *College Communication and Composition*, *32*, 444–455.

Cook, V. J. (1997). Monolingual bias in second language acquisition research. *Revista Canaria de Estudio Ingleses*, *34*, 35–50.

——. (1999). Going beyond the native speaker in language teaching. *TESOL Quarterly*, *33*(2), 185–209.

——. (Ed.). (2002). *Portraits of the L2 users*. Clevedon, England: Multilingual Matters.

——. (Ed.). (2004). *Effects of the second language on the first*. Clevedon, England: Multilingual Matters.

Cooper, J. (2004). Queering the contact zone. *JAC*, *24*(1), 23–45.

Cortes-Conde, F., & Boxer, D. (2002). Bilingual word-play in literary discourse: The creation of relational identity. *Language and Literature*, *11*(2), 137–151.

Couric, K. (2009, October 27). Author Sapphire talks about the new movie *Precious* inspired by her novel *Push*. CBS News. Retrieved January 1, 2012, from http://www.cbsnews.com/video/watch/?id=5426254n&tag=cbsnewsSectionsArea.69.

Coxhead, A., & Byrd, P. (2007). Preparing writing teachers to teach the vocabulary and grammar of academic prose. *Journal of Second Language Writing*, *16*(3), 129–147.

Craig, J. L. (2014). Teaching writing in a globally networked learning environment (GNLE): Diverse students at a distance. In T. M. Zawacki & M. Cox (Eds.), *WAC and second-language writers: Research towards linguistically and culturally inclusive programs and practices* (pp. 369–386). Anderson, SC: Parlor Press.

Craig, J., Poe, M., & Rojas, M. G. (2010). Professional communication education in a global context: A collaboration between the Massachusetts Institute of Technology, Instituto Tecnológico y de Estudios Superiores de Monterrey, Mexico, and Universidad de Quintana Roo, Mexico. *Journal of Business and Technical Communication, 24*(3), 267–295.

Crank, V. (2012). From high school to college: Developing writing skills in the disciplines. *WAC Journal, 23*(1), 49–63.

Crookes, G. (1993). Action research for second language teachers: Going beyond teacher research. *Applied Linguistics, 14*(2), 130–144.

Crowley, S. (1998). *Composition in the university: Historical and polemical essays.* Pittsburgh, PA: University of Pittsburgh Press.

Cruz, P. A. T. (2011). Code-switching, resistance, and reflection: Language awareness through Philippine literature in English. *Asian Englishes, 14*(2), 22–39.

Crystal, D. (2003). *English as a global language* (2nd ed.). Cambridge, England: Cambridge University Press.

———. (2008). *Txtng: The Gr8 Db8.* New York: Oxford University Press.

Cuccioletta, D. (2001). Multiculturalism or transculturalism: Towards a cosmopolitan citizenship. *London Journal of Canadian Studies, 17,* 1–11.

Dalke, A. F. (2002). *Teaching to learn/learning to teach: Meditations on the classroom.* New York: Peter Lang.

Davies, A. (2003). *The native speaker: Myth and reality.* Clevedon, England: Multilingual Matters.

———. (2013). *Native speakers and native users: Loss and gain.* New York: Cambridge University Press.

DeBose, C. (1992). Codeswitching: Black English and Standard English in the African-American linguistic repertoire. In C. Eastman (Ed.), *Codeswitching* (pp. 157–167). Clevedon, England: Multilingual Matters.

DeFrancis, J. (1984). *The Chinese language: Fact and fantasy.* Honolulu: University of Hawaii Press.

DeGenaro, W. (2014). "Where did all the white girls come from?": Difference and critical empathy in and out of the service learning classroom. *Open Words: Access and English Studies, 8*(1), 49–64.

Department of Comprehensive Statistics of the National Bureau of Statistics, PRC. (2005). *Xin Zhongguo Wushiwu Nian Tongji Ziliao Huibian* [China compendium of statistics, 1949–2005]. Beijing: Zhongguo tongji chubanshe.

Department of Education, PRC. (2010). tongji gongbao [educational statistics bulletin]. Retrieved June 1, 2010, from http://www.moe.edu.cn/edoas/website18/level2.jsp?tablename=1068.

DiGrazia, J., & Boucher, M. (2005). Writing InQueeries: Bodies, queer theory, and experimental writing class. *Composition Studies, 33*(2), 25–44.

Dill, V., & Stafford, D. (1997). Push: Teaching the children of neglect. *The Educational Forum, 61*(1), 36–45.

Dillard, J. L. (1973). *Black English*. New York: Vantage.

Dingo, R. A. (2012). *Networking arguments: Rhetoric, transnational feminism, and public policy writing*. Pittsburgh, PA: University of Pittsburgh Press.

———. (2013). Networking the macro and micro: Towards transnational literacy practices. *JAC, 33*(3–4), 529–552.

Donahue, C. (2009). "Internationalization" and composition studies: Reorienting the discourse. *College Composition and Communication, 61*(2), 212–243.

Drury, H. (2001). Short answers in first-year undergraduate science writing: What kind of genres are they? In M. Hewings (Ed.), *Academic writing in context: Implications and applications* (pp. 104–121). Birmingham, England: University of Birmingham Press.

Du Bois, W. E. B. (1994). *The souls of black folk*. Avenel, NJ: Gramercy Books.

Duffy, J. M. (2007). *Writing from these roots: Literacy in a Hmong-American community*. Honolulu: University of Hawaii Press.

Eastman, C. (Ed.). (1992). *Codeswitching*. Clevedon, England: Multilingual Matters.

Ede, L., & Lunsford, A. A. (1984). Audience addressed/audience invoked: The role of audience in composition theory and pedagogy. *College Composition and Communication, 35*, 155–171.

———. (1996). Representing audience: "Successful" discourse and disciplinary critique. *College Composition and Communication, 47*(2), 167–179.

Edwards, R. (2001). "The Metropol and the Mayster-Toun," Cosmopolitanism and late medieval literature. In V. Dharwadker (Ed.), *Cosmopolitan geographies: New locations in literature and culture* (pp. 33–62). London: Routledge.

Elbow, P. (2000). Vernacular Englishes in the writing classroom? Probing the culture of literacy. In C. Schroeder, H. Fox, & P. Bizzell (Eds.), *ALT DIS: Alternative discourses in the academy* (pp. 126–138). Portsmouth, NH: Boynton/Cook.

——. (2006). When margins are at the center. In S. J. Nero (Ed.), *Dialects, Englishes, creoles, and education* (pp. ix–xv). Mahwah, NJ: Lawrence Erlbaum.

Elias Fund. (n.d.). About the Elias Fund. Retrieved May 1, 2012, from http://www.eliasfund.org/about.

Engelson, A. (2011). *Writing the local-global: An ethnography of friction and negotiation in an English-using Indonesian Ph.D. program*. Open Access Dissertations. Paper 463. University of Massachusetts, Amherst. Retrieved from http://scholarworks.umass.edu/open_access_dissertations/463.

Enright, K. A., & Gilliland, B. (2011). Multilingual writing in an age of accountability: From policy to practice in U.S. high school classrooms. *Journal of Second Language Writing, 20*(3), 182–195.

Escolme, J. (2008). Meet Guo Xiaolu. Interview. Learning English Feature. BBC China. Retrieved July 1, 2011, from http://www.bbc.co.uk/china/learningenglish/specials/1020_guo_xialou/.

Ferris, D. R. (2007). Preparing teachers to respond to student writing. *Journal of Second Language Writing, 16*(3), 165–193.

——. (2014). Review: "English Only" and multilingualism in composition studies: Policy, philosophy, and practice. *College English, 77*(1), 73–83.

Ferris, D. R., & Hedgcock, J. S. (2005). *Teaching ESL composition: Purpose, process and practice* (2nd ed.). Mahwah, NJ: Lawrence Erlbaum.

Fine, R., & Cohen, R. (2002). Four Cosmopolitanism moments. In S. Vertovec & R. Cohen (Eds.), *Conceiving Cosmopolitanism: Theory, context, and practice* (pp. 137–162). Oxford: Oxford University Press.

Firth, A. (1996). The discursive accomplishment of normality: On "lingua franca" English and conversation analysis. *Journal of Pragmatics, 26*(2), 237–259.

Fishman, S. M., & McCarthy, L. (2002). *Whose goals? Whose aspirations?: Learning to teach underprepared writers across the curriculum*. Logan: Utah State University Press.

Fleckenstein, K. (1999). CyberEthos: Ethos as a cybernetic system. In C. J. Swearingen & D. Pruett (Eds.), *Rhetoric, the polis, and the global village* (pp. 191–197). Mahwah, NJ: Lawrence Erlbaum.

——. (2005). Cybernetics, ethos, and ethics: The plight of the bread-and-butter-fly. *JAC, 25*, 323–346.

Flores, N., & Schissel, J. L. (2014). Dynamic bilingualism as the norm: Envisioning a heteroglossic approach to standards-based reform. *TESOL Quarterly, 48*(3), 454–479.

Flower, L., Long, E., & Higgins, L. (2000). *Learning to rival: A literate practice for intercultural inquiry.* New York: Routledge.

Fortanet-Gómez, I. (2011, October 8). Critical components of integrating content and language in Spanish higher education. *Across the Disciplines, 8*(3). Retrieved April 12, 2012, from http://wac.colostate.edu/atd/clil/fortanet-gomez.cfm.

Fountain, T. K. (2014). *Rhetoric in the flesh: Trained vision, technical expertise, and the gross anatomy lab.* New York: Routledge.

Fox, H. (1994). *Listening to the world: Cultural issues in academic writing.* Urbana, IL: National Council of Teachers of English.

Fraiberg, S. (2010). Composition 2.0: Toward a multilingual and multimodal framework. *College Composition and Communication, 62*(1), 100–126.

Fránquiz, M. E., & Salinas, S. S. (2011). Newcomers developing English literacy through historical thinking and digitized primary sources. *Journal of Second Language Writing, 20*(3), 196–210.

Fredericksen, E. (2002). Language as power for Hispanic students in higher education. *Journal of Hispanic Higher Education, 1*(3), 211–224.

Fulwiler, T. (1986). Reflections: How well does writing across the curriculum work? In A. Young & T. Fulwiler (Eds.), *Writing across the disciplines: Research into practice* (pp. 235–246). Portsmouth, NH: Boynton/Cook.

Furukawa, A. (2006). SSS extensive reading method proves to be an effective way to learn. Retrieved May 1, 2011, from http://www.seg.co.jp/sss/information/SSSER-2006.htm.

Gagnier, R. (2010). *Individualism, decadence and globalization: On the relationship of part to whole, 1859–1920.* London: Palgrave Macmillan.

García, O. (2009). *Bilingual education in the 21st century: A global perspective.* Oxford, England: Wiley-Blackwell.

Gardner-Chloros, P. (2009). *Code-switching.* New York: Cambridge University Press.

Gee, J. P. (1990). *Social linguistics and literacies: Ideology in discourse* (2nd ed.). Philadelphia: Falmer.

——. (2007). *What video games have to teach us about learning and literacy.* New York: Palgrave.

Geisler, C. (1994). *Academic literacy and the nature of expertise: Reading, writing, and knowing in academic philosophy.* Hillsdale, NJ: Lawrence Erlbaum.

Gentil, G. (2005). Commitments to academic biliteracy: Case studies of Francophone university writers. *Written Communication, 22*, 421–471.

Geyh, P. E. (2001). An interview with Ha Jin. *Boulevard, 17*(3), 127–140.

Giaimo, G. (2010). Talking back through "talking black": African American English and agency in Walter Mosley's *Devil in a Blue Dress. Language and Literature, 19*(3), 235–247.

Gidden, A. (1990). *The consequences of modernity.* Cambridge, England: Polity.

Gidwani, V., & Sivaramakrishnan, K. (2004). Circular migration and rural cosmopolitanism in India. In F. Osella & K. Gardner (Eds.), *Migration, modernity, and social transformation in South Asia* (pp. 339–367). New Delhi/London: SAGE.

Gilroy, P. (1993). *The black Atlantic: Modernity and double consciousness.* London: Verso.

Gilyard, K. (1991). *Voices of the self: A study of language competence.* Detroit, MI: Wayne State University Press.

———. (1996). *Let's flip the script: An African American discourse on language, literature, and learning.* Detroit, MI: Wayne State University Press.

———. (1997). Cross-talk: Toward transcultural writing classrooms. In C. Severino, J. C. Guerra, & J. E. Butler (Eds.), *Writing in multicultural settings* (pp. 325–331). New York: Modern Language Association.

———. (2011). *True to the language game: African American discourse, cultural politics, and pedagogy.* New York: Routledge.

———. (2016). The rhetoric of translingualism. *College English, 78*(3), 284–289.

Glenn, C., & Ratcliffe, K. (Eds.). (2011). *Silence and listening as rhetorical arts.* Carbondale: Southern Illinois University Press.

Goffman, E. (1981). *Forms of talk.* Oxford, England: Blackwell.

Gorgorio, M., & Planas, M. (2001). Teaching mathematics in multilingual classrooms. *Education Studies in Mathematics, 47*(1), 7–33.

Graddol, D. (1997). *The future of English?* London: British Council.

Green, L. J. (2002). *African American English: A linguistic introduction.* Cambridge, England: Cambridge University Press.

Greene, K. J., Peña, E. D., & Bedore, L. M. (2012). Lexical choice and language selection in bilingual preschoolers. *Child Language Teaching and Therapy, 29*(1), 27–39.

Gregory, M., & Carroll, S. (1978). *Language and situation: Language varieties and their social contexts.* London: Routledge.

Grosjean, F. (1989). Neurolinguists, beware! The bilingual is not two monolinguals in one person. *Brain and Language, 36*(1), 3–15.

Guerra, J. C. (1997). The place of intercultural literacy in the writing classroom. In C. Severino, J. C. Guerra, & J. E. Butler (Eds.), *Writing in multicultural settings* (pp. 248–260). New York: Modern Language Association.

——. (2015). *Language, culture, identity and citizenship in college classrooms and communities.* New York: Routledge–National Council of Teachers of English.

Gumperz, J. J. (1972). Verbal strategies in multilingual communication. In R. D. Abrahams & R. C. Troike (Eds.), *Language and cultural diversity in American education* (pp. 184–196). Englewood Cliffs, NJ: Prentice-Hall.

Guo, X. (2007). *A concise Chinese-English dictionary for lovers.* New York: Anchor Books.

——. (2008). *Twenty fragments of a ravenous youth.* New York: Anchor Books.

——. (2009). *UFO in her eyes.* London: Chatto & Windus/Random House.

Gutiérrez, K., Baquedano-López, P., Tejeda, C. (1999). Rethinking diversity: Hybridity and hybrid language practices in the third space. *Mind, Culture, and Activity,* 6(4), 286–303.

Haas, C. (1994). Learning to read biology: One student's rhetorical development in college. *Written Communication, 11*(1), 43–84.

Hackert, S. (2012). *The emergence of the English native speaker: A chapter in nineteenth-century linguistic thought.* Berlin: De Gruyter Mouton.

Hale, J. K. (2005). *Milton's languages: The impact of multilingualism on style.* Cambridge, England: Cambridge University Press.

Hall, D. L., & Ames, R. T. (1995). *Anticipating China: Thinking through the narratives of Chinese and Western culture.* Albany, NY: SUNY Press.

Hall, R. M., & Rosner, M. (2004). Pratt and pratfalls: Revisioning contact zones. In A. A. Lunsford & L. Ouzgane (Eds.), *Crossing borderlands: Composition and postcolonial studies* (pp. 95–109). Pittsburgh, PA: University of Pittsburgh Press.

Hall, S. (1996). Cultural identity and diaspora. In P. Mongia (Ed.), *Contemporary postcolonial theory.* London: Arnold.

Halliday, M. A. K. (1970). Language structure and language function. In J. Lyons (Ed.), *New horizons in linguistics* (pp. 140–165). London: Penguin.

Halliday, M. A. K., & Hasan, R. (1976). *Cohesion in English.* London: Longman.

Han, Z., & Tarone, E. (2014). *Interlanguage: Forty years later.* Philadelphia: John Benjamins.

Hanson, J. (2013). Moving out of the monolingual comfort zone and into the multilingual world: An exercise for the writing classroom. In S. A. Canagarajah (Ed.), *Literacy as translingual practice: Between communities and classrooms*. (pp. 207–214). New York: Routledge.

Harbord, J. (2010, April 14). Writing in Central and Eastern Europe: Stakeholders and directions in initiating change. *Across the Disciplines, 7*. Retrieved April 12, 2012, from http://wac.colostate.edu/atd/articles/harbord2010.cfm.

Harder, P. (Ed.). (2009). *Angles on the English-speaking world, Vol. 9: English in Denmark: Language policy, internationalization and university teaching*. Copenhagen, Denmark: Museum Tusculanum Press.

Hasan, R. (1984). Coherence and cohesive harmony. In J. Flood (Ed.), *Understanding reading comprehension* (pp. 181–219). Newark, NJ: International Reading Association.

Hayhoe, R., Li, J., Lin, J., Zha, Q. (2011). *Portraits of 21st century Chinese universities: In the move to mass higher education*. Hong Kong: Springer.

Heath, S. B. (1981). Toward an ethnohistory of writing in American education. In M. F. Whiteman (Ed.), *Writing: The nature, development, and teaching of written communication, Vol. 1* (pp. 25–46). Hillsdale, NJ: Erlbaum.

Heidegger, M. (1993). Letter on humanism. In D. F. Krell (Ed.), *Basic writings* (2nd ed.), (pp. 213–265). New York: HarperCollins.

Held, D. (2010). *Cosmopolitanism: Ideals and realities*. Cambridge, England: Polity.

Heller, M. (2007). The future of "bilingualism." In M. Heller (Ed.), *Bilingualism: A social approach* (pp. 340–345). New York: Palgrave Macmillan.

Herrington, T. (2008). The Global Classroom Project: Multiple relationships in global partnering. In D. Starke-Meyerring & M. Wilson (Eds.), *Designing globally networked learning environments: Visionary partnerships, policies, and pedagogies* (pp. 37–51). Rotterdam, the Netherlands: Sense.

———. (2010). Crossing global boundaries: Beyond intercultural communication. *Journal of Business and Technical Communication, 24* (4), 516–539.

Hesford, W. S. (2006). Global turns and cautions in rhetoric and composition. *PMLA, 121*(3), 787–801.

———. (2011). *Spectacular rhetorics: Human rights visions, recognitions, feminisms*. Durham, NC: Duke University Press.

Hesford, W. S., & Kozol, W. (Eds.). (2005). *Just advocacy? Women's human rights, transnational feminisms, and the politics of representation*. New Brunswick, NJ: Rutgers University Press.

Hess, N. (1996). Code switching and style shifting as markers of liminality in literature. *Language and Literature*, 5(1), 5–18.

Hesse, D. (2010). The place of creative writing in composition studies. *College Composition and Communication*, 62(1), 31–52.

Higgins, C. (2009). *English as a local language: Post-colonial identities and multilingual practices*. Bristol, England: Multilingual Matters.

Hill, J. (1999). Language, race, and white public space. *American Anthropologist, 100*(3), 680–689.

Hirvela, A., & Belcher, D. (2007). Writing scholars as teacher educators: Exploring writing teacher education. *Journal of Second Language Writing, 16*(2), 125–128.

Holton, R. (1998). *Globalization and the nation-state*. Basingstoke, England: Palgrave.

——. (2005). *Making globalization*. Basingstoke, England: Palgrave Macmillan.

——. (2009). *Cosmopolitanisms: New thinking and new directions*. Basingstoke, England: Palgrave Macmillan.

Hornberger, N. (1989). Continua of biliteracy. *Review of Educational Research*, 59, 271–291.

Hornberger, N., & Skilton-Sylvester, E. (2003). Revisiting the continua of biliteracy: International and critical perspectives. In N. Hornberger (Ed.), *Revisiting the continua of biliteracy: A framework for educational research, policy, and practice in multilingual settings* (pp. 35–67). Clevedon, England: Multilingual Matters.

Horner, B. (2010). Introduction: From "English Only" to cross-language relations in composition. In B. Horner, M. Lu, & P. K. Matsuda (Eds.), *Cross-language relations in composition* (pp. 1–17). Carbondale: Southern Illinois University Press.

——. (2011). Writing English as a lingua franca. In A. Archibald, A. Cogo, & J. Jenkins (Eds.), *Latest trends in ELF research* (pp. 299–311). Cambridge, England: Cambridge Scholars Press.

Horner, B., & Kopelson, K. (Eds.). (2014). *Reworking English in rhetoric and composition: Global interrogations, local interventions*. Carbondale: Southern Illinois University Press.

Horner, B., Lu, M.-Z., & Matsuda, P. K. (Eds.). (2010). *Cross-language relations in composition*. Carbondale: Southern Illinois University Press.

Horner, B., Lu, M.-Z., Royster, J., & Trimbur, J. (2011). Language difference in writing: Toward a translingual approach. *College English*, 73(3), 303–321.

Horner, B., NeCamp, S., & Donahue, C. (2011). Toward a multilingual writing scholarship: From English only to a translingual norm. *College Composition and Communication, 63*(2), 269–300.

Horner, B., & Trimbur, J. (2002). English only and U.S. college composition. *College Composition and Communication, 53*(4), 594–630.

House, J. (1999). Misunderstanding in intercultural communication: Interactions in English as a lingua franca and the myth of mutual intelligibility. In C. Gnutzmann (Ed.), *Teaching and learning English as a global language* (pp. 73–89). Tübingen, Germany: Stauffenburg.

Howard-Pitney, D. (2005). *The African American Jeremiad: Appeals for justice in America*. Philadelphia: Temple University Press.

Hyde, M. J. (2004). Introduction: Rhetorically, we dwell. In M. J. Hyde, & C. O. Schrag (Eds.), *The ethos of rhetoric* (pp. xiii–xxviii). Columbia: University of South Carolina Press.

Hyland, K. (2007). Genre pedagogy: Language, literacy and L2 writing instruction. *Journal of Second Language Writing, 16*(3), 148–164.

Isocrates. (1982). *Antidosis*. (G. Norlin, Trans.). Cambridge, MA: Harvard University Press.

Jacquemet, M. (2005). Transidiomatic practices: Language and power in the age of globalization. *Language & Communication*, 25(3), 257–277.

James, M. A. (2007). Interlanguage variation and transfer of learning. *International Review of Applied Linguistics in Language Teaching, 45*(2), 95–118.

——. (2010). An investigation of learning transfer in English-for-general-academic-purposes writing instruction. *Journal of Second Language Writing, 19*(4), 183–206.

Jämtelid, K. (2002). *Texter och skrivande i en internationaliserad affärsvärld: Flerspråkig textproduktion vid ett svenskt storföretag* [Texts and writing in an internationalized business world: Multilingual text production in a global Swedish group]. Stockholm, Sweden: Almqvist & Wiksell International.

Janopoulos, M. (1992). University faculty tolerance of NS and NNS writing errors: A comparison. *Journal of Second Language Writing, 1*(2), 109–121.

——. (1995). Writing across the curriculum, writing proficiency exams, and the NNS college student. *Journal of Second Language Writing, 4*(1), 43–50.

Jäppinen, A. (2005). Thinking and content learning of mathematics and science as cognitional development in content and language integrated learning (CLIL): Teaching through a foreign language in Finland. *Language and Education, 19*(2), 148–169.

Jarratt, S. C. (1991). Feminism and composition: The case for conflict. In P. Harkin & J. Schilb (Eds.), *Contending with words: Composition and rhetoric in a postmodern age* (pp. 105–123). New York: Modern Language Association.

Jarratt, S. C., Losh, E., & Puente, D. (2006). Transnational identifications: Biliterate writers in a first-year humanities course. *Journal of Second Language Writing, 15*(1), 24–48.

Jenkins, J. (2000). *Phonology of English as an international language.* Oxford, England: Oxford University Press.

———. (2007). *English as a lingua franca: Attitude and identity.* Oxford, England: Oxford University Press.

———. (2011.) Accommodating (to) ELF in the international university. *Journal of Pragmatics, 43*(4), 926–936.

———. (2014). *English as a lingua franca in the international university: The politics of academic English language policy.* New York: Routledge.

Jin, H. (1999). *Waiting.* New York: Vintage.

———. (2008). *The writer as migrant.* Chicago: University of Chicago Press.

Johns, A. (1998). The visual and the verbal: A case study in macroeconomics. *English for Specific Purposes, 17*(2), 183–197.

Johnson, K. E. (2006). The sociocultural turn and its challenges for second language teacher education. *TESOL Quarterly, 40*(1), 235–257.

———. (2009). *Second language teacher education.* New York: Routledge.

Jordan, J. (2009). Second language users and emerging English designs. *College Composition and Communication, 61*(2), W310–W329.

———. (2012). *Redesigning composition for multilingual realities.* Urbana, IL: National Council of Teachers of English.

———. (2015). Material translingual ecologies. *College English, 77*(4), 364–382.

Jørgensen, J. N. (2008). Polylingual languaging around and among children and adolescents. *International Journal of Multilingualism, 5*(3), 161–176.

Jung, J. (2005). *Revisionary rhetoric, feminist pedagogy, and multigenre texts.* Carbondale: Southern Illinois University Press.

Jussawalla, F., & Jasenbrock, R. W. (Eds.). (1992). *Interviews with writers of the post-colonial world.* Jackson: University Press of Mississippi.

Kachru, B. (1982). Meaning in deviation: Toward understanding non-native English texts. In *The other tongue: English across cultures* (pp. 325–350). Oxford, England: Pergamon Press.

——. (1985). Standards, codification, and sociolinguistic realism: The English language in the outer circle. In R. Quirk and H. Widdowson (Eds.), *English in the World: Teaching and learning the language and literature* (pp. 11–30). Cambridge, England: Cambridge University Press.

——. (1987). The bilingual's creativity: discoursal and stylistic strategies in contact literature. In L. E. Smith (Ed.), *Discourse across cultures: Strategies in World Englishes* (pp. 125–140). Englewood Cliffs, NJ: Prentice Hall.

——. (1990). *The alchemy of English: The spread, functions, and models of non-native Englishes.* Urbana: University of Illinois Press.

——. (1992). World Englishes: Approaches, issues and resources. *Language Teaching, 25,* 1–14.

——. (1995). The speaking tree: A medium of plural canons. In J. E. Alatis (Ed.), *Georgetown University round table on language and linguistics 1994* (pp. 6–22). Washington, DC: Georgetown University Press.

——. (2005). *Asian Englishes: Beyond the canon.* Hong Kong: Hong Kong University Press.

Kam, A., & Meinema, Y. (2005). Teaching academic writing to international students in an interdisciplinary writing context: A pedagogical rough guide. *Across the Disciplines,* 2. Retrieved from http://wac.colostate.edu/atd/lds/kam_meinema.cfm.

Kang, O., & Rubin, D. L. (2009). Reverse linguistic stereotyping: Measuring the effect of listener expectations on speech. *Journal of Language and Social Psychology,* 28(4), 441–456.

Kaplan, R. B. (1966). Cultural thought patterns in intercultural education. *Language Learning, 16*(1), 1–20.

Kaur, J. (2011). Raising explicitness through self-repair in English as a lingua franca. *Journal of Pragmatics, 43*(11), 2704–2715.

Kawate, M., & Furukawa, A. (2005). Start with simple stories and enjoy reading. Retrieved April 1, 2008, from: http://www.seg.co.jp/sss/english/index.html.

Kell, C. (2013). Ariadne's thread: Literacy, scale and meaning making across space and time. *Working Papers in Urban Language & Literacies.* Paper 118. Retrieved from https://www.kcl.ac.uk/sspp/departments/education/research/ldc/publications/workingpapers/the-papers/WP118.pdf.

Kellman, S. G. (2000). *The translingual imagination.* Lincoln: University of Nebraska Press.

Kellman, S. G., & Lvovich, N. (2015). Introduction to the special issue. Literary translingualism: Multilingual identity and creativity [Special issue]. *L2 Journal*, *7*(1), 3–5.

Kendall, T., & Wolfram, W. (2009). Local and external language standards in African American English. *Journal of English Linguistics*, *37*(4), 305–330.

Kenner, C. (2000). Children writing in a multilingual nursery. In M. Martin-Jones & K. Jones (Eds.), *Multilingual literacies* (pp. 127–144). Amsterdam: John Benjamins.

Keohane, R. O., & Nye, J. S. (2000). Globalization: What is new? What's not? (And so what?). *Foreign Policy*, *118*, 104–109.

Kibler, A. (2010). Writing through two languages: First language expertise in a language minority classroom. *Journal of Second Language Writing*, *19*(3), 121–142.

———. (2011). "I write it in a way that people can read it": How teachers and adolescent L2 writers describe content area writing. *Journal of Second Language Writing*, *20*(3), 211–226.

King, K. (2006). Child language acquisition. In R. Fasold & J. Connor-Linton (Eds.), *An introduction to language and linguistics* (pp. 205–224). New York: Cambridge University Press.

Kirkpatrick, A. (2011). English as a medium of instruction in Asian education (from primary to tertiary): Implications for local languages and local scholarship. *Applied Linguistics Review*, *2*(1), 99–118.

Kirkpatrick, A., & Xu, Z. (2002). Chinese pragmatic norms and "China English." *World Englishes*, *21*(2), 269–280.

Kiuhara, S., Graham, S., & Hawken, L. S. (2009). Teaching writing to high school students: A national survey. *Journal of Educational Psychology*, *101*(1), 136–160.

Kong, S. (2010). Writing in late immersion biology and history classes in Hong Kong. *Writing & Pedagogy*, *2*(1), 13–38.

Kubota, R. (1997). A reevaluation of the uniqueness of Japanese written discourse. *Written Communication*, *14*(4), 460–80.

———. (1999). Japanese culture constructed by discourses: Implications for applied linguistics research and ELT. *TESOL Quarterly*, *33*, 9–35.

———. (2001a). Discursive constructions of images in U.S. classrooms. *TESOL Quarterly*, *35*(1), 9–38.

———. (2001b). Teaching World Englishes to native speakers in the United States. *World Englishes*, *20*(1), 47–64.

——. (2002). Japanese identities in written communication: Politics and discourses. In R. Donahue (Ed.), *Exploring Japaneseness: On Japanese enactments of culture and consciousness* (pp. 293–315). Westport, CT: Ablex.

——. (2014). The multi/plural turn, postcolonial theory, and neoliberal multiculturalism: Complicities and implications for applied linguistics. *Applied Linguistics*, 1–22. doi: 10.1093/applin/amu045.

Labov, W. (1970). The study of language in its social context. *Studium Generale, 23*, 30–87.

——. (1972). *Language in the inner city: Studies in the black English vernacular.* Philadelphia: University of Pennsylvania.

Laertius, D. (1972). *The lives of eminent philosophers, book 6.* Cambridge, MA: Harvard University Press. Online text in English at the Perseus Project. Retrieved from http://www.perseus.tufts.edu/hopper/text?doc=Perseus:text:1999.01.0258

Lam, W. S. E. (2009). Multiliteracies on instant messaging in negotiating local, translocal, and transnational affiliations: A case of an adolescent immigrant. *Reading Research Quarterly, 44*(4), 377–397.

Lamb, C. E. (1991). Beyond argument in feminist composition. *College Composition and Communication, 42*(1), 11–24.

Lambert, I. (2008). Representing Maori speech in Alan Duff's Once Were Warriors. *Language and Literature, 17*(2), 155–165.

——. (2011). Chris Abani's Graceland and Uzodinma Iweala's Beasts of No Nation: Nonstandard English, intertextuality and Ken Saro-Wiwa's Sozaboy. *Language and Literature, 20*(4), 283–294.

Lantolf, J. P. (Ed.). (2000). *Sociocultural theory and second language learning.* New York: Oxford University Press.

Latour, B. (1996). On interobjectivity. *Mind, Culture, and Activity, 3*(4), 228–245.

Lavelle, T., & Shima, A. (2014). Writing histories: Lingua Franca English in a Swedish graduate program. In T. M. Zawacki & M. Cox (Eds.), *WAC and second-language writers: Research towards linguistically and culturally inclusive programs and practices* (pp. 439–464). Anderson, SC: Parlor Press.

Lazerson, M. (2015, April 10). Beyond the Bologna Process. *The Chronicle of Higher Education*, pp. A45–A46.

Leander, K., & Boldt, G. (2012). Rereading "A pedagogy of multiliteracies": Bodies, texts, and emergence. *Journal of Literacy Research, 45*(1), 22–46.

Leander, K. M., & Lovvorn, J. F. (2006). Literacy networks: Following the circulation of texts, bodies, and objects in the schooling and online gaming of one youth. *Cognition and Instruction, 24*(3), 291–340.

Lee, C. K. M. (2002). Literacy practices in computer-mediated communication in Hong Kong. *The Reading Matrix*, 2(2), 1–25.

———. (2007a). Text-making practices beyond the classroom context: Private instant messaging in Hong Kong. *Computers and Composition*, *24*(3), 285–301.

———. (2007b). Affordances and text-making practices in online instant messaging. *Written Communication*, *24*(3), 223–249.

Lee, C. K. M., & Barton, D. (2011). Constructing glocal identities through multilingual writing practices on Flickr.com®. *International Multilingual Research Journal*, *5*(1), 39–59.

Lee, I. (2010). Writing teacher education and teacher learning: Testimonies of four EFL teachers. *Journal of Second Language Writing*, *19*(3), 143–157.

———. (2011). L2 writing teacher education for in-service teachers: Opportunities and challenges. *English in Australia*, *46*(1), 31–39.

———. (2013). Becoming a writing teacher: Using "identity" as an analytic lens to understand EFL writing teachers' development. *Journal of Second Language Writing*, *22*(3), 330–345.

Lee, J. S. (2004). Linguistic hybridization in K-pop: Discourse of self-assertion and resistance. *World Englishes*, *23*(3), 429–50.

Leki, I. (1992, Winter). Building expertise through sequenced writing assignments. *TESOL Journal*, 19–23.

———. (1998). *Academic writing: Exploring processes and strategies* (2nd ed.). New York: Cambridge University Press.

———. (2007). *Undergraduates in a second language: Challenges and complexities of academic literacy development*. Mahwah, NJ: Lawrence Erlbaum.

Lennon, B. (2000). Screening a digital visual poetics. *Configuration*, *8*(1), 63–85.

———. (2010). *In Babel's shadow: Multilingual literatures, monolingual states*. Minneapolis: University of Minnesota Press.

Leonard, R. L. (2013). Traveling literacies: Multilingual writing on the move. *Research in the Teaching of English*, *48*(1), 13–39.

———. (2014). Multilingual writing as rhetorical attunement. *College English*, *76*(3), 227–247.

Li, J. (2004). Pidgin and code-switching: Linguistic identity and multicultural consciousness in Maxine Hong Kingston's *Tripmaster Monkey*. *Language and Literature*, *13*(3), 269–287.

Li, Wei. (1994). *Three generations, two languages, one family: Language choice and language shift in a Chinese community in Britain*. Clevedon, England: Multilingual Matters.

Li, Wenzhong. (1993). China English and Chinese English. *Waiyu Jiaoxue Yu Yanjiu* [Foreign Language Teaching and Research], *4*, 18–24.

Lillis, T., & Curry, M. J. (2006). Professional academic writing by multilingual scholars: Interactions with literacy brokers in the production of English-medium texts. *Written Communication, 23*(1), 3–35.

Lippi-Green, R. (2012). *English with an accent* (2nd ed.). New York: Routledge.

Liu, L. (1995). *Translingual practice: Literature, national culture, and translated modernity-China, 1900–1937.* Stanford, CA: Stanford University Press.

Liu, Y. (2011). Power perceptions and negotiations in a cross-national email writing activity. *Journal of Second Language Writing, 20*(4), 257–270.

Lords, T. (2004). *Traci Lords: Underneath it all.* New York: Harper.

Lovejoy, K. B. (2003). Practical pedagogy for composition. In G. Smitherman, & V. Villanueva (Eds.), *Language diversity in the classroom: From intention to practice* (pp. 89–108). Carbondale: Southern Illinois University Press.

Lu, M.-Z. (1994). Professing multiculturalism: The politics of style in the contact zone. *College Composition and Communication, 45*(4), 442–458.

———. (2010). Living-English work. In Horner, B., Lu, M.-Z., & Matsuda, P. K. (Eds.), *Cross-language relations in composition* (pp. 42–56). Carbondale: Southern Illinois University Press.

Lu, M.-Z., & Horner, B. (2013). Translingual literacy, language difference, and matters of agency. *College English, 75*(6), 582–607.

Lueck, A., & Sharma, S. (2013). Writing a translingual script: Closed captions in the multilingual hearing classroom. *Kairos: A Journal of Rhetoric, Technology, and Pedagogy, 17*(3). Retrieved from http://kairos.technorhetoric.net/17.3/.

Lunsford, A., & Ouzgane, L. (Eds.). (2004). *Crossing borderlands: Composition and postcolonial studies.* Pittsburgh, PA: University of Pittsburgh Press.

Lyons, S. R. (2000). Rhetorical sovereignty: What do American Indians want from writing? *College Composition and Communication, 51*(3), 447–468.

MacLean, M., & Mohr, M. (1999). *Teacher-researchers at work.* Berkeley, CA: National Writing Project.

Mao, L. (2006). *Reading Chinese fortune cookie: The making of Chinese American rhetoric.* Logan: Utah State University Press.

Mao, L., & Young, M. (Eds.). (2009). *Representations: Doing Asian American rhetoric.* Logan: Utah State University Press.

Marko, T. (2012). Proyecto Boston Medellín as pedagogscape. Retrieved from http://mobility17.com/wp-content/uploads/2013/09/MarkoPBMas Pedagogscape.pdf.

Marko, T., et al. (2013). Here I am: A year in multilingual writing at Emerson College. Retrieved from http://emersontranslingual.wordpress.com/.

Marko, T., Osorio, M. E., Sepenoski, E., & Catalani, R. (2014). PROYECTO CARRITO: When the student receives an "A" and the worker gets fired: Disrupting the unequal political economy of translingual rhetorical mobility. *Literacy in Composition Studies*, 2(2), 21–43.

Marston, S., Jones, J. P., III, & Woodward, K. (2005). Human geography without scale. *Transactions of the Institute of British Geographers*, 30, 416–432.

Martin-Jones, M., & Jones, K. (Eds.). (2000). *Multilingual literacies: Reading and writing different worlds*. Amsterdam: John Benjamins.

Matsuda, A. (2003). The ownership of English in Japanese secondary schools. *World Englishes*, 22, 483–96.

——. (Ed.). (2012). *Principles and practices of teaching English as an international language*. Bristol, England: Multilingual Matters.

Matsuda, P. K. (1997). Contrastive rhetoric in context: A dynamic model of L2 writing. *Journal of Second Language Writing*, 6(1), 45–60.

——. (1999). Composition studies and ESL writing: A disciplinary division of labor. *College Composition and Communication*, 50(4), 699–721.

——. (2006). The myth of linguistic homogeneity in U.S. college composition. *College English*, 68(6), 637–651.

Matsuda, P. K., & Cox, M. (2004). Reading an ESL writer's text. In S. Bruce & B. Rafoth (Eds.), *ESL writers: A guide for writing center tutors* (pp. 39–47). Portsmouth, NH: Boynton/Cook.

Matsuda, P. K., Cox, M., Jordan, J., & Ortmeier-Hooper, C. (Eds.). (2006). *Second language writing in the composition classroom: A critical sourcebook*. Boston: Bedford/St. Martins.

Matsuda, P. K., Saenkhum, T., & Accardi, S. (2013). Writing teachers' perceptions of the presence and needs of second language writers: An institutional case study. *Journal of Second Language Writing*, 22, 68–86.

Matsumoto, Y. (2015). *Multimodal communicative strategies for resolving miscommunication in multilingual writing classroom*. Unpublished doctoral dissertation, The Pennsylvania State University, University Park.

Mauranen, A. (2006). Signaling and preventing misunderstanding in English as lingua franca communication. *International Journal of the Sociology of Language*, 177, 123–150.

———. (2012). *Exploring ELF: Academic English shaped by non-native speakers*. Cambridge. England: Cambridge University Press.

Mauranen, A., & Metsä-Ketelä, M. (Eds.). (2006). English as a Lingua Franca [Special issue]. *Nordic Journal of English Studies, 5*(2).

Mauranen, A., & Ranta, E. (Eds.). (2009). *English as a Lingua Franca: Studies and findings*. Newcastle, England: Cambridge Scholars Publishing.

Maylath, B., Vandepitte, S., Minacori, P., Isohella, S., Mousten, B., & Humbley, J. (2013). Managing complexity: A technical communication/translation case study in multilateral international collaboration. *Technical Communication Quarterly*, 22(1), 67–84.

Maylath, B., Vandepitte, S., & Mousten, B. (2008). Growing grassroots partnerships: Trans-Atlantic collaboration between American instructors and students of technical writing and European instructors and students of translation. In D. Starke-Meyerring & M. Wilson (Eds.), *Designing globally networked learning environments: Visionary partnerships, policies, and pedagogies* (pp. 52–66). Rotterdam, the Netherlands: Sense.

McComiskey, B. (Ed.). (2006). *English studies: An introduction to the discipline(s)*. Urbana-Champaign, IL: National Council of Teachers of English.

McDonald, M. A. (2005). The integration of social justice in teacher education: Dimensions of prospective teachers' opportunities to learn. *Journal of Teacher Education*, 56(5), 418–435.

McGinnis, T., Goodstein-Stolzenberg, A., & Costa Saliani, E. (2007). "indnpride": Online spaces of transnational youth as sites of creative and sophisticated literacy and identity work. *Linguistics and Education, 18*(3–4), 283–304.

Mejia, J. A. (2004). Arts of the U.S.-Mexico contact zone. In A. Lunsford & L. Ouzgane (Eds.), *Crossing borderlands: Composition and postcolonial studies* (pp. 171–198). Pittsburgh, PA: University of Pittsburgh Press.

Mendieta, E. (2009). From imperial to dialogical cosmopolitanism. *Ethics & Global Politics*, 2(3), 241–258.

Mercanti, S. (2009). *The rose and the lotus: Partnership studies in the works of Raja Rao*. New York: Rodopi.

Merritt, S. (2011). Crossing language (policy) boundaries: Development of bilingual first year writing courses. Paper presented at the Conference on College Composition and Communication, Atlanta, GA.

Mesthrie, R., & Bhatt, R. (2008). *World Englishes: The study of new linguistic varieties*. Cambridge, England: Cambridge University Press.

Meyer, S. L. (1993). Refusing to play the confidence game: The illusion of mastery in the reading/writing of texts. *College English*, *55*(1), 46–63.

Mignolo, W. (2000). The many faces of cosmopolis: Border thinking and critical cosmopolitanism. *Public Culture*, *12*(3), 721–748.

Mihut, L. A. (2014). Literacy brokers and the emotional work of mediation. *Literacy in Composition Studies*, *2*(1), 57–79.

Miller, C. R. (1984). Genre as social action. *Quarterly Journal of Speech*, *70*(2), 151–167.

Miller, T. (2010). *The evolution of college English: Literacy studies from the Puritans to the Postmoderns*. Pittsburgh, PA: University of Pittsburgh Press.

Modelski, G. (1972). *Principles of world politics*. New York: Free Press.

Moll, L. C., & Gonzalez, N. (1994). Lessons from research with language-minority children. *Journal of Reading Behavior*, *26*(4), 439–456.

Montes-Alcala, C. (2012). Code-switching in US-Latino novels. In M. Sebba, S. Mahootian, & C. Jonsson, C. (Eds.), *Language mixing and code-switching in writing: Approaches to mixed-language written discourse* (pp. 68–88). New York: Routledge.

Montgomery, M., & Fuller, J. (1996). Verbal -s in nineteenth-century African-American English. In Schneider, E. (Ed.), *Focus on the USA* (pp. 211–230). Philadelphia: John Benjamins.

Montgomery, M., Fuller, J., & Demarse, S. (1993). "The black men has wives and sweet harts [and third person -*s*] jest like the white men": Evidence for verbal -*s* from written documents on nineteenth-century African-American speech. *Language Variation and Change*, *5*(3), 335–357.

Moody, A. J. (2006). English in Japanese popular culture and J-Pop music. *World Englishes*, *25*(2), 209–222.

Moore, A. (2008). Rethinking scale as a geographical category: From analysis to practice. *Progress in Human Geography*, *32*(2), 203–225.

Moraga, C. (1983). *Loving in the war years: Lo que nunca pasó por sus labios*. Boston: South End Press.

——. (1993). *The last generation: Prose and poetry*. Boston: South End Press.

——. (1997). *Waiting in the wings: Portrait of a queer motherhood*. Ithaca, NY: Firebrand Books.

Mullen, B. V. (2004). *Afro-Orientalism*. Minneapolis: University of Minnesota Press.

Murate, K., & Jenkins, J. (2009). *Global Englishes in Asian contexts: Current and future debates*. London: Palgrave/Macmillan.

National Council of Teachers of English (2011). Resolution on the student's right to incorporate heritage and home languages in writing. Retrieved from http://www.ncte.org/positions/statements/homelanguages.

New London Group. (1996). A pedagogy of multiliteracies: Designing social futures. *Harvard Educational Review, 66*(1), 60–92.

Nunan, D. (1989). *Understand language classrooms: A guide for teacher-initiated action.* New York: Prentice-Hall.

Nussbaum, M. C. (2010). Patriotism and cosmopolitanism. In G. W. Brown, & D. Held (Eds.), *The cosmopolitanism reader* (pp. 155–162). Cambridge, England: Polity.

Orellana, M. F. (2015). *Immigrant children in transcultural spaces: Language, learning, and love.* New York: Routledge.

Ortmeier-Hooper, C. (2008). "English may be my second language, but I'm not 'ESL.'" *College Composition and Communication,* 59(3), 389–419.

——. (2013). *The ELL writer: Moving beyond basics in the secondary classroom.* New York: Teachers College Press.

Oswald, M. N. (2012). *Salomé's veils: Language, interpretation and translation.* Unpublished honors thesis, The Pennsylvania State University, University Park.

Page, B. (2007). Slow going: The mortuary, modernity and the hometown association in Bali-Nyonga, Cameroon. *Africa,* 77(3), 417–441.

Pandey, I. P. (2015). *South Asian in the Mid-South: Migrations of literacies.* Pittsburgh, PA: University of Pittsburgh Press.

Parks, S., Huot, D., Hamers, J., & H.-Lemonnier, F. (2005). "History of theatre" Web sites: A brief history of the writing process in a high school ESL language arts class. *Journal of Second Language Writing, 14*(4), 233–258.

Pennycook, A. (2007). *Global Englishes and transcultural flows.* London: Routledge.

——. (2010). *Language as a local practice.* New York: Routledge.

——. (2012). *Language and mobility: Unexpected places.* Bristol, England: Multilingual Matters.

Perry, T., & Delpit, L. (1998). *The real Ebonics debate: Power, language, and the education of African-American children.* Boston: Beacon Press.

Poe, M., & Craig, J. (2011). Modeling multivocality in a U.S.-Mexican collaboration in writing across the curriculum. *Journal of Academic Writing, 1*(1), 29–36.

Poe, M., Lerner, N., & Craig, J. (2010). *Learning to communicate in science and engineering: Case studies from MIT.* Cambridge, MA: MIT Press.

Polleck, J. N. (2011). Constructing dressing rooms in urban schools: Understanding family through book clubs with Latino and African American female adolescents. *Journal of Poetry Therapy, 24*(3), 139–155.

Pollock, S. (2002). Cosmopolitan and vernacular in history. In C. A. Breckenridge, S. Pollock, H. K. Bhabha, & D. Chakrabarty (Eds.), *Cosmopolitanism* (pp. 15–53). Durham, NC: Duke University Press.

Pollock, S., Bhabha, H, Breckenridge, C. A., & Chakrabarty, D. (2002). Cosmopolitanisms. In C. A. Breckenridge, S. Pollock, H. K. Bhabha, & D. Chakrabarty (Eds.), *Cosmopolitanism* (pp. 1–15). Durham, NC: Duke University Press.

Pough, G. D. (2006). "Each one, pull one": Womanist rhetoric and black feminist pedagogy in the writing classroom. In K. Ronald & J. Ritchie (Eds.), *Teaching rhetorica: Theory, pedagogy, practice* (pp. 66–81). Portsmouth, NH: Boynton/Cook.

Pratt, M. L. (1991). Arts of the contact zone. *Profession*, 91, 33–40.

Preece, S. (2011). Universities in the Anglophone centre: Sites of multilingualism. *Applied Linguistics Review*, 2, 121–145.

Prendergast, C. (2008). *Buying into English: Language and investment in the new capitalist world*. Pittsburgh, PA: University of Pittsburgh Press.

Prior, P. (1998). *Writing/disciplinarity: A sociohistoric account of literate activity in the academy*. Mahwah, NJ: Lawrence Erlbaum.

Rafoth, B. (2015). *Multilingual writers and writing centers*. Logan: Utah State University Press.

Raguseo, C. (2010). Twitter fiction: Social networking and microfiction in 140 characters. *TESL-EJ, 13*(4). Retrieved August 30, 2011, from http://www.tesl-ej.org/wordpress/issues/volume13/ej52/ej52int/.

Rampton, M. B. H. (1995). *Crossing: Language and ethnicity among adolescents*. London: Longman.

Rao, R. (1967). *Kanthapura*. New York: New Directions.

Ratcliffe, K. (2006). *Rhetorical listening: Identification, gender, whiteness*. Carbondale: Southern Illinois University Press.

Reiss, H. (Ed.). (1970). *Kant's political writings*. Cambridge, England: Cambridge University Press.

Reynolds, N. (1993). Ethos as location: New sites for understanding discursive authority. *Rhetoric Review, 11*(2), 325–338.

——. (2004). *Geographies of writing: Inhabiting places and encountering differences*. Carbondale: Southern Illinois University Press.

Richards, K. (2003). *Qualitative inquiry in TESOL*. Basingstoke, England: Palgrave Macmillan.

Richardson, E. (2003). *African American literacies.* New York: Routledge.

Rickford, J. R., & Rickford, R. J. (2000). *Spoken soul: The story of Black English.* New York: John Wiley and Sons.

Roberts, F., & Cimasko, T. (2008). Evaluating ESL: Making sense of university professors' responses to second language writing. *Journal of Second Language Writing, 17*(3), 125–143.

Robinson, S. K. (2010, October 14). RSA animate—changing education paradigms. RSA (Royal Society for the encouragement of Arts, Manufactures and Commerce). Video lecture. Retrieved August 4, 2012, from www.youtube.com/watch?v=zDZFcDGpL4U.

Rodriguez, R. (1982). *Hunger of memory: The education of Richard Rodriguez.* New York: Bantam.

Rosenwald, L. A. (2008). *Multilingual America: Language and the making of American literature.* Cambridge, England: Cambridge University Press.

Royster, J. J. (1996). When the first voice you hear is not your own. *College Composition and Communication, 47*(1), 29–40.

Rubin, D. L. (1992). Nonlanguage factors affecting undergraduate's judgments of nonnative English-speaking teaching assistants. *Research in Higher Education, 33,* 511–531.

Rubin, D. L., & Smith, K. (1990). Effects of accent, ethnicity, and lecture topics on undergraduates' perceptions of nonnative English-speaking teaching assistants. *International Journal of Intercultural Relations, 14,* 337–353.

Russell, D. R., & Yanez, A. (2003). "Big picture people rarely become historians": Genre systems and the contradictions of general education. In C. Bazerman & D. R. Russell (Eds.), *Writing selves/writing societies: Research from activity perspectives* (pp. 331–362). Fort Collins, CO: The WAC Clearinghouse.

Ryan, M., & Barton, G. (2014). The spatialized practices of teaching writing in Australian elementary schools: Diverse students shaping discoursal selves. *Research in the Teaching of English, 48*(2), 303–329.

Samuel, E., & Wane, N. (2005). "Unsettling relations": Racism and sexism experienced by faculty of color in a predominantly white Canadian university. *Journal of Negro Education, 74*(1), 76–87.

Sánchez, M. E. (1986). *Contemporary Chicana poetry: A critical approach to an emerging literature.* Berkeley: University of California Press.

Sapp, D. (2004). Global partnerships in business communication. *Business Communication Quarterly, 67*(3), 267–280.

Sapphire. (1997). *Push.* New York: Vintage.

Schaafsma, D. (1993). *Eating on the street: Teaching literacy in a multicultural society.* Pittsburgh, PA: University of Pittsburgh Press.

Schendl, H., & Wright, L. (2011). *Code-switching in early English.* Berlin: De Gruyter Mouton.

Schieffelin, B. B., & Ochs, E. (1986). *Language socialization across cultures.* New York: Cambridge University Press.

Schmidt, M. (2011). The limitations of code switching in Chicano/a literature. *Young Scholars in Writing, 8,* 40–51.

Schneider, B. (2005). Uncommon ground: Narcissistic reading and material racism. *Pedagogy,* 5(2), 195–212.

Schneider, E. (1989). *American earlier Black English: Morphological and syntactic variables.* Tuscaloosa: University of Alabama Press.

Schoene, B. (2010). *The cosmopolitan novel.* Edinburgh: Edinburgh University Press.

Scholte, J.-A. (2005). *Globalization: Critical perspectives.* Basingstoke, England: Palgrave.

Schroeder, C., Fox, H., & Bizzell, P. (Eds.). (2002). *ALT DIS: Alternative discourses and academy.* Portsmouth, NH: Boynton/Cook.

Schwartzward, R. (2008). Lines drawn and redrawn: How does the national matter? *ADE Bulletin, 126,* 33–37.

Scollon, R., & Scollon, S. W. (2004). *Nexus analysis: Discourse and the emerging Internet.* London: Routledge.

Sebba, M., Mahootian, S., & Jonsson, C. (Eds.). (2012). *Language mixing and code-switching in writing: Approaches to mixed-language written discourse.* New York: Routledge.

Seeley, C. (1991). *A history of writing in Japan.* Leiden, the Netherlands: E. J. Brill.

Seidlhofer, B. (2001). Closing a conceptual gap: the case for a description of English as a lingua franca. *International Journal of Applied Linguistics, 11,* 133–158.

——. (2003). *A concept of international English and related issues: From "real English" to "realistic English."* Strasbourg, France: Council of Europe.

——. (2004). Research perspectives on teaching English as a lingua franca. *Annual Review of Applied Linguistics, 24,* 209–239.

——. (2011). *Understanding English as a lingua franca.* Oxford, England: Oxford University Press.

Selinker, L. (1972). Interlanguage. *International Review of Applied Linguistics, 10,* 209–241.

Selinker, L., & Douglas, D. (1985). Wrestling with "context" in interlanguage theory. *Applied Linguistics*, 6, 190–204.

Seloni, L. (2013). Understanding how preservice teachers develop a working knowledge of second language writing: Toward a socioculturally oriented postmethod pedagogy in teacher education. In L. de Oliveira & T. Silva (Eds.), *Second language writing in the secondary classroom: Experiences, issues, and perspectives* (pp. 166–189). New York: Routledge.

Selzer, L. (2010). Barack Obama, the 2008 presidential election, and the new cosmopolitanism: Figuring the black body. *MELUS*, 35(4), 15–37.

Severino, C. (1993). The sociopolitical implications of response to second language and second dialect writing. *Journal of Second Language Writing*, 2(3), 187–201.

Severino, C., Guerra, J. C., & Butler, J. E. (Eds.). (1997). *Writing in multicultural settings*. New York: Modern Language Association.

Shapiro, M. J. (2001). Sounds of nationhood. *Millennium*, 30(3), 583–601.

Shell, M., & Sollors, W. (Eds.). (2000). *The multilingual anthology of American literature*. New York: New York University Press.

Shi, L. (2002). How Western-trained Chinese TESOL professionals publish in their home environment. *TESOL Quarterly*, 36(4) 625–634.

Shi, L., Wang, W., & Xu, J. (2005). Publication culture of foreign language education journals in China. *TESOL Quarterly*, 39(4), 765–776.

Silva, T. (1993). Toward an understanding of the distinct nature of L2 writing: The ESL research and its implications. *TESOL Quarterly*, 27(4), 657–677.

Silva, T., Leki, I., & Carson, J. (1997). Broadening the perspective of mainstream composition studies: Some thoughts from the disciplinary margins. *Written Communication*, 14(3), 398–428.

Singh, N., & Boughton, P. D. (2005). Measuring website globalization: A cross-sectional country and industry level analysis. *Journal of Website Promotion*, 1(3), 3–20.

Skehan, P. (2008). Interlanguage and language transfer. In B. Spolsky & F. M. Hult (Eds.), *The handbook of educational linguistics* (pp. 411–423). Oxford, England: Blackwell.

Skerrett, A., & Bomer, R. (2013). Recruiting languages and lifeworlds for border-crossing compositions. *Research in the Teaching of English*, 47(3), 313–337.

Skinner, J. (1998). *The stepmother tongue: An introduction to new Anglophone fiction*. New York: Palgrave Macmillan.

Smitherman, G. (1985). *Talkin and testifyin: The language of Black America*. Detroit, MI: Wayne State University Press.

——. (1999). *Talkin that talk: Language, culture and education in African America*. New York: Routledge.

——. (2000). *Black talk: Words and phrases from the hood to the Amen corner*. New York: Mariner Books.

Smitherman, G., & Villanueva, V. (Eds.). (2003). *Language diversity in the classroom: From intention to practice*. Carbondale: Southern Illinois University Press.

Sommer, D. (2004). *Bilingual aesthetics: A new sentimental education*. Durham, NC: Duke University Press.

Spack, R. (1997a). The acquisition of academic literacy in a second language: A longitudinal case study. *Written Communication, 14*(1), 3–62.

——. (1997b). The rhetorical construction of multilingual students. *TESOL Quarterly, 31*(4), 765–774.

Sridhar, S. N., & Sridhar, K. K. (1980). The syntax and psycholinguistics of bilingual code-mixing. *Canadian Journal of Psychology, 34*(4), 407–416.

Stanlaw, J. (2004). *Japanese English: Language and cultural contact*. Hong Kong: Hong Kong University Press.

Staples, S., Kang, O., & Wittnerb, E. (2013). Considering interlocutors in university discourse communities: Impacting U.S. undergraduates' perceptions of ITAs through a structured contact program. *English for Specific Purposes, 35*(4), 54–65.

Starke-Meyerring, D. (2005). Meeting the challenges of globalization: A framework for global literacies in professional communication programs. *Journal of Business and Technical Communication, 19*(4), 468–499.

Starke-Meyerring, D., & Andrews, D. (2006). Building a shared virtual learning culture: An international classroom partnership. *Business Communication Quarterly, 69*(1), 25–49.

Stavans, I. (2001). *On borrowed words: A memoir of language*. New York: Viking Penguin.

Street, B. V. (1984). *Literacy in theory and practice*. New York: Cambridge University Press.

——. (1993). *Cross-cultural approaches to literacy*. New York: Cambridge University Press.

——. (2003). What's new in new literacy studies? *Current Issues in Comparative Education, 5*(2), 1–14.

Strickland, S. (2006). Writing the virtual: Eleven dimensions of e-poetry. *Leonardo Electronic Almanac, 14*(5). Retrieved September 1, 2009, from http://leoalmanac.org/journal/Vol_14/lea_v14_n05–06/sstrickland.asp.

Subtirelu, N. C. (2015). "She does have an accent but…": Race and language ideology in students' evaluations of mathematics instructors on RateMyProfessors.com. *Language in Society, 44*(1), 35–62.

Sue, D. W., Bucceri, J., Lin, A. I., Nadal, K. L., & Torino, G. C. (2007). Racial microaggressions and the Asian American experience. *Cultural Diversity and Ethnic Minority Psychology, 13*(1), 72–81.

Surma, A. (2013). *Imagining the cosmopolitan in public and professional writing*. New York: Palgrave Macmillan.

Swales, J. (1990). *Genre analysis*. New York: Cambridge University Press.

Szerszynski, B., & Urry, J. (2002). Cultures of cosmopolitanism. *Sociological Review, 50*(4), 461–481.

Tardy, C. (2009). *Building genre knowledge*. West Lafayette, IN: Parlor Press.

Tarone, E. (1979). Interlanguage as chameleon. *Language Learning, 29*(1), 181–191.

Tesdell, L. S. (2013). Innovation in the distributed technical communication classroom. In K. C. Cook & K. Grant-Davie (Eds.), *Online education 2.0: evolving, adapting, and reinventing online technical communication* (pp. 257–270). Amityville, NY: Baywood.

Thomas, L. (1990). A sense of community: Blues music as primer for urbanization. *Popular Music and Society, 14*(2), 77–86.

Trier, J. (2007). The 400 Blows as cinematic literacy narrative. *Teacher Education Quarterly, 34*(3), 35–51.

Trimbur, J. (2010). Linguistic memory and the uneasy settlement of U.S. English. In B. Horner, M.-Z. Lu, & P. K. Matsuda (Eds.), *Cross-language relations in composition* (pp. 21–41). Carbondale: Southern Illinois University Press.

Uitermark, J. (2002). Be-scaling, "scale fragmentation," and the regulation of antagonistic relationships. *Progress in Human Geography, 26*(6), 743–765.

Ulmer, G. L. (2012). *Avatar emergency*. Anderson, SC: Parlor Press.

Unger, D. (2008). Persons of letters: Creative writing and internationalizing the English curriculum. *ADE Bulletin, 126*, 46–51.

Vaish, V. (2008). *Biliteracy and globalization*. Clevedon, England: Multilingual Matters.

Venuti, L. (1996). Translation and the pedagogy of literature. *College English, 58*(3), 327–344.

Vertovec, S. (1997). Three meanings of "diaspora," exemplified among South Asian religions. *Diaspora, 6*, 277–299.

Verzellaa, M., & Tommasob, L. (2014). Learning to write for an international audience through cross-cultural collaboration and text-negotiation. *Changing English, 21*(4), 310–321.

Vieira, K. (2013). On the social consequences of literacy. *Literacy in Composition Studies, 1*(1), 26–32.

Villamil, O. S., & de Guerrero, M. C. M. (2005). Constructing theoretical notions of L2 writing through metaphor conceptualization. In N. Bartels (Ed.), *Applied linguistics and language teacher education* (pp. 79–90). New York: Springer.

Villanueva, V. (1993). *Bootstraps: From an American academic of color.* Urbana, IL: National Council of Teachers of English.

———. (1997). Maybe a colony: And still another critique of the composition community. *Journal of Advanced Composition, 17*(2), 183–190.

Vygotsky, L. S. (1978). *Mind in society: The development of higher psychological processes.* Cambridge, MA: Harvard University Press.

———. (1986). *Thought and language.* Cambridge, MA: MIT Press.

Walker, A. (1982). *The color purple.* New York: Washington Square Press.

Wallace, A. (2011). Alexandra Wallace "Asians in the Library" @ UCLA. Youtube video. Retrieved from http://www.youtube.com/watch?v=QkQ5-7Ii3aU.

Wan, A. J. (2014). *Producing good citizens: Literacy training in anxious times.* Pittsburgh, PA: University of Pittsburgh Press.

Wang, B. (2013). Comparative rhetoric, postcolonial studies, and transnational feminisms: A geopolitical approach. *Rhetoric Society Quarterly, 43*(1), 226–242.

Wang, C., Niu R., & Zheng. X. (1999). Yi xie chu xue: Yixiang yingyu xiezuo jiaoxue gaige de shiyan [Improving English learning through writing: An experiment in the reform of English writing instruction]. *Waiyu Jiaoxue Yu Yanjiu* [Foreign Language Teaching and Research], *4*, 43–49.

Wang, M., & Li, J. (1993). An investigation on English discourse patterns used by Chinese students. *Waiyu Jiaoxue Yu Yanjiu* [Foreign Language Teaching and Research], *4*, 59–64.

Watkhaolarm, P. (2005). Think in Thai, write in English: Thainess in Thai English literature. *World Englishes, 24*(2), 145–158.

Waxer, L. (2001). Llego la salsa: The rise of salsa in Columbia and Venezuela. In L. Waxer (Ed.), *Situating salsa: Global markets and local meanings in Latin popular music* (pp. 219–246). New York: Routledge.

Weigle, S. C. (2007). Teaching writing teachers about assessment. *Journal of Second Language Writing, 16*(3), 194–209.

Wells, G. (1999). *Dialogic inquiry: Toward a sociocultural practice and theory of education*. Cambridge, England: Cambridge University Press.

Werbner, P. (1999). Global pathways and working class cosmopolitans: The creation of transnational worlds. *Social Anthropology, 7*(1), 17–35.

———. (2006). Vernacular cosmopolitanism. *Theory, Culture, and Society, 23*(2–3), 496–498.

Wertsch, J. (1991). *Voices of the mind: A sociocultural approach to mediated action*. Cambridge, MA: Harvard University Press.

Wetzl, A. M. (2013). World Englishes in the mainstream composition course: Undergraduate students respond to WE writing. *Research in the Teaching of English, 48*(2), 204–227.

Wible, S. (2006). Pedagogies of the "students' right" era: The language curriculum research group's project for linguistic diversity. *College Composition and Communication, 57*(3), 442–478.

Wilcox, K. C. (2011). Writing across the curriculum for secondary school English language learners: A case study. *Writing & Pedagogy, 3*(1), 79–111.

Wilkinson, R. (Ed.). (2004). *Integrating content and language: Meeting the challenge of a multilingual higher education*. Maastricht, the Netherlands: Universitaire Pers.

Willard-Traub, M., & Dressen-Hammouda, D. (2014). Revising voice and identity through internet-mediated, intercultural peer review. HAL open access archive. Retrieved from http://hal.archives-ouvertes.fr/hal-01013711/.

Wittman, E. O., & Windon, K. (2010). Twisted tongues, tied hands: Translation studies and the English major. *College English, 72*(5), 449–469.

Wolff, J. M. (Ed.). (2002). *Professing in the contact zone: Bringing theory and practice together.* Urbana, IL: National Council of Teachers of English.

Wolfram, W. (2003). Reexamining the development of African American English: Evidence from isolated communities. *Language, 79*(2), 282–316.

Worden, D. (2015a). *The development of L2 writing teachers' pedagogical content knowledge in teaching activity.* Unpublished doctoral dissertation, The Pennsylvania State University, University Park.

———. (2015b). Developing writing concepts for teaching purposes: Preservice L2 writing teachers' developing conceptual understanding of parallelism. *Journal of Second Language Writing, 30*, 19–30.

Xu, Z. (2010). *Chinese English: Features and implications*. Hong Kong: Open University of Hong Kong Press.

Yang, G. (2010). *The power of the Internet in China: Citizen activism online.* New York: University of Columbia Press.

Yao, S. G. (2010). *Foreign accents: Chinese American verse from exclusion to postethnicity.* Oxford, England: Oxford University Press.

Yi, Y. (2010). Adolescent multilingual writers' transitions across in- and out-of-school writing contexts. *Journal of Second Language Writing, 19*(1), 17–32.

Yildiz, Y. (2012). *Beyond the mother tongue: The postmonolingual condition.* New York: Fordham University Press.

You, X. (2006). The Way, multimodality of ritual symbols, and social change: Reading Confucius's Analects as a rhetoric. *Rhetoric Society Quarterly, 36*(4), 425–448.

——. (2008). Rhetorical strategies, electronic media, and China English. *World Englishes, 27*(2), 233–249.

——. (2010). *Writing in the devil's tongue: A history of English composition in China.* Carbondale: Southern Illinois University Press.

——. (2011). Chinese white-collar workers and multilingual creativity in the diaspora. *World Englishes, 30*(3), 409–427.

You, X., & You, X. (2013). American content teachers' literacy brokerage in multilingual university classrooms. *Journal of Second Language Writing, 22*(3), 260–276.

Young, A. (2006). *Teaching writing across the curriculum* (4th ed.). Upper Saddle River, NJ: Prentice Hall.

Young, M. (2004). *Minor re/visions: Asian American literacy narratives as a rhetoric of citizenship.* Carbondale: Southern Illinois University Press.

Young, V. A. (2004). Your average nigga. *College Composition and Communication, 55*(4), 693–715.

——. (2007). *Your average nigga: Performing race literacy and masculinity.* Detroit, MI: Wayne State University.

Young, V. A., & Martinez, A. Y. (Eds.). (2011). *Code-meshing as world English: Pedagogy, policy, performance.* Urbana, IL: National Council of Teachers of English.

Zamel, V. (1995). Strangers in academia: The experience of faculty and ESL students across the curriculum. *College Composition and Communication, 46*, 506–521.

——. (1997). Toward a model of transculturation. *TESOL Quarterly, 31*, 341–352.

Zamel, V., & Spack, R. (Eds.). (2004). *Crossing the curriculum: Multilingual learners in college classrooms.* Mahwah, NJ: Lawrence Erlbaum.

Zawacki, T. M. (1992). Recomposing as a woman: An essay in different voices. *College Composition and Communication*, *43*(1), 32–38.

Zawacki, T. M., & Habib, A. S. (2010). "Will our stories help teachers understand?": Multilingual students talk about identity, academic writing, and expectations across academic communities. In M. Cox, J. Jordan, C. Ortmeier-Hooper, & G. G. Schwartz (Eds.), *Reinventing identities in second language writing* (pp. 54–76). Urbana, IL: National Council of Teachers of English.

Zawacki, T. M., Hajabbasi, E., Habib, A., Antram, A., & Das, A. (2007). *Valuing written accents: Non-native students talk about identity, academic writing and meeting teachers' expectations*. Fairfax, VA: George Mason Diversity Research Group.

Zhang, H. (2002). Bilingual creativity in Chinese English: Ha Jin's *In the Pond*. *World Englishes*, *21*(2), 305–315.

Zheng, C. (2004). *Yi xie cu xue: Yingyu xiechangfa de linian yu caozuo* [Improving English learning through writing: Theory and practice of the length approach]. Beijing: Kexue Chubanshe [Science Press].

——. (2008). *Yingyu xiezuo tongyong jiaocheng* [A general course of English composition]. Beijing: Kexue Chubanshe [Science Press].

Zheng, C., Du, Y., & Wu, Z. (2013). *Zhongmei xuesheng yingyu kuayang hudong: xingdong yanjiu yu yuliao fenxi* [Chinese and American student cross-Pacific interactions in English: Action research and data analysis]. Beijing: Kexue Chubanshe [Science Press].

Zhu, W. (2004). Faculty views on the importance of writing, the nature of academic writing, and teaching and responding to writing in the disciplines. *Journal of Second Language Writing, 13* (1), 29–48.

Zisselsberger, M., Assaf, L. C., & Singh, S. (2012). Delving into third space: Supporting multilingual and multicultural students' writing. *Writing & Pedagogy*, *4*(1), 69–97.

Index

Xiaoye You is an associate professor of English and Asian studies at the Pennsylvania State University, United States, and a Yunshan chair professor at Guangdong University of Foreign Studies, China. He is the recipient of the 2011 CCCC Outstanding Book Award for *Writing in the Devil's Tongue: A History of English Composition in China* (Southern Illinois University Press).